The Textual History
of the Greek New Testament

Society of Biblical Literature

Text-Critical Studies

Editor
Sidnie White Crawford

Number 8

THE TEXTUAL HISTORY
OF THE GREEK NEW TESTAMENT

The Textual History of the Greek New Testament

Changing Views
in Contemporary Research

Edited by
Klaus Wachtel
and
Michael W. Holmes

Society of Biblical Literature
Atlanta

THE TEXTUAL HISTORY OF THE GREEK NEW TESTAMENT

Copyright © 2011 by the Society of Biblical Literature

All rights reserved. No part of this work may be reproduced or transmitted in any form or by any means, electronic or mechanical, including photocopying and recording, or by means of any information storage or retrieval system, except as may be expressly permitted by the 1976 Copyright Act or in writing from the publisher. Requests for permission should be addressed in writing to the Rights and Permissions Office, Society of Biblical Literature, 825 Houston Mill Road, Atlanta, GA 30329 USA.

Library of Congress Cataloging-in-Publication Data

The textual history of the Greek New Testament / edited by Klaus Wachtel and Michael W. Holmes.
    p. cm. — (Society of Biblical Literature text-critical studies ; no. 8)
    Proceedings of a colloquium held in 2008 in M?nster, Germany.
    Includes bibliographical references.
    ISBN 978-1-58983-624-2 (paper binding : alk. paper) — ISBN 978-1-58983-625-9 (electronic format)
    1. Bible. N.T.—Criticism, Textual—Congresses. I. Wachtel, Klaus. II. Holmes, Michael W. (Michael William), 1950-
  BS2325.T49 2011
  225.4'86—dc23

2011042791

Printed on acid-free, recycled paper conforming to
ANSI /NISO Z39.48–1992 (R1997) and ISO 9706:1994
standards for paper permanence.

CONTENTS

Abbreviations vii

Introduction
Klaus Wachtel and Michael W. Holmes 1

1 Is "Living Text" Compatible with "Initial Text"?
  Editing the Gospel of John
  D. C. Parker 13

2 Original Text and Textual History
  Holger Strutwolf 23

3 The Need to Discern Distinctive Editions
  of the New Testament in the Manuscript Tradition
  David Trobisch 43

4 Conceptualizing "Scribal" Performances: Reader's Notes
  Ulrich Schmid 49

5 Working with an Open Textual Tradition:
  Challenges in Theory and Practice
  Michael W. Holmes 65

6 Traditional "Canons" of New Testament Textual Criticism:
  Their Value, Validity, and Viability–or Lack Thereof
  Eldon Jay Epp 79

7 What Should Be in an *Apparatus Criticus*? Desiderata
  to Support a Thoroughgoing Eclectic Approach
  to Textual Criticism
  J. K. Elliott 129

8 Contamination, Coherence, and Coincidence
  in Textual Transmission
  Gerd Mink 141

Conclusions
  Klaus Wachtel 217

ABBREVIATIONS

AGLB	Vetus latina: die Reste der altlateinischen Bibel: Aus der Geschichte der lateinischen Bibel
ANTF	Arbeiten zur neutestamentliche Textforschung
BETL	Bibliotheca ephemeridum theologicarum lovaniensium
Bib	*Biblica*
BT	*The Bible Translator*
BZNW	Beihefte zur Zeitschrift für die neutestamentliche Wissenschaft
CBET	Contributions to Biblical Exegesis and Theology
CCSL	Corpus Christianorum, Series Latina
CCSG	Corpus Christianorum. Series graeca
CPG	*Clavis patrum graecorum*. Edited by M. Geerard. 5 vols. Turnhour: Brepols, 1974–87.
CSEL	Corpus scriptorum ecclesiasticorum latinorum
EKKNT	Evangelisch-katholischer Kommentar zum Neuen Testament
ETL	*Ephemerides theologicae lovanienses*
ExpTim	*Expository Times*
GCS	Die griechische christliche Schriftsteller der ersten drei Jahrhunderte
GNT⁴	*The Greek New Testament*. Edited by Kurt Aland et al. 4th rev. ed. Stuttgart: Deutsche Bibelgesellschaft, 2001.
HibJ	*Hibbert Journal*
HSCP	*Harvard Studies in Classical Philology*
HTR	*Harvard Theological Review*
ICC	International Critical Commentary
JBL	*Journal of Biblical Literature*
JECS	*Journal of Early Christian Studies*
JGRChJ	*Journal of Greco-Roman Christianity and Judaism*
JSNT	*Journal for the Study of the New Testament*
JTS	*Journal of Theological Studies*
KEK	Kritisch-exegetischer Kommentar über das Neue Testament

NA²⁷	Nestle, Eberhard, and Erwin Nestle. *Novum Testamentum Graece*. Edited by Kurt Aland and Barbara Aland. 27th rev. ed. Stuttgart: Deutsche Bibelstiftung, 1993.
NICNT	New International Commentary on the New Testament
NovT	*Novum Testamentum*
NovTSup	Supplements to Novum Testamentum
NTGF	New Testament in the Greek Fathers
NTOA	Novum Testamentum et orbis antiquus
NTS	*New Testament Studies*
NTTS	New Testament Tools and Studies
NTTSD	New Testament Tools, Studies, and Documents
PG	J.-P. Migne, *Patrologia cursus completus: Series graeca*. 162 vols. Paris: J.-P. Migne, 1857–86.
RB	*Revue biblique*
SBLTCS	Society of Biblical Literature Text-Critical Studies
SD	Studies and Documents
SNTSMS	Society for New Testament Studies Monograph Series
StPatr	*Studia Patristica*
TSAJ	Texte und Studien zum antiken Judentum
TZ	*Theologische Zeitschrift*
WBC	Word Biblical Commentary
WUNT	Wissenschaftliche Untersuchungen zum Neuen Testament

INTRODUCTION

THE TEXTUAL HISTORY OF THE GREEK NEW TESTAMENT: CHANGING VIEWS IN CONTEMPORARY RESEARCH

Klaus Wachtel and Michael W. Holmes

In August 2008 the Institute for New Testament Textual Research and the German Bible Society convened in Münster a colloquium on the topic of "The Textual History of the Greek New Testament: Changing Views in Contemporary Research." Internationally renowned scholars representing a broad range of quite different views and methodological approaches gathered to discuss basic issues of New Testament textual criticism today. The first day of the colloquium featured the presentation and discussion of a series of invited papers, while the second day was devoted to an extensive introduction to the theory and practice of the Coherence-Based Genealogical Method (CBGM) by its developer, Gerd Mink.[1] Mink subsequently expanded his contribution about contamination and coherence so that it includes much of the presentation he gave on the second day. Thus, the present volume documents the presentations from both days of the colloquium.[2]

The colloquium was initiated by the editors of the *Novum Testamentum Graecum: Editio Critica Maior* (ECM), the core project of the Münster Institut für Neutestamentliche Textforschung, to discuss a decisive phase

---

1. A comprehensive reproduction of his contribution can be found at http://www.uni-muenster.de/NTTextforschung/cbgm_presentation/.

2. Our sincere gratitude is due to Ryan Wettlaufer for reviewing the English of contributions by German authors.

of their work with partners and colleagues. The appearance in 2005 of the fourth installment of the ECM brought to completion the critical text and apparatus of Part IV of the ECM, comprising the Catholic Letters. An accompanying study volume, the core of which will be a textual commentary on the Catholic Letters, is currently being prepared. In the course of this work, the editorial decisions taken so far will be reviewed by means of the CBGM. Mink devised the CBGM as a method for the analysis of the manuscript transmission with the aim of reconstructing the initial text, that is, the form of text from which the transmission started. Thanks to the continuing work of the Institute since the appearance of the first installment in 1997, the revision can now be based on the full evidence for all the Catholic Letters, and this may lead to different results in some instances.

For the ECM user—who was first introduced to the concept of "coherence" in the second installment (2000), and then to the "Coherence-Based Genealogical Method" as such in the third installment (2003)—it will be much easier to comprehend the CBGM because now there is an online version of it that allows for a reproduction of the tables and graphs utilized for the method. The new application ("Genealogical Queries") is available at http://intf.uni-muenster.de/cbgm/en.html.

In view of these circumstances—the completion of Part IV of the ECM, the availability online of key results of the CBGM, and the ongoing review of editorial decisions embodied in Part IV as the editors work on the accompanying study volume—it seemed a propitious time to discuss the ECM's achievements, its methods, and associated questions with interested partners and colleagues.

1. The Initial Text: Construction or Reconstruction?

The concept of editing or reconstructing the original text is no longer a matter of course. What status can be claimed for the text of a critical edition? Is it at all justified to call it a reconstruction or recovery of a text no longer extant, or is it nothing more than a projection of our own thinking on the material that the transmission preserved for us? In view of contemporary discussions, it may be both appropriate and necessary to treat this subject more extensively here than would usually be required to introduce the contributions of David Parker and Holger Strutwolf.

The distinction made in the ECM between the "initial text" (*Ausgangstext*), on the one hand, and the original text as composed by the author, on the other, may be seen by some as a recourse to Karl Lachmann, who, according to his 1830 "Rechenschaft," was not yet aiming for the true reading but for the oldest among widespread variants in his *Editio Maior* of the New Testament.³

Lachmann's method⁴ consists of "a complex of criteria for *recensio*":

1. rejection of the vulgate (i.e., the Byzantine text) and the requirement that the edited text should be entirely based on the manuscripts as determined by methodical recensio;
2. "distrust for manuscripts of the Humanist period";
3. reconstruction of the textual history and the genealogical relations linking the manuscripts;
4. mechanical determination of which reading goes back to the archetype according to clearly defined criteria (*stemma codicum*).

According to Lachmann, the reconstruction of the initial text would ideally result from a *recensio sine interpretatione*,⁵ that is, without any internal criteria being applied. He distinguished two main classes of tradition of the Greek New Testament, Eastern and Western, in analogy with Bengel's Asian and African *nationes*.⁶ He regarded readings shared by both classes as having equal value, regardless of whether the attestation from both supported just one or several variants. In practice, however, Lachmann usually followed the Eastern text, because very often the Western readings were transmitted in Latin only.⁷

But if a reading is attested by only a part of one class against agreement of the other part with witnesses of the other class, then it was rejected, even if—and this shows how strictly Lachmann followed the principle of reconstructing just the text form that was widespread in the fourth century—there was reason to believe that it was the genuine one.⁸

---

3. Karl Lachmann, "Rechenschaft über seine Ausgabe des Neuen Testaments," *Theologische Studien und Kritiken* 3 (1830): 817–45, repr. in *Kleinere Schriften* (2 vols.; Berlin: Reimer, 1876; repr., Berlin and New York: de Gruyter, 1974), 250–72; cf. 826: ". . . ich bin . . . noch gar nicht auf die wahre Lesart aus, die sich freilich gewiss oft in einer einzelnen Quelle erhalten hat, ebenso oft aber auch gänzlich verloren ist, sondern nur auf die älteste unter den erweislich verbreiteten."

4. See Sebastiano Timpanaro, *The Genesis of Lachmann's Method* (ed. and trans. Glenn W. Most; Chicago and London: University of Chicago Press, 2005), 115–18.

5. Karl Lachmann, ed., *Novum Testamentum Graece et Latine*, vol. 1 (Berlin: G. Reimer, 1842), v. On the discrepancy between claim and reality in this regard in Lachmann's actual editorial work, see Timpanaro, *Genesis*, 88–89.

6. See Timpanaro, *Genesis*, 85.

7. Lachmann, *Kleinere Schriften*, 2:258.

8. Ibid., 257: "Was beiden gemeinschaftlich ist, sei es eins oder schwanken beide Klassen in gleicher Art, die eine oder die mehreren Lesarten zeigen sich als verbreitet und sind des Textes würdig: für gleich begründet gilt mir die Lesart

Fifty years after Lachmann's "Rechenschaft," the edition brought forward by Westcott and Hort finally overcame the reign of the Textus Receptus in New Testament scholarship.[9] By its very title, *The New Testament in the Original Greek*, it signals the editors' confidence that it is possible to bridge the gap between the earliest attainable text and the authorial text. They devote an entire chapter of their *Introduction* to the question "whether there is good ground for confidence that the purest text transmitted by existing documents is strictly or at least substantially identical with the text of the autographs" and conclude that there is in fact "approximate sufficiency of existing documents for the recovery of the genuine text, notwithstanding the existence of some primitive corruptions."[10]

This Hortian confidence has been characteristic of New Testament textual criticism throughout the twentieth century, sometimes more cautiously, sometimes less so. Thus, Bruce M. Metzger states in the concluding paragraph of his *Text of the New Testament*: "Although in very many cases the textual critic is able to ascertain without residual doubt which reading must have stood in the original, there are not a few other cases where he can come only to a tentative decision based on an equivocal balancing of probabilities. Occasionally none of the variant readings will commend itself as original."[11] Kurt and Barbara Aland reach a similar conclusion: "Only in very rare instances does the tenacity of the New Testament tradition present an insoluble tie between two or more alternative readings."[12]

Yet towards the end of the century, two important publications gave evidence of a change of perspective. One is David Parker's monograph

---

der einen Klasse und die ihr entgegengesetzte der andern: verwerflich ist (wenn auch vielleicht einzig wahr), für die nur ein Theil der einen von beiden Klassen zeugt" ("Every reading shared by both families, whether it is the only reading attested or both families vary in the same way, thereby proves itself to have been widespread [*verbreitet*] and is worth accepting into the text; a reading of the one family and a different one of the other family have equal authority for me; a reading attested only by one part of one of the two families is to be eliminated (even if perhaps it is the only genuine one)" [translation from Timpanaro, *Genesis*, 85]).

9. B. F. Westcott and F. J. A. Hort, *The New Testament in the Original Greek*, vol. 1, *Text*; vol. 2, *Introduction*; and *Appendix* (Cambridge and London: Macmillan, 1881; 2nd ed., 1896).

10. Westcott and Hort, *Introduction*, 271, 276.

11. Bruce M. Metzger, *The Text of the New Testament: Its Transmission, Corruption, and Restoration* (New York and London: Oxford University Press, 1964), 246 (= 3rd enl. ed., 1992).

12. Kurt Aland und Barbara Aland, *The Text of the New Testament* (2nd ed.; trans. E. F. Rhodes; Grand Rapids: Eerdmans; Leiden: Brill, 1989), 280; trans. of *Der Text des Neuen Testaments* (2nd erg. und erw. Aufl.; Stuttgart: Deutsche Bibelgesellschaft, 1989), 282.

The Living Text of the Gospels,[13] and the other one is Eldon Epp's essay "The Multivalence of the Term 'Original Text' in New Testament Textual Criticism."[14]

The latter reminds us of the gap between the earliest attainable text and what the author actually wrote. Epp assigns four levels of meaning to the term "original text." First, it can denote a *"predecessor textform"* or *"pre-canonical original"* that was used in the process of producing the canonical text form, for example, Q for the Synoptic Gospels. Second, "original text" may mean the text of the author on which the canonical text form is based, yet without being identical to it. One has to take redactional or editorial activities into account that added certain features to the text as it left the desk of the author. Third, the canonical text form may be regarded as the original. Finally, an "interpretive text-form," the exemplar of a distinct strand of transmission that was subjected to editorial activity, can be seen as "original" with regard to the group of manuscripts descending from it.

One may be tempted to accuse Epp of ignoring the well-established boundaries between redaction criticism, textual criticism, and different levels of the latter. His "canonical text-form" appears to be what is commonly called the archetype, while the "interpretive text-form" refers to the hyparchtype in philological terms. But this obviously is a strategy on his part to point out that the term "original text" requires a clear definition of its reference. It is time to consider the use of more clearly differentiating terminology.

One may begin with the traditional distinction between the archetype of a tradition and the authorial text that continues in common usage in classical philology to this day. Though in much of New Testament textual criticism as practiced during the twentieth century this distinction has been ignored or overlooked (or occasionally denied), methodologically it is no less important for New Testament textual criticism than it is for classical, as (to name only one example) Günther Zuntz has so fruitfully demonstrated.[15]

Recently a third term has been proposed to describe the text form of New Testament writings that the editors of the ECM aim (and claim) to reconstruct: the "initial text." The term goes back to the German *"Aus-*

---

13. David C. Parker, *The Living Text of the Gospels* (Cambridge: Cambridge University Press, 1997).

14. Eldon Jay Epp, "The Multivalence of the Term 'Original Text' in New Testament Textual Criticism," *HTR* 92 (1999): 245–81; repr. in *Perspectives on New Testament Textual Criticism: Collected Essays, 1962–2004* (NovTSup 116; Leiden: Brill, 2005), 551–93.

15. Günther Zuntz, *The Text of the Epistles: A Disquisition upon the* Corpus Paulinum (Schweich Lectures, 1946; London: Oxford University Press for the British Academy, 1953).

gangstext," coined by Gerd Mink to designate the text established in the *Editio Critica Maior*. In his seminal study of "problems of a highly contaminated tradition" he defines "initial text" as follows: "The initial text is a hypothetical, reconstructed text, as it presumably existed, according to the hypothesis, before the beginning of its copying."[16]

Then Mink distinguishes the initial text from the text of the author, on the one hand, and, surprisingly perhaps, from the archetype of the manuscript tradition, on the other hand. It may be useful to explain the latter difference more extensively, because it is methodologically as important as the distinction from the text of the author. An archetype by definition is a manuscript (now lost) from which all extant manuscripts descend. As editors of the New Testament, we would be happy if we could reconstruct this manuscript's text reliably. Yet even if such a text could be recovered, it would not necessarily mean that the authorial text had been recovered. It is important to note at this point that the archetype already is the result of transmission bridging the span between the start of the tradition as attested by extant witnesses, on the one hand, and the authorial exemplar, on the other hand. We do not know what exactly happened to the text in this span of time, which might be called the initial phase of transmission. Some features of our manuscripts, such as the presence of titles for books and the *nomina sacra*, are signs of editorial activity in the initial phase.[17] There is also textual evidence (such as early patristic citations) that is likely to antedate the archetype of the extant manuscript tradition.[18] It is likely that oral tradition had an impact on written forms of the text, as Parker says in his contribution to the present volume. The author himself may have revised his text while copies of the unrevised form circulated already.[19] The initial reading may have been lost completely so that an emendation is necessary (see, e.g., 2 Pet 3:10 in the ECM). In short, an edi-

---

16. Gerd Mink, "Problems of a Highly Contaminated Tradition, the New Testament: Stemmata of Variants as a Source of a Genealogy for Witnesses," in *Studies in Stemmatology II* (ed. Pieter van Reenen, August den Hollander, and Margot van Mulken; Amsterdam and Philadelphia: John Benjamins, 2004), 25.

17. David Trobisch, *The First Edition of the New Testament* (Oxford and New York: Oxford University Press, 2000); trans. of *Die Endredaktion des Neuen Testaments: Eine Untersuchung zur Entstehung der christlichen Bibel* (NTOA 31; Göttingen: Vandenhoeck & Ruprecht, 1996).

18. See, e.g., William L. Petersen, "What Text Can New Testament Textual Criticism Ultimately Reach?" in *New Testament Textual Criticism, Exegesis, and Early Church History: A Discussion of Methods* (ed. Barbara Aland and Joël Delobel; CBET 7; Kampen: Kok Pharos, 1994), 136–52.

19. So W. A. Strange, *The Problem of the Text of Acts* (SNTSMS 71; Cambridge and New York: Cambridge University Press, 1992).

tion of the initial text will incorporate readings that antedate the archetype. For methodological reasons, therefore, it is helpful to distinguish three possible stages: (1) authorial text, (2) "initial" text, and (3) archetypal text.

It is clear that there is no evidence that could prove that the resulting "initial" text ever existed in exactly the reconstructed form. The reconstruction remains hypothetical, although it claims to get closer to the authorial text than the archetype. Indeed, "[t]he simplest working hypothesis must be," according to Mink, "that there are no differences between the original [i.e. authorial] and the initial text."[20]

Mink is quite right to adopt this working hypothesis; the hypothesis, however, cannot be converted to an assumption or conclusion without further investigation. Here is where the classical step of *examinatio* (Maas) comes into play: once the earliest recoverable form of text (i.e., the "initial text") has been identified, it must be examined to determine if its readings also qualify as authorial. This is exactly what Westcott and Hort were doing when they raised the question of how reliable their reconstruction of the text was. At the end of their examination they identified some sixty-five instances of what they termed "primitive corruption"—places where the transmitted text did not preserve, in their estimation, the original text.[21] One must investigate, rather than assume, the nature of the relationship between "initial text" and "original text."

David Parker's position regarding the quest for the original text of the New Testament may be characterized by the following statement from his monograph: "The attempt to discern earlier forms of text, from which those known to us are descended, is an essential task in the critical studies of Christian origins. It does not follow that it is also necessary to recover a single original text."[22] In his conference paper Parker shows how the term "initial text" relieves the editor from the claim to restore *the* original. The initial text in fact is the result of attempting to discern the earliest attainable form(s) of text while the difference from the text of the author is carefully observed.

Holger Strutwolf stresses the aspect of methodological approximation to the authorial text by the very title of his contribution: "Original Text and Textual History." He emphasizes that the efforts to reconstruct the initial text are oriented toward the original as written by the author, although it must not be treated as an extant artifact. Like Parker, Strutwolf

---

20. Mink, "Problems," 26.
21. See Westcott and Hort, *Introduction*, 288–310, esp. 279–82 (for specific readings, see the *Appendix*).
22. Parker, *Living Text*, 208.

has a deep respect for the manuscripts that actually came down to us, but for him the preeminent goal of textual criticism still is a reconstruction of the New Testament text that conforms as closely as possible to the text of the author.

2. Causes and Forms of Variation

David Trobisch argues that, very much like a printed edition of our day, a New Testament manuscript is a product to which several persons contributed. Regarding the text and its arrangement these are, apart from the author, the publisher, the editor, the scribe (or typesetter) and readers (and correctors). What gave the pages of a manuscript their final form is the result of the cooperation of these persons. A most important consequence of this observation refers to the question of what we are actually trying to reconstruct as the initial text. As in his monograph of the same title, Trobisch argues that it is "The First Edition of the New Testament." He points out that this edition has to be carefully distinguished from the text of the author. Yet, on the other hand, it was the author's text that was arranged for the edition, in the case of Paul's epistles probably with the author's interaction. Thus, it is methodologically important to differentiate categorically the edition and the authorial text, but Trobisch's theory is obviously compatible with the aim to approximate the author's text as closely as possible.

In the present paper, however, Trobisch focuses on another aspect. Editorial traits can also be used to identify distinct manuscript traditions such as that represented by codices D, F, and G of the Pauline epistles. In this context Trobisch asks how to deal with the possibility that there may have existed more than one edition of single New Testament books (like Acts, notably) or of collections of New Testament books.

Ulrich Schmid draws attention to important distinctions between the persons who influenced the composition of the text with its variants in the manuscript tradition. First, a scribe must not be confused with an editor who reserved the right to correct the text where it appeared necessary. Second, marginal additions are not necessarily meant to be editorial or scribal corrections. In many cases they may be readers' notes that crept into the text when a later scribe found them in the exemplar he had to copy and assumed that they were corrections to be incorporated into the next copy of the manuscript.

How important these distinctions are is shown by the theories of "orthodox corruption" that usually assign editorial activity to scribes. But their primary task obviously was to produce faithful copies of their exemplars. Their ethos was, according to a nearly proverbial maxim that is cited also at the end of the Apocalypse (Rev 22:19), neither to add to nor to delete anything from the text being copied.[23]

Schmid demonstrates how readers' notes could intrude into the transmitted text. He refers to three intertextually motivated additions whose attestations show different aggregate states of attestation. The first example is a reading in the margin of $\mathfrak{P}^{75}$ from a later hand that was not integrated into the text of any preserved manuscript (Luke 17:14). The second example is the interjection of the spear incident at Matt 27:49 that occurs in the running text of several venerable witnesses such as codices Vaticanus and Sinaiticus, but not in the mainstream tradition. Finally, there is the reference to Isa 53:12 in Mark 15:27 in the Byzantine tradition against a range of old witnesses.

3. Contamination and Coherence

In his programmatic 1995 essay "Reasoned Eclecticism in New Testament Textual Criticism," Michael Holmes sums up the *status quaestionis* as follows: "It is not the eclectic method itself that is at fault, but our lack of a *coherent* view of the transmission of the text."[24] There could not be a better motto for a dialogue with the developer of the *coherence method*, which set out to remedy precisely this lack. It would be short-circuiting the discussion, however, to assume that Mink's method could provide the solution to the problem stated by Holmes. Holmes has in mind a rewriting of the history of the text, a better description of the transmission and its strands following the model of Zuntz's work on the Pauline epistles. Mink's coherence method takes all available historical information into account to assess the variants, but its own contribution is a structure of the transmission derived from the totality of textual assessments. Consequently, a more coherent view of the history of the text, for example, as a phenomenon of cultural history, is not within the immediate scope of the CBGM. It sequences the textual transmission in terms of ancestry and descent, and thus it results in a chronological order of successive generations of witnesses, but it does not address the question how they align with the history of copying the New Testament writings in the framework of Christian culture.

---

23. The maxim is a topos already in classical times; see C. Schäublin, "Μήτε προσθεῖναι μήτ' ἀφελεῖν," *Museum Helveticum* 31 (1974): 144–49.

24. Michael W. Holmes, "Reasoned Eclecticism in New Testament Textual Criticism," in *The Text of the New Testament in Contemporary Research: Essays on the Status Quaestionis* (ed. Bart D. Ehrman and Michael W. Holmes; SD 46; Grand Rapids: Eerdmans, 1995), 350.

One virtue of Holmes's discussion of "open" or "contaminated" traditions is the clarification of terms describing the phenomenon. His suggestion to avoid pejorative terms such as "contamination" may help to guide us to a more productive way to deal with the problems traditionally labeled in this manner. In fact, it is not a realistic aim to purge the tradition of mixture. If we uphold Paul Maas's ideal of reconstructing the archetype *more geometrico*, we will indeed find confirmed his dictum that there is no cure for contamination.[25] But Giorgio Pasquali, in his lengthy review of Maas's brief treatise, presented abundant evidence for his thesis that no rich transmission of a text from antiquity is ever free from horizontal influence of the strands of transmission upon each other.[26] The real question can only be about how to analyze and assess the tradition in spite of such interdependencies.

Holmes sees the remedy in a reasoned eclecticism based on more precise knowledge (or at least an acknowledged hypothesis) about the textual history. He wants to improve the outcomes of reasoned eclecticism by improving this knowledge. Mink introduces a new methodological tool into textual criticism: the analysis and interpretation of coherence, both pre-genealogical and genealogical. Holmes puts the focus on assessing individual variant passages (what Kurt Aland termed the "local-genealogical method"). But the challenge of such a procedure has always been this: How does one relate the individual choices to the larger whole? Does the choice made at any one point of variation "make sense" or "cohere" with those made elsewhere? Precisely here is where the CBGM makes its contribution: it extrapolates the results of all individual assessments to derive tendencies from these and thereby come to an overall picture, the structure of the transmission in light of which individual assessments can then be reassessed. Mink demonstrates that coherence can be utilized as a new class of evidence that can guide us along the way to a far more discriminating application of the external criteria supplied by the extant manuscripts.

4. The Canons of New Testament Textual Criticism

More than thirty years ago, Eldon Jay Epp published an essay entitled "The Eclectic Method in New Testament Textual Criticism: Solution or

---

25. Paul Maas, *Textual Criticism* (Oxford: Clarendon, 1958), 49; trans. of *Textkritik* (3rd ed.; Leipzig: Teubner, 1957; 1st ed., 1927).

26. Giorgio Pasquali, review of Paul Maas, *Textkritik*, *Gnomon* 5 (1929): 417–35, 498–521.

Symptom?"[27] He arrived at the diagnosis that eclecticism is in fact symptomatic of the basic problem of our discipline: the lack of "objective" criteria (in the Lachmannian or genealogical sense) for determining originality of readings. This circumstance has not changed; given the fundamentally "open" character of the New Testament textual tradition (see Holmes's essay), there is no possibility of proving that the reading that brings the most weight onto the scales of textual criticism really renders the original wording of the author. Can this ever change? The original manuscripts as they left the authors' desks are lost. Even if we had them, we would still not be able to check the extent to which the authors themselves may have introduced variants into the transmission. We have to face the categorical gap between authorial and initial text again. We also need to be aware that textual criticism cannot measure and weigh its evidence like physical objects but has to understand and interpret it: it is an art, not a science, to paraphrase Metzger's well-known dictum.[28] We have to base our conclusions on probabilities rather than on deductive logic (à la Lachmann). Hence, Epp insistently reminds us of the fact that text-critical decisions are part of the hermeneutical process and that "the exegete becomes the final arbiter." This means that it is all the more important to analyze the evidence methodically and to describe text-critical problems as objectively as possible. In this regard the formulation of clear-cut criteria or probabilities as offered in Epp's paper is indispensable.

Keith Elliott is well known as an advocate of 'thoroughgoing eclecticism' as developed by his teacher George D. Kilpatrick. This method dispenses with conclusions about the quality of witnesses for the assessment of readings. According to Kilpatrick and Elliott, knowledge of the author's style is decisive. If a reading fits the stylistic pattern, it does not matter in which manuscript, version, or citation it is preserved. So one may be tempted to ask what relevance a critical apparatus can have for thoroughgoing eclecticism. Yet Elliott was one of the editors of the Luke volumes of the International Greek New Testament Project featuring an extensive critical apparatus, and in his contribution to the present volume he advocates as full an apparatus as possible. Like other editors, thoroughgoing eclectics need a critical apparatus for documentary purposes. It presents the evidence that was sifted and at the same time shows that the reading selected for the text has support in the extant tradition. Elliott seems to share the optimistic view of Hort, Aland, and others that the ini-

---

27. Eldon J. Epp, "The Eclectic Method in New Testament Textual Criticism: Solution or Symptom?" *HTR* 69 (1976): 211-57; repr. in *Perspectives on New Testament Textual Criticism: Collected Essays, 1962–2004* (NovTSup 116; Leiden: Brill, 2005), 125–73.

28. See Metzger, *Text*, v.

tial reading must be preserved in some source. Moreover, the apparatus is important for finding passages without variants, because without them there is no basis of firm examples that enable the editor to survey the features of the author's style. At any rate, thoroughgoing eclecticism rejects conclusions based on the quality of witnesses. This is the corollary of the supposition that the initial reading can be found in any witness regardless of its relationship with others.

5. Summary

To be sure, it is evident that a reconstruction of the initial text of our transmission is not of like importance for all contributors. However, each of them confirms from his particular perspective that a reconstruction of the earliest attainable text is useful and feasible. In sum, the present volume offers an overview of current perspectives on methodology in striving for this goal.

1
IS "LIVING TEXT" COMPATIBLE WITH "INITIAL TEXT"? EDITING THE GOSPEL OF JOHN

D. C. Parker

What sort of creature is a textual critic meant to be? On the one hand, we have inherited a tradition of individual scholars working on their own who look at the materials and reach their own judgments; on the other, we can complete major critical editions only by working together in teams, and that requires finding methodologies and interpretations on which we can all agree. Where there were teams in the past, they tended to be dominated by strong individuals (for example, and conspicuously, the names of Wolfram von Soden's large team of assistants have vanished from view[1]). Today, there are several reasons why we need to make our editions with a more creative attitude of teamwork. One is that here the growth of specialization produces better results. Not only do we need technical experts to help us produce databases and websites and to generate editions. We also need, for example, experts in particular versions: the days when an editor used his Syriac or his Coptic to form a judgment on its relation to a Greek variant are, one hopes, gone for good. We should have learned that we need someone with a thorough knowledge of the version to advise us on how best to incorporate it in the apparatus.

There is another enormous benefit in working in a team to make an edition: we have no room for giving full play to our prejudices and idiosyncrasies. We have to justify our opinions to our colleagues, make a serious evaluation of their and everyone else's theories, and screen out arguments and views that turn out to be so individualistic that they do

---

1. An exception is Eduard van der Golz, whose researches on Codex 1739 were published under his name.

not seem to inhabit the same world as everybody else's. But it also carries with it a risk, namely, that we will end up in a too-conformist world, a world of consensus textual criticism, in which we only say the boring things that we are all agreed upon anyway. To avoid this, we need also to be self-critical within our groups and partnerships as well as self-critical individually.[2]

These were the thoughts that prompted the title of this paper. It is prompted by the last twenty years of my life in textual criticism. In 1997, my book *The Living Text of the Gospels* was published.[3] Since 1987, ten years before then, I have been one of the editors of the International Greek New Testament Project, with our goal an edition of the Gospel of John. Back in the late 1980s and half of the 1990s, what we had in mind was a series of stages in which we worked toward an edition like the two volumes of Luke, namely, a thesaurus of readings against a base text (the Textus Receptus).[4] The first of those stages, an edition of the papyri, came out in 1995, and we then moved on to the majuscules.[5] So long as we were doing that, the theoretical and practical challenges of making a critical text were something we did not have to think about. But in 1997 all that changed. What happened was that in the momentous SBL meeting in San Francisco, at which the first fascicle of the *Editio Critica Maior* was launched, the IGNTP and the Institut hosting this happy event agreed to work together. In a very short period of time we had abandoned the concept of an edition of John as a thesaurus of readings and had begun moving toward the current situation, in which we have the franchise, as one might say, to provide the Gospel of John in the *Editio Critica Maior*. We

---

2. I once wrote that committees were better for compiling the evidence, but for reconstructing a critical text an individual was to be preferred. See "The Development of Textual Criticism since B. H. Streeter," *NTS* 24 (1977): 149–62, here 159; repr. in *Manuscripts, Texts, Theology: Collected papers 1977–2007* (ANTF 40; Berlin: de Gruyter, 2009), 151–66, here 163. It has to be said that at that stage in my career my experience of both activities was rather limited. It is certainly worth adding that an editorial committee has to be balanced, both in its range of skills and in its dynamics.

3. David C. Parker, *The Living Text of the Gospels* (Cambridge: Cambridge University Press, 1997).

4. *The New Testament in Greek*, vol. 3, *The Gospel According to St. Luke, edited by the American and British Committees of the International Greek New Testament Project* (2 vols.; Oxford: Oxford Univeristy Press, 1984–87).

5. *The New Testament in Greek IV: The Gospel According to St. John, edited by the American And British Committees of the International Greek New Testament Project*, vol. 1, *The Papyri* , ed. W. J. Elliott and D. C. Parker (NTTS 20; Leiden: Brill, 1995); vol. 2, *The Majuscules*, ed. by U. B. Schmidt with W. J. Elliott and D. C. Parker (NTTS 37; Leiden: Brill, 2007).

are therefore in a quite different position from where we were until 1997, since we are needing to construct the initial text that will stand at the head of the page. We, and therefore I, can no longer remain detached from the challenges faced by the critical editor. Moreover, the more technical aspects of the task are changed, since compiling an apparatus against a target fixed from the outset, such as the Textus Receptus, is simpler than setting it under a text that is itself in the process of development.

Personally, I am therefore faced with the imperative of addressing the relationship between the theories about the development about the textual history of the Gospels as I set them out in *The Living Text* and the requirement to establish a critical text. Are the two compatible? Am I poacher turned gamekeeper? Will my *Living Text* theories turn out to show the task of which I am now a part to be impossible? Will the application of the Coherence-Based Genealogical Method to the Johannine materials show flaws in my *Living Text* arguments? Will we be able to construct a convincing initial text or, more to the point, what will that initial text actually be?

Let me at this point set out a definition of the initial text. It is the text from which the readings in the extant manuscripts are genealogically descended. It is *not* an authorial text. The relationship between it and earlier forms of the text is another matter entirely, which may interest us as historians and exegetes but is outside the editor's remit. An obvious example is any one of the various questions about the literary history of the Fourth Gospel: the ordering of chs. 5 and 6, or the status of the last chapter. There are good arguments in favor of the text having been rearranged, and of ch. 21 being a later addition. But none of these issues is significant for the reconstruction of the initial text, because so far as I am aware there is no variation in the documents to suggest that either of these two phenomena may be observed in the genealogy of the tradition as we have it.

Now let me set out a couple of observations about *The Living Text of the Gospels* as I consider it today. First and foremost, I stand on the basic observation that I made there: that there is a significant body of textual variation in the Gospels that should be understood as a process of interpretation of the Gospel tradition. This process was a part of that tradition's transmission in early Christianity. By describing some of this variation and commenting on its significance, I was drawing attention to the elephant sitting in the corner of the room that is New Testament research, and even venturing to try to start a conversation with it.[6] To anyone who wants to

---

6. For discussion of the reasons why scholarship has largely ignored the fact and the motivation of this process, and for the development of approaches that take account of it, see Eldon Jay Epp, "The Multivalence of the Term 'Original

challenge my theories, I ask them to consider the body of material and to come up with a better explanation for it. It is worth noting that the motivation for the book was not solely text-critical. As you might say, it was not just a text-critical room in whose corner the elephant was sitting. Most of my conversations about the material were held with theologians, not textual critics, and my aim was to raise broader issues about the significance of our discipline, and especially of the variant readings, for theology, not least the way the Gospels are used in the churches. So I tried to do three things. The first is fairly obvious: to describe a number of variants and to discuss why they have a significance beyond the interests of textual criticism. The third was to offer an explanation of the phenomenon of such variants. I found it in a description of the nature of early Christian tradition, which I characterized with a Pauline tag as being devoted to the spirit rather than the letter of what Jesus had said and done. At the risk of being grossly repetitive, I used the quotation from Papias, who said that he considered the voice that liveth and abideth to be superior to things that were written.[7]

In a passage which is particularly important for the discussion of the Initial Text, I wrote:

> In the beginning there were traditions about Jesus. Then there were Gospels, a part of these streams of tradition. Later still, four Gospels were placed together, and the question of the accuracy of the traditions became subordinate to the claim for the authority of the writings. Yet, even then, the character of all manuscript copying meant that there was a continuing interplay between the Scripture—the text copied—and the tradition—the person engaged in the process of copying in and for the church. That is, we have a double interaction of Scripture and tradition in the copying: the one arising out of the fluidity of the early period, the other out of the inevitably provisional character of all manuscript copies.[8]

I presented a general theory of how the variant readings may have arisen, but apart from offering a few quotations, I did not do very much to offer any detailed evidence. I took my stand on the fact of the variation,

---

Text' in New Testament Textual Criticism," *HTR* 92 (1999): 245–81; repr. in idem, *Perspectives on New Testament Textual Criticism: Collected Essays, 1962–2004* (NovTSup 116; Leiden and Boston: Brill, 2005), 551–93, with Added Notes (592–93); David C. Parker, *An Introduction to the New Testament Manuscripts and Their Texts* (Cambridge: Cambridge University Press, 2008), 185–89; idem, "Textual Criticism and Theology," *ExpTim* 118 (2007): 583–99; repr. in idem, *Manuscripts, Texts, Theology. Collected Papers 1977–2007* (ANTF 40; Berlin and New York: de Gruyter, 2009), 323–33, esp. 323–26.

7. Parker, *Living Text*, 203–4.
8. Ibid., 204.

and since I could not think of any other explanation, I let my case rest on that. To be honest, I also thought it unlikely that the evidence was available, because if I was right then early Christians will have taken their attitude to the text so much for granted that they never discussed it. To be fair to myself, I did also argue that the theory gave a plausible explanation of the strange character of the surviving Gospel books themselves: not parchment rolls, not papyrus rolls, but something that had never had much of a tryout and that seemed to leave the texts written on them in a literary and religious shadow land, somewhere between literary texts and documents and dealing with the divine in a workaday format.[9] With regard to some of the variants themselves, I did sometimes offer an explanation of how they might have arisen, but I did not spend much time on this.

But I cannot resist saying that, for the essential theory of the book, this does not matter one way or the other. The fact is that, for whatever reason they appeared, the variant readings do exist. And since they exist, they inevitably change the sense of the texts they are within. And that offers a completely different, free. and non-textbound way of reading the texts that I believe is important, regardless of the historical context in which they happened. It does not even matter so much which of the alternative readings in any place of variation is the oldest. Of course, that textual history can help us to understand them, but the important point is the forms and the differences between them.

Remember also that I was considering always—and invite you to consider also—the ever-green question of the history of the Gospel text in the second century. Since the discovery of $\mathfrak{P}^{66}$ and $\mathfrak{P}^{75}$ we have forms of text that date from around the year 200 or somewhat before. The latter, in the Gospel of Luke, contains a form of text very similar to that of Codex Vaticanus, so that it appears that both are derived independently from a similar source. The question is, Where does this form of text come from? Does it have a history that perhaps spanned the second century and came from the subapostolic age or even earlier? I reckoned that the variation we find in our witnesses—the kind of *really interesting* variation I wrote about, I mean—came from the earliest period. I do not mean that every variation in Codex Bezae happened in the second century. But I do take as a good (though admittedly rather rare) example the survival in a couple of Byzantine manuscripts of a wording in the Lord's Prayer, "Thy Holy Spirit come upon us and cleanse us," which may reflect the wording as it was known to Tertullian and even possibly to Marcion (though the precise wording of his text remains highly doubtful). Here would be an example of a reading

---

9. Ibid., 186–88.

preserved in an eleventh- and a twelfth-century manuscript dating from well before the known date of the $\mathfrak{P}^{75}$-B text.[10]

And here we come to the possible crunch between my theory and reconstructing an initial text. If the oldest text we have is on this side of the second-century gulf, then what do we do with this reading, which is a variation predating the initial text? This example is unfortunately not from the Fourth Gospel, so let me try to explore this issue in terms of the text we are editing. In the passage that I have already quoted, I wrote: "In the beginning there were traditions about Jesus. Then there were Gospels, a part of these streams of tradition. Later still, four Gospels were placed together."[11]

I am not stating anything very revolutionary in suggesting that an important stage in the history of the traditions we are discussing came when the Four Gospel collection was formed. There is a codicological issue: Did the formation of this group happen after the development of the multi-quire codex? It is certainly striking that even in the third century, $\mathfrak{P}^{45}$ was put together in the rather rare format of single-leaf quires. What else was necessary at this stage? In what ways were the four texts standardized? This is only the first of many questions: Is the initial text a form of the collected Gospels? Should we follow Günther Zuntz's theories for the Pauline Letters and insist that the editor's task is to reconstruct the collected edition, not the individual works behind it?[12] But, just as Zuntz was mistaken to reckon with only a single edition of Paul, is it an error to suggest that there was only one collected edition of the Gospels? And if so, are our witnesses descended from a single collected edition, or are there traces of more than one edition behind it?[13]

But if we are editing the collected edition in its earliest recoverable form, are we going to find forms of the text in the surviving witnesses that are not descended from the initial text? We do not have to think very hard before finding such a problem in John, namely, the passage 7:53–8:11.

---

10. Ibid., 66–68.

11. Ibid., 204.

12. Günther Zuntz, *The Text of the Epistles: A Disquisition upon the* Corpus Paulinum (Schweich Lectures, 1946; London: Oxford University Press for the British Academy, 1953), 14.

13. For more on theories of collected editions, see David Trobisch, *Die Entstehung der Paulusbriefsammlung: Studien zu den Anfängen christlicher Publizistik* (NTOA 10; Freiburg: Universitätsverlag; Göttingen: Vandenhoeck & Ruprecht, 1989); idem, *Paul's Letter Collection: Tracing the Origins* (Minneapolis: Fortress, 1994); idem, *Die Paulusbriefe und die Anfänge der christlichen Publizistik* (Munich: Kaiser, 1994); idem, *The First Edition of the New Testament* (New York and Oxford: Oxford University Press, 2000); Theo K. Heckel, *Vom Evangelium des Markus zum viergestaltigen Evangelium* (WUNT 120; Tübingen: Mohr Siebeck, 1999).

Is it a part of the initial text or isn't it? And if it is not, what do we do with it? The interesting thing about a longer passage like this is that it also contains its own textual history. That is, there is also an initial text of this to be reconstructed, even if it is not a part of *the* initial text, and this initial text requires a critical apparatus. Or does one just jettison it if one decides it does not belong to the initial text?

What I have said about John 7:53–8:11 applies also to 5:3–4. These passages pose a particular challenge. But while the story of the angel visiting the waters is a detail, the episode of the woman has an extra layer of complexity, not just because of its age and length but because of its apparent character as a preexistent literary unit. Perhaps the answer is to edit it in a separate fascicle, as a part of the Gospel tradition but not part of the Gospel of John. This is a simple and stylish solution to the problem, which will be adopted in the *Editio Critica Maior*. There will be a supplementary fascicle in which are edited those larger passages in the Gospels that are not part of the initial text but did become integral to later forms of the text. Everything added after Mark 16:8 evidently requires similar treatment. In such a fascicle, the initial text of these special cases will be reconstructed, and the textual transmission set out.

When the editorial process moves on from John to Paul, similar questions may arise, for example, with regard to the addresses of several epistles and the ending of Romans. One may also ask whether certain readings in Deutero-Pauline letters might be the result of attempts to bring their thought or character into conformity with the authentic letters, in the formation of the corpus. If this were the case, then there might be a mismatch between the desire for the exegete to have access to older forms of the text and a critical edition setting out the text as it is found in the collected version.

I suspect that someone is going to tell me that I have misunderstood the nature of the initial text and that, in trying to find a specific date for it, such as late second century, I am confusing a logical text-critical process with a historical inquiry. I still plead the need to ask the historical question, if not when editing, then very soon after. But the point will still be well made. The Coherence-Based Genealogical Method, and with it the initial text provide a framework for interpreting the development of the tradition downward in time. That is to say, it is a way of explaining what happened after it but not what might have gone before. It offers the possibility of rationally interpreting the surviving tradition, not of speculating about earlier phases—or only when the only logical explanation for a variant is a reading no longer attested.

It is worth pausing at this point to reflect on the question of the value for exegetes of our methodology, raised in the two preceding paragraphs. The exegete is eager to be given an authorial text. The initial text is not such a text. What should we do to bridge the gulf? Does exegetical method, in particular, its study of authorial style, thought ,and text, offer a tool for making the initial text into an authorial text? If it does, is this process a suitable matter for textual criticism? It is worth observing that the boundaries are certain to be obscured, since textual critics use judgments on style and thought in comparing readings in order to reconstruct the textual history. But only rarely does such analysis depart beyond the readings known in the extant witnesses. Using similar techniques to restore an authorial text from an initial text would consist solely of emendations. It is interesting to note in this connection that most of what are known as conjectural emendations have been the work of literary critics far more than of textual critics.[14] On the other hand, how useful are exegetes in the task of reconstructing an initial text? The textual scholar has to reckon with the fact that such a text, based on a period of transmission extending over (in the case of the Gospels) at least a century, will already show signs of what its readers rather than its author thought it should contain.[15]

This is not to diminish the value of the Coherence-Based Genealogical Method. It is a broad church. And it needs to be. One matter of which textual scholars should always be aware is the danger of creating the traditions in their own image. It is sometimes said that academics studying the historical Jesus concentrate too much on the sayings at the expense of the actions, because they are sayers not doers. Likewise, textual critics can treat the tradition solely as a written tradition, because they spend their lives with texts. One of the contentions of *The Living Text of the Gospels* is that

> [t]he oral tradition is often seen as ending at some point in the early church, so that we today are wholly dependent on the written text. But it is not so. One should think instead of an unbroken oral tradition extending unbroken from the lips and actions of Jesus, since people have never stopped talking about the things he said and did. Sometimes the oral tradition has been influenced by the written tradition, and sometimes the influence has been in the opposite direction. The written and oral tradition have accompanied, affected, and followed one another.[16]

Putting this into text-critical language, one might say that contamination is caused not only by the interference of written variants from another

---

14. Jan Krans, *Beyond What Is Written: Erasmus and Beza as Conjectural Critics of the New Testament* (NTTS 35; Leiden and Boston: Brill, 2006).

15. Where $\mathfrak{P}^{45}$, $\mathfrak{P}^{66}$, $\mathfrak{P}^{75}$, or some smaller fragment is concerned. For much of the text, the earliest witnesses remain parchment codices copied at least two and a half centuries after the composition of the Gospels.

16. Parker, *Living Text*, 210.

branch of the tradition but also by the conscious or unconscious importation of forms of oral forms of the text. It is comforting to know that the Coherence-Based Genealogical Method has provided a tool for dealing with contamination, a problem that had seemed insuperable. When *The Living Text* was written, most scholars were still accepting the view that the genealogical method was of very limited significance. Today, we have not only the Coherence-Based Genealogical Method but also phylogenetic analysis, which between them have arguably made what is loosely called Lachmannian stemmatics work for the first time.

Finally, let me conclude with a point on which *The Living Text* and the initial text are totally agreed, namely, the impossibility of the attempt to recover a single original text.[17]

We would agree also, I believe, that the reconstruction of the initial text does nothing to weaken the historical worth of the forms of text derived from it. While the initial text makes sense of the extant tradition, saying that philology demonstrates the tradition to be derived from this once-extant form, it also follows that the initial text makes no sense on its own but can be rightly understood only when the subsequent developments from which it is reconstructed are considered. The *Editio Critica Maior* is described as "the textual history of the first thousand years." The importance of this history is precisely what I was arguing: "the attempt to recover early text forms is a necessary part of that reconstruction of the history of the text without which . . . nothing can be understood."[18]

That is, it offers a consideration of the living textual tradition.

---

17. Ibid., 209.
18. Ibid., 211.

2
ORIGINAL TEXT AND TEXTUAL HISTORY

Holger Strutwolf

In the last two decades the quest for the original text of the Greek New Testament has become problematic in the eyes of many scholars. The traditional definition of the goal of textual criticism—the recovery or reconstruction of the original text, that is, the text that the author wrote or wanted to have written down if he dictated his text to a secretary—was the unanimous consensus of the discipline from the beginning.[1] This seemingly self-evident approach to textual criticism has been challenged by some of the leading scholars in this field of research.

One cannot doubt that there are certain problems connected with the traditional approach. While the interest of New Testament textual criticism has focused merely on the reconstruction of the original text, other questions of equal importance have been neglected. The manuscripts

---

1. "Ziel bleibt die Gewinnung des Textes, wie ihn die Verfasser der Neutestamentlichen Schriften beabsichtigten" (Ernst von Dobschütz, *Eberhard Nestle's Einführung in das Griechische Neue Testament* [Göttingen: Vandenhoeck & Ruprecht, 1923], 143). As B. F. Westcott and F. J. A. Hort state in their classic formulation: "textual criticism is always negative, because its final aim is virtually nothing more than the detection and rejection of error." Its task is defined as "recovering an exact copy of what was actually written on parchment or papyrus by the author of the book or his amanuensis" (*The New Testament in the Original Greek*, vol. 2, *Introduction, Appendix* [Cambridge and London: Macmillan, 1881; 2nd ed., 1896], 3). Frederic G. Kenyon describes the aim of textual criticism as "the ascertainment of the true form of a literary work, as originally composed and written down by its author" by the use of later and thus corrupted manuscripts because of the loss of the autograph (*Handbook to the Textual Criticism of the New Testament* [London: Macmillan, 1926], 1–2). Cf. Kurt Aland and Barbara Aland, *The Text of the New Testament: An Introduction to the Critical Editions and to the Theory and Practise of Modern Textual Criticism* (2nd ed.; trans. Erroll F. Rhodes; Leiden: Brill, 1989), 280.

have been used only as reservoirs of readings that might be of interest for the quest for the original text. The manuscript tradition as such, the history of the text, the living process of its transmission, the historical and theological influences that stirred or at least influenced this transmission, the impact that this transmission in turn had on the history of the church and its theology were all not of central interest. Typical of this contempt of the manuscript tradition as such are the famous words of the outstanding scholar and philologist Carel Gabriel Cobet (1813-1889) that the more recent manuscript should not be collated but should be burned (*comburendi non conferendi*), which are cited with approval by Paul Maas in his volume *Textkritik*.[2]

For the majority of scholars today it is quite obvious that this contempt of the manuscript tradition and the lack of interest in the variants as such are no longer acceptable, but there are still other problems with the quest for the original text.

Eldon Jay Epp has pointed out the multivalence of the term "original text" in New Testament textual criticism by distinguishing a "predecessor text-form," an "autographic text-form," a "canonical text-form," and an "interpretive text-form."[3] Are we able to reconstruct the text of the author, or are we left with a later state of the textual tradition, the state of text that was produced when the Gospels and the Letters of Paul were put together into the "canonical edition" or even a later redaction or recension? Concerning the Gospels, we have to ask ourselves: Is there really a distinct line to be drawn between the oral or written tradition and an author? One has to admit that there are kinds of literature in which such a clear distinction does not exist. In the Hekhalot texts, the Egyptian tomb texts, and also in medieval texts, the editors are faced with the problem that such an entity as "the text of the author" cannot be fixed, because it never existed.[4]

Apart from these problems we also have to deal with the objection that the quest for the original text is overemphasized in traditional textual criticism, while the history of the text and the use of the variants and the different text forms as "windows" into this history have been underem-

---

2. Paul Maas, *Textkritik* (4th ed.; Leipzig: Teubner, 1960), 33.

3. Eldon Jay Epp, "The Multivalence of the Term 'Original Text' in New Testament Textual Criticism," *HTR* 92 (1999): 245–81.

4. See Peter Schäfer, *Hekhalot-Studien* (TSAJ 19; Tübingen: Mohr Siebeck, 1988), 63–64 ("Zum Problem der redaktionellen Identität von Hekhalot Rabbati"); Martin Baisch, *Textkritik als Problem der Kulturwissenschaft* (Trends in Medieval Philology 9; Berlin: de Gruyter, 2006), 14–53; Joachim Bumke, *Die vier Fassungen der Nibelungenklage: Untersuchungen zur Überlieferungsgeschichte und Textkritik der höfischen Epik im 13. Jahrhundert* (Quellen und Forschungen zur Literatur- und Kulturgeschichte 8; Berlin: de Gruyter, 1996), 390–455.

phasized. Bart Ehrman seems to hold that there is an opposition between these two tasks of textual criticism when he writes: "Given these historical concerns, there may indeed be scant reason to privilege the 'original' text over forms of the text that developed subsequently."[5]

This is also the question I want to deal with in my present paper: Is the quest for the original text obsolete? Or does it still make sense to search for the one and only original reading that the author of the text had in mind when he produced his text? Is the text we can reconstruct by means of textual criticism really the original text, in the sense of an autographic text? Is the concept of an author's text still a useful category for New Testament textual research?

Let me discuss these questions by using two examples that are well known and often treated: the version of the Lord's Prayer in the Gospel of Luke (Luke 11:2–3)[6] and the Matthean version of the Jesus logion concerning the exclusive goodness of God (Matt 19:17).

1. The Lord's Prayer according to Luke (Luke 11:2–3)

The facts concerning this Lukan passage and its relation to the Matthean parallel are well known, so that I have only to summarize them. On the one hand, the manuscripts 𝔓[75] and B/03—surely the two oldest witnesses of the text—and three manuscripts from the High Middle Ages (1192, 1210, and 1342) offer a short version of the prayer wherein God is addressed only as Father, instead of the Matthean "Our Father in heaven." Moreover, it consists of only five demands:

Πάτερ, ἁγιασθήτω τὸ ὄνομά σου·
ἐλθέτω ἡ βασιλεία σου·
τὸν ἄρτον ἡμῶν τὸν ἐπιούσιον δίδου ἡμῖν τὸ καθ' ἡμέραν·
καὶ ἄφες ἡμῖν τὰς ἁμαρτίας ἡμῶν, καὶ γὰρ αὐτοὶ ἀφίομεν παντὶ
   ὀφείλοντι ἡμῖν·
καὶ μὴ εἰσενέγκῃς ἡμᾶς εἰς πειρασμόν.

---

5. Bart D. Ehrman, "The Text as Window: New Testament Manuscripts and the Social History of Early Christianity," in *The Text of the New Testament in Contemporary Research: Essays on the Status Quaestionis* (ed. Bart D. Ehrman and Michael W. Holmes; SD 46; Grand Rapids: Eerdmans, 1995), 361 n. 1.

6. Joël Delobel, "The Lord's Prayer in the Textual Tradition: A Critique of Recent Theories and Their View on Marcion's Role," in *The New Testament in Early Christianity: La réception des écrits néotestamentaires dans le christianisme primitif* (ed. Jean-Marie Sevrin; BETL 86. Leuven: Leuven University Press, 1989), 293–309; David C. Parker, *The Living Text of the Gospels* (Cambridge: Cambridge University Press, 1997), 60–74.

This short form of the Lord's Prayer is cited also by Origen[7] and supported by the Sinaitic Syriac and the Vulgate.

The majority of the manuscripts, on the other hand, offer a longer version that assimilates Luke's text of the Lord's Prayer to the text of Matthew. Codex Alexandrinus (A/02) and Codex Ephraemi rescriptus (C/04) are the oldest witnesses of the longer text, which obviously is an assimilation to the Matthean parallel: ἡμῶν ὁ ἐν τοῖς οὐρανοῖς is added according to the text of Matthew, as well as the text of the third and the last demand: γενηθήτω τὸ θέλημά σου, ὡς ἐν οὐρανῷ καὶ ἐπὶ τῆς γῆς· and ἀλλὰ ῥῦσαι ἡμᾶς ἀπὸ τοῦ πονηροῦ.

Matt 6:9–11	Luke 11:2–4 (according to A 02)
Πάτερ ἡμῶν ὁ ἐν τοῖς οὐρανοῖς,	Πάτερ <u>ἡμῶν ὁ ἐν τοῖς οὐρανοῖς</u>,
ἁγιασθήτω τὸ ὄνομά σου·	ἁγιασθήτω τὸ ὄνομά σου·
ἐλθέτω ἡ βασιλεία σου·	ἐλθέτω ἡ βασιλεία σου·
γενηθήτω τὸ θέλημά σου,	<u>γενηθήτω τὸ θέλημά σου,</u>
ὡς ἐν οὐρανῷ καὶ ἐπὶ γῆς·	<u>ὡς ἐν οὐρανῷ καὶ ἐπὶ τῆς γῆς·</u>
τὸν ἄρτον ἡμῶν τὸν ἐπιούσιον δὸς ἡμῖν σήμερον·	τὸν ἄρτον ἡμῶν τὸν ἐπιούσιον δίδου ἡμῖν τὸ καθ' ἡμέραν·
καὶ ἄφες ἡμῖν τὰ ὀφειλήματα ἡμῶν,	καὶ ἄφες ἡμῖν τὰς ἁμαρτίας ἡμῶν,
ὡς καὶ ἡμεῖς ἀφήκαμεν τοῖς ὀφειλέταις ἡμῶν·	καὶ γὰρ αὐτοὶ ἀφίομεν παντὶ ὀφείλοντι ἡμῖν·
καὶ μὴ εἰσενέγκῃς ἡμᾶς εἰς πειρασμόν,	καὶ μὴ εἰσενέγκῃς ἡμᾶς εἰς πειρασμόν,
ἀλλὰ ῥῦσαι ἡμᾶς ἀπὸ τοῦ πονηροῦ.	<u>ἀλλὰ ῥῦσαι ἡμᾶς ἀπὸ τοῦ πονηροῦ.</u>

While in the majority text the assimilations to the Matthean form of the Lord's Prayer mainly consist of the interpolation of the aforesaid passages, the text of Codex Bezae (D/05) is far more assimilated to the Matthean form of the text:

Matt 6:9–11 (according to Codex Bezae)	Luke 11:2–4 (according to Codex Bezae)
Πάτερ ἡμῶν ὁ ἐν τοῖς οὐρανοῖς,	Πάτερ <u>ἡμῶν ὁ ἐν τοῖς οὐρανοῖς</u>,
ἁγιασθήτω τὸ ὄνομά σου·	ἁγιασθήτω τὸ ὄνομά σου·
ἐλθέτω ἡ βασιλεία σου·	ἐφ' ἡμᾶς ἐλθέτω σου ἡ βασιλεία·

---

7. The text is cited by Origen, *De oratione* 18.1 (340, 20-24 Koetschau), who was quite aware of the differences between the Lukan and the Matthaean form: πάτερ, ἁγιασθήτω τὸ ὄνομά σου· ἐλθέτω ἡ βασιλεία σου· τὸν ἄρτον ἡμῶν τὸν ἐπιούσιον δίδου ἡμῖν τὸ καθ' ἡμέραν· καὶ ἄφες ἡμῖν τὰς ἁμαρτίας ἡμῶν, καὶ γὰρ αὐτοὶ ἀφίεμεν παντὶ τῷ ὀφείλοντι ἡμῖν· καὶ μὴ εἰσενέγκῃς ἡμᾶς εἰς πειρασμόν.

γενηθήτω τὸ θέλημά σου,   <u>γενηθήτω τὸ θέλημά σου,</u>
ὡς ἐν οὐρανῷ καὶ ἐπὶ γῆς·   <u>ὡς ἐν οὐρανῷ καὶ ἐπὶ τῆς γῆς·</u>
τὸν ἄρτον ἡμῶν τὸν ἐπιούσιον δὸς ἡμῖν   τὸν ἄρτον ἡμῶν τὸν ἐπιούσιον δὸς ἡμῖν
σήμερον·   σήμερον·
καὶ ἄφες ἡμῖν τὰ ὀφειλήματα ἡμῶν,   καὶ ἄφες ἡμῖν τὰ ὀφειλήματα ἡμῶν,
ὡς καὶ ἡμεῖς ἀφήκαμεν τοῖς ὀφειλέταις   ὡς καὶ ἡμεῖς ἀφίομεν τοῖς ὀφειλέταις
ἡμῶν·   ἡμῶν·
καὶ μὴ εἰσενέγκῃς ἡμᾶς εἰς πειρασμόν,   <u>καὶ μὴ εἰσενέγκῃς ἡμᾶς εἰς πειρασμόν,</u>
ἀλλὰ ῥῦσαι ἡμᾶς ἀπὸ τοῦ πονηροῦ.   <u>ἀλλὰ ῥῦσαι ἡμᾶς ἀπὸ τοῦ πονηροῦ.</u>

The addition of ἐφ᾿ ἡμᾶς before ἐλθέτω σου ἡ βασιλεία surely is a theological interpretation that has to do with the problems Tertullian is dealing with in *De oratione* 5: "'Thy kingdom come' has also reference to that whereto 'Thy will be done' refers—in us, that is. For when does God not reign, in whose hand is the heart of all kings?"[8]

I think there can be little doubt that the longer text forms are later developments of the short form, due to the tendency of harmonization between Synoptic parallels. The alternative hypothesis would be that the longer version of the Lord's Prayer was abbreviated because of theological bias, for example, by the Marcionite redaction of the Gospel of Luke. This is much less convincing, however, since it seems very unlikely that the edition of Marcion, being easy to discern from other editions of the New Testament and considered heretical, should have had such a great influence on the text of the ecclesiastical Four Gospel tradition as this theory presupposes.

So if we agree that the short form of the Lord's Prayer is older than the long form and, since we have no other evidence that there ever was an older form of the Lukan pericope in question, that the long form evolved from the short form, then I think the hypothesis that we have reconstructed the oldest available text of the Lukan Gospel at this place of variation is a sound one. Already Bengel in the apparatus of his edition[9] considered this option. In his apparatus the omission of ἡμῶν ὁ ἐν τοῖς οὐρανοῖς, . . . γενηθήτω τὸ θέλημά σου, ὡς ἐν οὐρανῷ καὶ ἐπὶ τῆς γῆς, and ἀλλὰ ῥῦσαι ἡμᾶς ἀπὸ τοῦ πονηροῦ is marked with a γ, the symbol for a reading that

---

8. Translation by S. Thelwall. In Alexander Roberts, ed., *The Ante-Nicene Fathers: Translations of the Writings of the Fathers down to A.D. 325* (Edinburgh, 1867; repr. Grand Rapids: Eerdmans, 1987), 3:681–91.

9. Η ΚΑΙΝΗ ΔΙΑΘΗΚΗ. *Novum Testamentum Graecum ita adornatum ut textus probatarum editionum medullam margo variantium lectionum in suas classes distributarum locorumque parallelorum delectum, apparatus subiunctus criseos sacrae Millianae praesertim compendium, limam, supplementum ac fructum exhibeat inserviente* Io. Alberto Bengelio (Tubingae, 1734). In his discussion of the *variae lectiones* in the appendix (pp. 533–34), Bengel also argues for the great value of the short version of the prayer. Here he is also discussing the variant of Gregory of Nyssa and says that it is a "*glossa vetus.*"

is at least of equal value as compared with the majority reading. Griesbach then was the first who dared to put the short version of the Lukan Lord's Prayer into the text of a critical edition.[10]

There is, however, more evidence concerning the text of the Lord's Prayer that I have not yet taken into account. It may lead us a step behind the text of Luke's Prayer of the Lord as reconstructed from 𝔓[75], B/03, and others. I am speaking about the well-known variant attested in two minuscules, 700 from the eleventh century and 162 from 1153,[11] but also by Gregory of Nyssa[12] and Maximus Confessor.[13] Manuscript 700 reads, in

---

10. *Novum Testamentum Graece. Textum ad fidem codicum versionum et patrum emendavit et lectionis varietatem adiecit* Io. Iac. Griesbach, vol. 1, *Evangelia et acta apostolorum completens* (Halae, 1777), 176. Griesbach also notes in his apparatus the reading of Gregory of Nyssa, and cites the remark of Germanus of Constantinople: ἡ βασιλεία τοῦ θεοῦ τὸ πνεῦμά ἐστι τὸ ἅγιον.

11. Manuscript 162 (Città del Vaticano, Bibl. Vat., Barb. gr. 449) has all the characteristics of a purely Byzantine manuscript in every other respect. According to *Text und Textwert* it agrees with the majority text at more than 95% of the test passages in the Synoptic Gospels (*Text und Textwert der griechischen Handschriften des Neuen Testaments, IV: Die Synoptischen Evangelien*, 1. *Das Markusevangelium* [ed. Kurt Aland†, and Barbara Aland in collaboration with Klaus Wachtel and Klaus Witte; 2 vols.; ANTF 26–27; Berlin and New York: de Gruyter, 1998]; 2. *Das Matthäusevangelium* [ed. Kurt Aland†, Barbara Aland, and Klaus Wachtel in collaboration with Klaus Witte; 2 vols.; ANTF 28–29; Berlin and New York: de Gruyter, 1999]; 3. *Das Lukasevangelium* [ed. Kurt Aland†, Barbara Aland, and Klaus Wachtel in collaboration with Klaus Witte; 2 vols.; ANTF 30–31; Berlin and New York: de Gruyter, 1999]). It is quite astonishing to find such a peculiar old reading in such a manuscript.

12. Ὁ δὲ ἐφεξῆς λόγος τὴν βασιλείαν τοῦ θεοῦ εὔχεται ἐλθεῖν. Ἆρα νῦν ἀξιοῖ γενέσθαι βασιλέα τὸν τοῦ παντὸς βασιλέα, τὸν ἀεὶ ὄντα ὅπερ ἐστίν, τὸν πρὸς πᾶσαν μεταβολὴν ἀμετάθετον, τὸν οὐκ ἔχοντα εὑρεῖν κρεῖττον εἰς ὃ μεταβήσεται; Τί οὖν βούλεται ἡ εὐχὴ τὴν τοῦ θεοῦ βασιλείαν ἐκκαλουμένη; ... Ἦ τάχα, καθὼς ἡμῖν ὑπὸ τοῦ Λουκᾶ τὸ αὐτὸ νόημα σαφέστερον ἑρμηνεύεται, ὁ τὴν βασιλείαν ἐλθεῖν ἀξιῶν τὴν τοῦ ἁγίου πνεύματος συμμαχίαν ἐπιβοᾶται; οὕτω γὰρ ἐν ἐκείνῳ τῷ εὐαγγελίῳ φησίν, ἀντὶ τοῦ, Ἐλθέτω ἡ βασιλεία σου, Ἐλθέτω τὸ ἅγιον πνεῦμά σου ἐφ' ἡμᾶς καὶ καθαρισάτω ἡμᾶς. Gregory of Nyssa, *De oratione dominica* III (ed. Johannes F. Callahan, *Gregorii Nysseni De oratione dominica. De beatudinibus* [Gregorii Nysseni Opera 7.2; Leiden: Brill, 1992], 37.8–12, 39.15–19).

13. Πάτερ ἡμῶν ὁ ἐν τοῖς οὐρανοῖς, ἁγιασθήτω τὸ ὄνομά σου· ἐλθέτω ἡ βασιλεία σου. Εὐθὺς καθηκόντως θεολογίας ἐν τούτοις ἀπάρξασθαι διδάσκει τοὺς προσευχομένους ὁ κύριος καὶ τὴν πῶς ὕπαρξιν τῆς τῶν ὄντων ποιητικῆς αἰτίας μυσταγωγεῖ, κατ' οὐσίαν τῶν ὄντων αἴτιος ὤν· Πατρὸς γὰρ καὶ ὀνόματος Πατρὸς καὶ βασιλείας Πατρὸς δήλωσιν ἔχει τῆς προσευχῆς τὰ ῥητά, ἵν' ἀπ' αὐτῆς διδαχθῶμεν τῆς ἀρχῆς τὴν μοναδικὴν σέβειν τριάδα ἐπικαλεῖσθαί τε καὶ προσκυνεῖν· ὄνομα γὰρ τοῦ θεοῦ καὶ Πατρὸς οὐσιωδῶς ὑφεστώς ἐστιν ὁ μονογενὴς Υἱὸς καὶ βασιλεία τοῦ θεοῦ καὶ Πατρὸς οὐσιωδῶς ἐστιν ὑφεστῶσα τὸ Πνεῦμα τὸ ἅγιον—ὃ γὰρ ἐνταῦθα Ματθαῖος φησὶ βασιλείαν, ἀλλαχοῦ τῶν εὐαγγελιστῶν ἕτερος Πνεῦμα κέκληκεν ἅγιον, φάσκων· Ἐλθέτω σου τὸ Πνεῦμα τὸ ἅγιον καὶ καθαρισάτω ἡμᾶς—οὐ γὰρ ἐπίκτητον ὁ Πατὴρ ἔχει τὸ ὄνομα, οὔτε μὴν ὡς ἀξίαν ἐπιθεωρουμένην αὐτῷ

place of the second demand "Thy kingdom come," ἐλθέτω τὸ πνεῦμά σου τὸ ἅγιον ἐφ' ἡμᾶς καὶ καθαρισάτω ἡμᾶς, while MS 162 has ἐλθέτω σου τὸ πνεῦμα τὸ ἅγιον καὶ καθαρισάτω ἡμᾶς.[14]

That this reading was already known to or even created by Marcion, as many scholars think, is far from certain, as Joël Delobel demonstrated nearly twenty years ago.[15] Although it seems quite obvious that Marcion's Gospel contained the Lord's Prayer in the short version and that in his version of this prayer the first demand was about the Holy Spirit to come,[16] we have no evidence for the thesis of Adolf von Harnack that the Marcionite first demand had the form we find in the MSS 700 and 162 and in Gregory and Maximus.[17] After all, in the Marcionite Gospel the plea for the coming of the Holy Spirit replaces the first demand, while in the other witnesses under discussion it replaces the second! This is a strong argument for the thesis that the plea for the coming of the Holy Spirit—whatever form it had in the beginning—is a secondary gloss to the text of the Lukan Gospel that was inserted independently into the text, one time replacing the first demand of the Lord's Prayer, while another time replacing the second.

In any case, this reading seems to be an old one and is of some value. It must have been widespread in antiquity although now it is preserved

---

νοοῦμεν τὴν βασιλείαν· οὐκ ἦρκται γὰρ τοῦ εἶναι, ἵνα καὶ τοῦ πατὴρ ἢ βασιλεὺς εἶναι ἄρξηται, ἀλλ' ἀεὶ ὤν, ἀεὶ καὶ πατήρ ἐστι καὶ βασιλεύς, μήτε τοῦ εἶναι, μήτε τοῦ πατὴρ ἢ βασιλεὺς εἶναι τὸ παράπαν ἠργμένος. Εἰ δὲ ἀεὶ ὤν, ἀεὶ καὶ πατήρ ἐστι καὶ βασιλεύς, ἀεὶ ἄρα καὶ ὁ Υἱὸς καὶ τὸ Πνεῦμα τὸ ἅγιον οὐσιωδῶς τῷ Πατρὶ συνυφεστήκασιν, ἐξ αὐτοῦ τε ὄντα καὶ ἐν αὐτῷ φυσικῶς ὑπὲρ αἰτίαν καὶ λόγον, ἀλλ' οὐ μετ' αὐτὸν γενόμενα δι' αἰτίαν ὕστερον· ἡ γὰρ σχέσις συνενδείξεως κέκτηται δύναμιν, τὰ ὧν ἐστί τε καὶ λέγεται σχέσις, μετ' ἄλληλα θεωρεῖσθαι μὴ συγχωροῦσα. Maximus Confessor, *Expositio orationis dominicae* 230–257 (ed. P. van Deun. *Maximi confessoris opuscula exegetica duo* [CCSG 23; Turnhout: Brepols, 1991]).

14. "Thy Holy Spirit come over us and cleanse us." (The transposition of σου does not change the meaning.)

15. J. Delobel, *The Lord's Prayer*, 295–98. The history of research is brilliantly reconstructed by G. Schneider, "Die Bitte um das Kommen des Geistes im lukanischen Vaterunser (Lk 11,2 v.l.)." in *Studien zum Text und zur Ethik des Neuen Testaments: Festschrift zum 80. Geburtstag von Heinrich Greeven* (ed. Wolfgang Schrage; BZNW 47; Berlin and New York: de Gruyter, 1986), 344-373.

16. In a polemical context arguing against Marcion's distinction of the two Gods, Tertullian alludes to the Lord's Prayer as Marcion had it in his Gospel (*Marc.* 4.26.3–5): Denique sensus orationis quem Deum sapiant recognose. Cui dicam, Pater? . . . A quo spiritum sanctum postulem? . . . Eius regnum optabo venire quem numquam regem gloriae audivi, an in cuius manu etiam corda sunt regnum? Quis dabit mihi panem cotidianum? . . . Quis mihi delicta dimittet? . . . Quis non sinet nos deduci in temptationem?

17. Adolf von Harnack, *Marcion: Das Evangelium vom fremden Gott. Eine Monographie zur Geschichte der Grundlegung der katholischen Kirche* (1924; repr., Darmstadt: Wissenschaftliche Buchgesellschaft, 1960), 207*-208*.

in only a few witnesses. For while Maximus Confessor may be dependent on Gregory of Nyssa,[18] Gregory in his commentary cites the reading known from MS 700 as *the* text of the Gospel of Luke: οὕτω γὰρ ἐν ἐκείνῳ τῷ εὐαγγελίῳ φησὶν, ἀντὶ τοῦ, Ἐλθέτω ἡ βασιλεία σου, Ἐλθέτω τὸ ἅγιον πνεῦμά σου ἐφ' ἡμᾶς καὶ καθαρισάτω ἡμᾶς. ("So he says in his Gospel instead of 'Thy Kingdom come': 'Thy Holy Spirit come over us and clean us.'")

Several prominent authors argued for the authenticity of this logion,[19] because it stands in strong contrast to the tendency of harmonization of the Lukan text to the text of Matthew. However one might decide this question, one thing seems to be quite clear: as far as I can see, all the scholars that have dealt with this logion arguing for or against its Lukan authenticity agree on one point: it is a reinterpretation of the demand "Thy kingdom come," reflecting a more spiritual and less apocalyptic understanding of the Lord's Prayer. In which phase of the textual history of the Gospel of Luke, however, did this reinterpretation take place? Is it a creation of the author of the Gospel of Luke, or was it introduced by later scribes or editors?

I think that there are strong arguments for the view that "Thy Kingdom come" and not "Thy Holy Spirit come over us and clean us" was written by the author of the Gospel, with the latter being introduced into the tradition sometime later by a scribe or redactor. If we look at the form of the Lord's Prayer in $\mathfrak{P}^{75}$ and B/03, we see that these two manuscripts are almost free of any tendency to assimilate the text of Luke to the text of Matthew. The impression one gets by looking at the transmission of the Lord's Prayer is strongly confirmed by the survey of the influence of the Synoptic parallels on the textual tradition in general by the Institute in Münster, which will be published in the near future. On the basis of full collations of more than 150 manuscripts in 39 Synoptic pericopes the degree of influence from Synoptic parallels can be assessed for each manuscript. The use of this tool reveals that the manuscripts $\mathfrak{P}^{75}$ and B/03 are almost free of any tendency to align Synoptic texts to each other. Hence, it is quite improbable that such an influence could have been at work in both manuscripts or in the tradition from which they stem in Luke 11:2, to the effect that an original "Thy Holy Spirit come over us and clean us" would

---

18. "A similar statement by Maximus Confessor is doubtless borrowed from Gregory" (Westcott and Hort, *Appendix*, 60).

19. Delobel ("Lord's Prayer," 298 n. 16, following G. Schneider, "Die Bitte," 358) gives a list of defenders of the originality of the logion of MS 700 containing such prominent names as "Resch, Blass, Harnack, Spitta, Paslack, G. Klein, J. Weiss, Loisy, Leisegang, Streeter, Klostermann, Greeven, Lampe, Grässer, Leaney, Ott, Freundenberger."

have been replaced by "Thy Kingdom come," thus assimilating an older text to the Synoptic parallel.

On the other hand, we might suspect that theological reasons led to the insertion of a plea for the Holy Spirit instead of the kingdom of God. Tertullian and Origen in their exegesis of the phrase "Thy Kingdom come" interpret the coming of the kingdom as the coming of God into the hearts of the believers, because these patristic writers are obviously uneasy about the apocalyptic concept of God beginning his reign over the world only in the future, while they are both convinced that God was always the almighty king over the whole creation.

> Thy Kingdom Come. According to the word of our Lord and Savior, the Kingdom of God does not come observably, nor shall men say "Lo it is here," or "Lo it is there," but the Kingdom of God is within us; for the utterance is exceedingly near in our mouth and in our heart. It is therefore plain that he who prays for the coming of the kingdom of God prays with good reason for rising and fruit bearing and perfecting of God's kingdom within him. For every saint is ruled over by God and obeys the Spiritual laws of God, and conducts himself like a well-ordered city; and the Father is present with him, and Christ rules together with the Father in the perfected Soul, according to the saying that I mentioned shortly before: We will come unto him and make abode with him. By God's kingdom I understand the blessed condition of the mind and the settled order of wise reflection.(Origen, *On Prayer* 25.1)[20]

Indeed, in Origen's thinking the dwelling of God in the souls of believers can happen only by the coming of the Holy Spirit into their souls and by the purifying effect of this process. Theological considerations such as this may have led a scribe or a reader of Luke to add a comment in the margin of the manuscript saying that the coming of the kingdom consists in the coming of the Holy Spirit into the soul of the believer. Later, this marginal note may have moved into the text, perhaps because it was interpreted as a correction.

If—as many scholars think—the replacement of "Kingdom of God" with "Holy Spirit" is a theologically motivated change, then it was made by a theologian who had difficulty accepting the idea of the coming of the kingdom of God, understood in a too-realistic and apocalyptic way. This surely is not the case with the author of the Third Gospel (cf. Luke 4:43; 6:20; and especially 10:9). So there is good reason to assume that the plea

---

20. Trans.William A. Curtis; GCS 3. See also *Christian Classics Ethereal Library* (n.d.), online at http://www.ccel.org/ccel/origen/prayer.xvi.html. The online version, however, numbers this section as "XV.1" rather than "XXV.1" as per the GCS edition and other English translations.

for the Holy Spirit originates neither from the text as written by Luke nor from the source of Luke, the so-called *Logienquelle* Q, but was made by a later scribe.

These considerations show that the concept of an original text of the Gospels is not obsolete but is still useful and even necessary. Even if we should concentrate our research merely on the history of the New Testament text, the quest for the original text would remain of vital interest for the reconstruction of this history, because studying the emergence of variants as phenomena of reception history requires a distinction between prior and secondary states of text. In his book *The Living Text of the Gospels* David Parker has very convincingly shown, for example, how different generations of scribes have "written on Luke's page,"[21] but even his approach proves how important the quest for the original text still is, because in order to find out how later generations wrote on Luke's page, it is indispensable to know what was written on Luke's page originally.

But there is yet another challenge for the traditional view concerning the concept of an "original text." The late William L. Petersen insisted on taking the so-called secondary witnesses more seriously. He argued that in some important cases the original text could be detected only by going beyond the limits of the New Testament manuscript tradition, taking into account early versions and citations of the early fathers even if their readings are not supported by any manuscript evidence.[22]

2. Matthew 19:17

I will deal with the example that Petersen used in his paper as an instance where the original text has not survived in the manuscript tradition but only in secondary witnesses such as patristic citations and early versions. We are talking about citations and allusions to Matt 19:17 in the writings of Justin Martyr. While the text in GNT[4] and NA[27] simply states εἷς ἐστιν ὁ ἀγαθός, "one is the good one," Justin cited a longer version of the

---

21. Parker, *Living Text*, 174.
22. William L. Petersen, "What Text Can New Testament Textual Criticism Ultimately Reach?" in *New Testament Textual Criticicism, Exegesis, and Early Church Historiy: A Discussion of Methods* (ed. Barbara Aland and Joël Delobel; CBET 7; Kampen: Kok Pharos, 1994),136–51. For the following discussions with Petersen's position, see also Joseph Verheyden, "Assessing Gospel Quotations in Justin Martyr," in *New Testament Textual Criticism and Exegesis: Festschrift J. Delobel* (ed. Adelbert Denaux; BETL 161; Leuven: Leuven University Press, 2002), 361–77. In the same volume, Petersen repeated and elaborated his position: William L. Peterson, "The Genesis of the Gospels," 33–66; see esp. p. 62, where he comes to this conclusion: "To be brutally frank, we know next to nothing about the shape of the 'autograph' gospels; indeed, it is questionable if one can even speak of such a thing."

same text: εἷς ἐστιν ὁ ἀγαθός, ὁ πατήρ μου ὁ ἐν τοῖς οὐρανοῖς, "one is good, my father in the heavens" (Justin, *Dial*. 101.2).

What Petersen considers very significant in this case is the broad attestation of this variant reading in the time of Justin and shortly after. Petersen gives a list of witnesses that support the reading of Justin:

> Tatian, *Diatessaron*: ḥsad (h)u lam ṭobo abo dba-šmayo ("One is good, it is said, the Father who is in heaven.")[23]
> Irenaeus (*Haer*. 1.20.2): εἷς ἐστιν ἀγαθός, ὁ πατήρ ἐν τοῖς οὐρανοῖς.
> Hippolytus (*Haer*. 5.7.26): εἷς ἐστιν ἀγαθός, ὁ πατήρ μου ὁ ἐν τοῖς οὐρανοῖς.
> Clement of Alexandria (*Strom*. 5.10.63.8): εἷς ἀγαθός, ὁ πατήρ.
> Clementine Homilies 16.3.4: ὁ γὰρ ἀγαθός εἷς ἐστιν, ὁ πατήρ ὁ ἐν τοῖς οὐρανοῖς.
> Vetus Latina MS e [Beuron 2]: *Unus est bonus, pater*.

Some of these quotations are older than our Greek New Testament manuscripts—Justin's *Dialogue with Trypho* was composed in the middle of the second century—and therefore Petersen suggests that the quotations represent a text form that is older and closer to the original than the text form extant in the manuscripts. He argues for the authenticity of Justin's text by pointing out that the NA[27] and GNT[4] text can be seen as resulting from orthodox corruption, to use Bart Ehrman's term.

If we follow Petersen, the reading supported by Justin and other early witnesses could be understood as championing an adoptionist Christology, picturing Jesus as a mere human being and declaring that only the Father is God and therefore good, or at least as presenting clearly subor-

---

23. According to Ephraem Syrus, *Commentary on the Diatessaron* 15.9; see Dom Louis Leloir ed., *Saint Éphrem, Commentaire de l'Evangile concordant, Texte syriaque (Manuscrit Chester Beatty 709)* (Dublin: Figgis, 1963), 138–51. In the context of ch. 15 of his commentary Ephrem is commenting on Mark 10:17–24 as he found it in the *Diatessaron*. But in the course of his commenting he perpetually is mixing and confusing the parallels of Synoptic passages. (For the sake of convenience I cite the Latin translation of Leloir verbatim). In 15.1 he begins with a citation of Mark 10:17 (*Cur vocas me bonum?*), but then slips to Matt 19:17 (*Si vis vitam intrare, serva mandata*). In 15.2 Ephrem quotes: *Unus est bonus . . . sed adiecit Pater* (Matt 19:17), then *Magister bone . . . Non est aliquis bonus, ut putasti, nisi unus Deus Pater. . . Non est bonus, nisi unus, Pater, qui in caelo*. In 15.6 he cites: *Non est bonus, nisi unus . . . Mandata cognoscisne?* (Mark 10:19). In 15.8 we find: *Magister bone . . . Et respexit in eum cum amore* (Mark 10:21) . . . *Unus est bonus* (Matt 19:17). And in 15.9 we find the following citations: *Non est bonus nisi unus . . . Unus est bonus, Pater, qui in caelo est*. As a result of this observation I find it not very safe to assume that Tatian really is a witness for the strange reading of Matt 19:17, but rather Ephrem is producing this reading in his commentary.

dinationist views. The view that only the Father in heaven is in full possession of divinity while the Son is not was widely accepted in the early church, but was—according to Petersen--not acceptable anymore after the ecumenical synod of Nicaea. That is why the older text, still attested by Justin, was altered to the more orthodox form, so that Jesus answered the question about the essence of goodness: "Why do you ask me about the Good, one is good." This change removed the antithesis between the Father being the only one to be called good and the Son, who consequently would not share this goodness.

If Petersen's argument was convincing, the reading of the great uncials (Codices Sinaiticus, Vaticanus, Bezae, L and Θ) adopted by most modern editors as the original text would be the result of an orthodox corruption. In this special case, orthodox corruption would not only have changed the text of many manuscripts but would also have erased the original reading from the whole manuscript tradition.

What is strange about this theory is that the supported orthodox reading, which is supposed to have pushed away the reading that later came under suspicion of heresy, did not become the majority reading. Quite the contrary, it is attested only by very few, but very old and good witnesses,[24] while the majority of manuscripts support a reading that is far from sounding more orthodox. In fact, the majority reading appears as heretical and dogmatically incorrect as the text of Justin.

The majority of the manuscripts at Matt 19:17 read: Τί με λέγεις ἀγαθόν; οὐδεὶς ἀγαθὸς εἰ μὴ εἷς ὁ θεός ("Why do you call me good? No one is good, except one, God!").[25] How could a formulation so unorthodox and dangerous as this one, one that makes the difference—one could say, the contrast—between Jesus and God even stronger than the citation of Justin Martyr, -not only survive in the process of transmission by the orthodox church, but also become the majority reading?

I think this example shows that dogmatic reasons were not responsible for the victory of the majority reading in the process of transmission. In all probability, it results simply from the influence of the Synoptic

---

24. Matthew 19:17: Τί με ἐρωτᾷς περὶ τοῦ ἀγαθοῦ; is read by 01.03.019.038.1.22.70 0.892.2372. εἷς ἐστιν ὁ ἀγαθός is attested by 01.03^{C1}.019.038.892*.1424^{mg}, while 03* has ἐστιν ὁ ἀγαθός, and 05.1.22.700.791. 2372 read εἷς ἐστιν ἀγαθός. Origen (*Comm. Matt.* 15.10 [GCS 40:373.28–378.9)] cites Matt 19:17 this way: Τί με ἐρωτᾷς περὶ τοῦ ἀγαθοῦ; εἷς ἐστιν ὁ ἀγαθός, noting the different wording of this logion in the Markan (Mark 10:17) and Lukan (Luke 18:19) parallels: Τί με λέγεις ἀγαθόν; οὐδεὶς ἀγαθὸς εἰ μὴ εἷς ὁ θεός.

25. John Chrysostom (*Hom. Matt.* 1.90 [CPG 4424; PG 58:603.13ff.]) is the first patristic witness for the majority reading of Matt 19:17, while Eusebius (*Praep. ev.* 11.21.1f. [GCS 43:2, 47:7–18]) is a witness for another form of conflation of the Synoptic parallels: Τί με ἐρωτᾷς περὶ τοῦ ἀγαθοῦ; οὐδεὶς ἀγαθὸς εἰ μὴ εἷς ὁ θεός.

parallels in Luke and Mark. While Matthew changed the text of Mark, the influence of the Synoptic parallels had the effect that this Matthean change was undone in the end. So Matt 19:17 became identical to the parallel texts of Luke and Mark.

Further, I think it was the same mechanism of Synoptic assimilation that also led to the text of Matt 19:17 in Justin's citation[26]:

Matt 19:16–17	Justin. *Dial.* 101.2	Luke 18:18–19	Mark 10:17–18	Justin, *1 Apol.* 16.7
Καὶ ἰδοὺ εἷς προσελθὼν αὐτῷ εἶπεν, Διδάσκαλε, τί ἀγαθὸν ποιήσω ἵνα σχῶ ζωὴν αἰώνιον;	λέγοντος αὐτῷ τινος· <u>Διδάσκαλε ἀγαθέ</u>, ἀπεκρίνατο	Καὶ ἐπηρώτησέν τις αὐτὸν ἄρχων λέγων, <u>Διδάσκαλε ἀγαθέ</u>, τί ποιήσας ζωὴν αἰώνιον κληρονομήσω;	Καὶ ἐκπορευομενου αὐτοῦ εἰς ὁδὸν προσδραμὼν εἷς καὶ γονυπετήσας αὐτὸν ἐπηρώτα αὐτόν, <u>Διδάσκαλε ἀγαθέ</u>, τί ποιήσω ἵνα ζωὴν αἰώνιον κληρονομήσω;	καὶ προσελθόντος αὐτῷ τινος καὶ εἰπόντος: <u>Διδάσκαλε ἀγαθέ</u>,
ὁ δὲ εἶπεν αὐτῷ, Τί με ἐρωτᾷς περὶ τοῦ ἀγαθοῦ; <u>εἷς ἐστιν ὁ ἀγαθός.</u>	<u>Τί με λέγεις ἀγαθόν; εἷς ἐστιν ἀγαθός,</u> ὁ πατήρ μου ὁ ἐν τοῖς οὐρανοῖς.	εἶπεν δὲ αὐτῷ ὁ Ἰησοῦς, <u>Τί με λέγεις ἀγαθόν;</u> οὐδεὶς ἀγαθὸς εἰ μὴ εἷς ὁ θεός.	ὁ δὲ Ἰησοῦς εἶπεν αὐτῷ, <u>Τί με λέγεις ἀγαθόν;</u> οὐδεὶς ἀγαθὸς εἰ μὴ εἷς ὁ θεός.	ἀπεκρίνατο λέγων: <u>Οὐδεὶς ἀγαθὸς εἰ μὴ μόνος ὁ θεός</u>, ὁ ποιήσας τὰ πάντα.

Justin first follows Luke in Διδάσκαλε ἀγαθέ, and then conflates the Lukan Τί με λέγεις ἀγαθόν; and the Matthean εἷς ἐστιν ἀγαθός and ends up in the typical Matthean formulation: ὁ πατήρ μου ὁ ἐν τοῖς οὐρανοῖς.

We can observe the tendency of Justin to read the parallel pericopes in a Synoptic and harmonizing way, thereby producing a mixture of the Matthean and Lukan texts, a tendency that is not only at work here, but is typical of the way Justin deals with the text of the Synoptic Gospels in general. In many of his Gospel citations we find him combining and mingling cola and parts of verses from Luke and Matthew into the artful compositions of his Gospel citations. In this paper I will give only one other example of this kind of treatment in the works of Justin, his use of Matt 1:20–21//Luke 1:31–32 in two places in his *Apology*:

---

26. See Arthur J. Bellinzoni, *The Sayings of Jesus in the Writings of Justin Martyr* (NovTSup 17; Leiden: Brill, 1967), 17–20.

Justin, 1 Apol. 33.8	Justin, 1 Apol. 33.5	Matt 1:20–21	Luke 1:30–32	Matt 1:18
ὅθεν καὶ <u>ὁ ἄγγελος πρὸς τὴν παρθένον εἶπε</u>·	καὶ ὁ ἀποσταλεὶς δὲ <u>πρὸς αὐτὴν τὴν παρθένον</u> κατ' ἐκεῖνο τοῦ καιροῦ ἄγγελος θεοῦ εὐηγγελίσατο αὐτὴν εἰπών·	ταῦτα δὲ αὐτοῦ ἐνθυμηθέντος ἰδοὺ <u>ἄγγελος</u> κυρίου κατ' ὄναρ ἐφάνη αὐτῷ λέγων, Ἰωσὴφ υἱὸς Δαυίδ, μὴ φοβηθῇς παραλαβεῖν Μαριὰμ τὴν γυναῖκά σου,	καὶ <u>εἶπεν ὁ ἄγγελος αὐτῇ</u>, Μὴ φοβοῦ, Μαριάμ, εὗρες γὰρ χάριν παρὰ τῷ θεῷ·	Τοῦ δὲ Ἰησοῦ Χριστοῦ ἡ γένεσις οὕτως ἦν. μνηστευθείσης τῆς μητρὸς αὐτοῦ Μαρίας τῷ Ἰωσήφ,
	<u>Ἰδοὺ συλλήψῃ ἐν γαστρὶ ἐκ πνεύματος ἁγίου</u>	τὸ γὰρ ἐν αὐτῇ γεννηθὲν <u>ἐκ πνεύματός</u> ἐστιν <u>ἁγίου</u>.	<u>καὶ ἰδοὺ συλλήμψῃ ἐν γαστρὶ</u>	πρὶν ἢ συνελθεῖν αὐτοὺς εὑρέθη <u>ἐν γαστρὶ</u> ἔχουσα <u>ἐκ πνεύματος ἁγίου</u>.
	<u>καὶ τέξῃ υἱὸν καὶ υἱὸς ὑψίστου κληθήσεται</u>,		<u>καὶ τέξῃ υἱόν</u>,	
<u>Καὶ καλέσεις τὸ ὄνομα αὐτοῦ Ἰησοῦν· αὐτὸς γὰρ σώσει τὸν λαὸν αὐτοῦ ἀπὸ τῶν ἁμαρτιῶν αὐτῶν.</u>	<u>καὶ καλέσεις τὸ ὄνομα αὐτοῦ Ἰησοῦν, αὐτὸς γὰρ σώσει τὸν λαὸν αὐτοῦ ἀπὸ τῶν ἁμαρτιῶν αὐτῶν,</u> ὡς οἱ ἀπομνημονεύσαντες πάντα τὰ περὶ τοῦ σωτῆρος ἡμῶν Ἰησοῦ Χριστοῦ ἐδίδαξαν, οἷς ἐπιστεύσαμεν.	<u>καὶ καλέσεις τὸ ὄνομα αὐτοῦ Ἰησοῦν, αὐτὸς γὰρ σώσει τὸν λαὸν αὐτοῦ ἀπὸ τῶν ἁμαρτιῶν αὐτῶν.</u>	<u>καὶ καλέσεις τὸ ὄνομα αὐτοῦ Ἰησοῦν.</u> οὗτος ἔσται μέγας καὶ υἱὸς ὑψίστου κληθήσεται, καὶ δώσει αὐτῷ κύριος ὁ θεὸς τὸν θρόνον Δαυὶδ τοῦ πατρὸς αὐτοῦ.	

In this exhibit we not only see Justin's tendency to mix the Synoptic parallels in citing the Gospel text, but we can also make another interesting observation: In both passages Justin introduces his citations as the words the angel said to Mary, although in citing Matt 1:21 (καὶ καλέσεις τὸ ὄνομα αὐτοῦ Ἰησοῦν, αὐτὸς γὰρ σώσει τὸν λαὸν αὐτοῦ ἀπὸ τῶν ἁμαρτιῶν αὐτῶν) he is using the very words that, according to Matthew, the angel spoke to Joseph in a vision! I think that when Justin used the conflation of Lukan and Matthean passages he was not aware that he was citing two promises that in their original setting were addressed to two different persons. This observation is a strong argument for the assumption that Justin is falling back on an existing collection of scriptural testimonies produced in a scholarly environment.

This way of dealing with the New Testament text presupposes a large amount of textual and scholarly work with the aim of getting back behind the different texts to the one Gospel of Jesus. This sort of handling of the text of the Gospels hints at the sociological background of this enterprise. The *Sitz im Leben* of the citations of Justin and their textual form appear to have been the school of Justin in Rome, where the texts were not only used for theological argumentation but were also reworked for this purpose.[27]

The list of witnesses points in the same direction. Most of them by far are found in the works of early Christian teachers who were heads of free Christian schools functioning after the model of the philosophical schools—Clement of Alexandria and Tatian. In addition, the Markosians and the Gnostics cited by Hippolytus worked as teachers in a scholarly environment.

This list of witnesses also reveals that this special kind of reworking of the text of the New Testament is not a peculiarity of certain theological groups that later were called heretical. Moreover, it has nothing to do with certain theological preferences—as if heretics and orthodox were more prone to this kind of tampering with the text. It has to do, rather, with the *Sitz im Leben* of such *florilegia* in Christian schools. Exponents of free theological schools, be they Gnostics, such as the Marcosians of Irenaeus and the Naassenes of Hippolytus, or the ecclesiastical counterparts of the heretics, such as Clement of Alexandria, show the same way of handling the text they found in their manuscripts.

Let me make my point by referring to the Gnostics cited by Hippolytus. He himself was no longer the exponent of a free Christian school, but the self-confident bishop of the church of Rome. He fought against Gnostics and other heretics in his antiheretical chief work *Refutatio omnium haeresium*, written in 220 C.E., citing and paraphrasing many original Gnostic documents that are now lost. This material is usually called "the gnostic *Sondergut*" of Hippolytus. What makes this material so valuable for our purpose is that the majority of the texts derive from one and the same Gnostic Christian school, where they were produced, used, commented on, or reworked. Examining the biblical citations in Hippolytus's accounts of different heretical schools, we can take an in-depth look into a Gnostic school. We learn how a certain Christian Gnostic school in the time of Justin Martyr dealt with the text of the New Testament. Their way of handling the text is quite similar to what we have observed Justin doing with his New Testaments citations.

Thus, it is not accidental that the shape Matt 19:17 assumed in the report of Hippolytus about the Naassenes is akin to the text of Justin:

---

27. See Bellinzoni, *Sayings*, 141: "Justin and his pupils apparently used the synoptic gospels as their primary source and composed church catechisms and vade mecums by harmonizing material from the synoptic gospels."

Matt 19:17	Hipp., Haer.5.7.26	Mark 10:17	Luke 18:19
Τί με ἐρωτᾷς περὶ τοῦ ἀγαθοῦ;	τί με λέγεις ἀγαθόν;	<u>Τί με λέγεις ἀγαθόν;</u>	<u>Τί με λέγεις ἀγαθόν;</u>
<u>εἷς ἐστιν ὁ ἀγαθός.</u>	εἷς ἐστιν ἀγαθός,	οὐδεὶς ἀγαθὸς εἰ μὴ εἷς ὁ θεός.	οὐδεὶς ἀγαθὸς εἰ μὴ εἷς ὁ θεός.
1	ὁ πατήρ μου ὁ ἐν τοῖς οὐρανοῖς·		
ὅτι <u>τὸν ἥλιον αὐτοῦ ἀνατέλλει ἐπὶ</u> πονηροὺς καὶ ἀγαθοὺς <u>καὶ βρέχει ἐπὶ</u> δικαίους καὶ ἀδίκους.	ὃς ἀνατέλλει τὸν ἥλιον αὐτοῦ ἐπὶ δικαίους καὶ ἀδίκους καὶ βρέχει ἐπὶ ὁσίους καὶ ἁμαρτωλούς		

The source Hippolytus is using has produced a textual mixture of Matt 19:17 and the Lukan parallel, just as Justin did. It then goes on citing Matt 5:45, where we read, "the father in heaven makes his sun rise on the evil and the good." I think the combination of Matt 19:17 and Matt 5:45 is the reason for the addition of "the father in heaven" (ὁ πατήρ μου ὁ ἐν τοῖς οὐρανοῖς), providing a bridge between the verses. It is possible that the addition of "the father in heaven" in Justin's citation has a similar background.

Support for this view can be found in a citation of Matt 19:17 in Clement of Alexandria: «οὐδεὶς ἀγαθός, εἰ μὴ ὁ πατήρ μου ὁ ἐν τοῖς οὐρανοῖς» ἐπὶ τούτοις αὖθις «ὁ πατήρ μου» φησὶν «ἐπιλάμπει τὸν ἥλιον τὸν αὐτοῦ ἐπὶ πάντας» (*Paed.* 1.8.72.2–3 [Stählin 132.13–15]). This combination of Matt 19:17 with Matt 5:45 found in Hippolytus and Clement appears to have already been part of a given tradition.

In any case, we find in Hippolytus's source the same harmonizing kind of citation and redaction of Gospel texts, combining Matthean wording with Lukan parallels.

What we find here is not a precanonical text form but a secondary testimony for the so called canonical text. To me it seems quite obvious that Justin Martyr already knew and used the so called canonical edition of the New Testament.[28] In many of his citations of the Gospels we find a school

---

28. Although Oskar Skarsaune ("Justin and His Bible," in *Justin Martyr and His Worlds* [ed. Sara Parvis and Paul Foster; Minneapolis: Fortress, 2007], 53–76) writes, "In conclusion . . . it seems to me that Justin is to be placed before, not after, the grand edition of the Christian Bible postulated by Trobisch" (p. 75), he gives strong arguments for the dependence of Justin on a "protocanonical collection" of New Testament writings, containing the four Gospels as well as the letters of

text based on the text of the Four Gospel collection and forming a collection of proof-texts for pedagogical and apologetic purposes, an example of Eldon Epp's "interpretive text-form." These texts, however, were not written first on the pages of Matthew, Mark, or Luke but had their *Sitz im Leben* in the school traditions and their handbooks, which were not only used in the school of Justin but were probably also exchanged between different schools. Such *florilegia* may have had an influence on the New Testament manuscript tradition later on.

Looking at the harmonizing citations of Justin and his followers, we find them to be very old and valuable witnesses of the text that underlies their theological and exegetical work, but these citations give no hints to a "predecessor text" of the Gospels. They derive from the entity I would still be inclined to call the initial text, and thereby they give us insights into the earliest history of the tradition and thus help us to get as close as possible to the original text!

3. Conclusions

The exploration of the history of the living text of the Gospel leads us back to the concept of an "original text." If I speak as a textual critic, I am using the term "original text" to denote the author's text of a certain writing: the short form of the Lord's Prayer without the additions coming from the Gospel of Matthew could be or probably is the original text of this oration in the Gospel of Luke. In the context of the literary work known to us as the Gospel of Luke, this form of the text is the oldest available form of that prayer. The same is true for the text of Matt 19:17 as supported by the old and trustworthy witnesses and thus accepted by most modern critical editions. This is the text that textual criticism can reach by using all the available evidence from manuscripts, early translations, and citations. This passage certainly is a reliable example of the hypothetical reconstruction we call the initial text.

In the *Editio Critica Maior*, the evaluation of the manuscript tradition by means of the Coherence-Based Genealogical Method[29] leads to a

---

Paul (pp. 72–76). If Justin speaks of "the Memoirs" that the apostles produced, "which are called Gospels" (*1 Apol.* 66.3) and lets Trypho speak about the "so-called Gospel" of the Christians (*Dial.* 10.2), while on the other hand he knows that these "Memoirs" were written down by the apostles "and their followers" (*Dial.* 103.8), it seems quite obvious that Justin "already knew the concept of four Gospels, two of which had direct apostolic authorship (Matthew and John) and two of which were written by followers of the apostles: Mark by Peter's follower and Luke by Paul's" (Skaursaume, 72). But this concept presupposes the existence of the "canonical edition"!

29. See Gerd Mink, "Eine umfassende Genealogie der neutestamentli-

hypothesis concerning the initial text (in German the *"Ausgangstext"*) of this whole tradition. To say something about the status of this *"Ausgangstext"* in the process of analyzing the textual flow in the manuscript tradition may be of some value for the discussion of the problems concerning the notion of "original text."

In this method the quest for the initial text that lies behind the whole tradition as it is known today and as it is represented by all the relevant manuscripts, the early versions, and the citations is intrinsically tied to the reconstruction of the history of transmission in its totality. We begin our research with the status quo of today and try to bring this complete evidence into a genealogical order, so that stemmatology can be used to display the textual flow within the New Testament tradition.

Starting from local genealogies of those units of variation for which philological reasoning allows a reasonable and safe decision on the priority or posteriority of readings, we are able to conceive a picture of the textual flow between the manuscripts—or rather the states of text represented by the manuscripts—that contain these readings. So the sum of philological decisions leads, on the one hand, to a first and still incomplete hypothesis concerning the initial text of the tradition and, on the other hand, to a picture of the textual flow between the states of text. The information about the relationships between the different states of the text and their coherence may, in a second methodological step, lead to a modification of our picture of the relations between the readings we have established with the first evaluation. The second phase also gives us the opportunity to reconsider the cases where decisions were not possible before. So the knowledge concerning the textual flow within the manuscript transmission has an influence on the hypothesis about the initial text. The reconstruction of the initial text on the basis of a developing picture of the textual history is an iterative process. By means of this pro-

---

chen Überlieferung," *NTS* 39 (1993): 481–99; idem, "Editing and Genealogical Studies: The New Testament," *Literary and Linguistic Computing* 15 (2000): 51–56; idem, "Was verändert sich in der Textkritik durch die Beachtung genealogischer Kohärenz?" in *Recent Developments in Textual Criticism: New Testament, Other Early Christian and Jewish Literature. Papers Read at a Noster Conference in Münster, January 4–6, 2001* (ed. Wim Weren and Dietrich-Alex Koch; Studies in Theology and Religion 8; Assen: Royal Van Gorcum, 2003), 39–68; idem, "Problems of a Highly Contaminated Tradition, the New Testament: Stemmata of Variants as a Source of a Genealogy for Witnesses," in *Studies in Stemmatology II* (ed. Pieter van Reenen, August den Hollander, and Margot van Mulken; Amsterdam and Philadelphia: John Benjamins, 2004), 13–85. The method can now also be used online (http://intf.uni-muenster.de/cbgm/en), and there is a very instructive introduction by Gerd Mink available (www.uni-muenster.de/NTTextforschung/ cbgm_presentation/download.html).

cess we can expect to reach a plausible hypothesis concerning the initial text from which the whole tradition started and which best explains the multiple text forms existing in this tradition.

I think we have good reason to be confident that in the majority of the places of variation we can reconstruct the initial text of our manuscript tradition; we already are very close to that goal, especially where the *Editio Critica Maior* exists. But, on the other hand, we still have to ask what state of text we have reconstructed as a starting point of our existing manuscript tradition.

I therefore opt for the view that, in most cases, we can get back to the beginning of our manuscript tradition, which according to David Trobisch's theory would bring us as far back as the middle of the second century,[30] as long as we have no reliable data that lead us behind the canonical redaction of the New Testament. However, as long as we have no evidence that suggests a radical break in the textual transmission between the author's text and the initial text of our tradition, the best hypothesis concerning the original text still remains the reconstructed archetype to which our manuscript tradition and the evidence of early translations and the citations point.

In most cases we are able to produce a valid and stable hypothesis about the original text where there are variant readings in the text of the Greek New Testament. The reconstruction of the original text of the New Testament is of vital theological and historical interest: we want to know what Paul really wrote to the Romans and what was the original form of the Gospel of Luke. The quest for the original text does not as such involve contradictions and logical impossibilities. The goal may be much harder to achieve than was believed before, but why should we not try to get as far back to the roots as possible?

---

30. David Trobisch, *Die Endredaktion des Neuen Testaments: Eine Untersuchung zur Entstehung der christlichen Bibel* (NTOA 31; Freiburg: Universitätsverlag;,Göttingen: Vandenhoeck & Ruprecht, 1996); idem, *The First Edition of the New Testament* (Oxford: Oxford University Press, 2000).

3
THE NEED TO DISCERN DISTINCTIVE EDITIONS OF THE NEW TESTAMENT IN THE MANUSCRIPT TRADITION

David Trobisch

The role of printed critical editions of literary works written and published in antiquity is twofold. On the one hand, they are expected to present a scholarly reconstruction of the initial text, and, on the other hand, they have to document the manuscript evidence used to reconstruct the initial text.

A few decades ago the manuscript evidence of the New Testament was accessible to the scholar only through printed photographs of a handful of the most important codices. With the advent of digital photography and the inexpensive dissemination of visual information through the Internet, however, the ultimate goal of making images of every page of every manuscript accessible anywhere in the world is within reach today.[1]

In the past, critical editions had to be selective about the places where variants were noted, and they had to concentrate on the witnesses considered crucial to the history of the text. By doing so, editions gave scholars a rudimentary sense of what the manuscript evidence looked like. In the near future, however, one will have access to the data through electronic editions, and it will not be necessary to limit the collation of readings to only a few places and only a selection of manuscripts. No printed edition will be able to provide this kind of access to the evidence. So what will the role of printed critical editions like the *Editio Critica Maior* become? In the

---

1. David Trobisch, "From New Testament Manuscripts to a Central Electronic Database," in *Bible and Computer: The Stellenbosch AIBI-6 Conference. Proceedings of the Association Internationale Bible et Informatique 'From Alpha to Byte,'* (ed. Johann Cook; Leiden: Brill, 2002), 427–33.

following I suggest that their role will be to describe not only the initial text but to provide information about the editorial features of different editions as they are documented in the manuscripts.

Although it is undoubtedly accurate that the transmission of a literary work over time is the transmission of an initial text, it is at the same time true that this text is packaged in ever-changing ways as it is handed down from generation to generation and that the editorial package considerably modifies the message of the text.

Any page of a printed modern translation of the New Testament will contain textual and nontextual elements that originated at different stages during the production and transmission of literature. Some of these elements will have been provided by the translator, but typesetters, editors, publishers, and readers will have left their mark as well. Manuscripts that were published in antiquity, that is, that were produced in numbers and with the intent to be distributed to a reading public, show comparable textual and nontextual features.[2]

Looking at the end of Paul's letter to the Romans in a printed translation of the New Testament, one might find any or all of the following elements: a footnote, which reflects the work of contemporary editors; verse numbers, which originated in the sixteenth century; the famous doxology Rom 16:25–27, which is missing in some manuscripts and might be the result of second-century editors; the layout of the page and the page numbers, reflecting redactional decisions of the publisher of the print edition; perhaps marks and notes added by readers, if the examined exemplar was used heavily; and the "text" itself, a translation from the Greek reflecting modern vernacular and thought.

Likewise a page from an ancient manuscript will contain editorial elements reflecting the work of scribe, editor, and publisher in addition to the text of the author. Variants may originate on each of these levels: authors in antiquity have sometimes overseen more than one edition of their own works, creating significant variants in the manuscript traditions.[3] Readers might add marginal notes that could find their way into the text as the next scribe copies the manuscript. Scribes are aware that they make mistakes and might create new variants by attempting to cor-

---

2. For images of examples in printed editions and in manuscripts, see David Trobisch, "Structural Markers in New Testament Manuscripts with Special Attention to Observations in Codex Boernerianus (G 012) and Papyrus 46 of the Letters of Paul," in *Layout Markers in Biblical Manuscripts and Ugaritic Tablets* (ed. Marjo C.A. Korpel and Josef M. Oesch; Pericope: Scripture as Written and Read in Antiquity 5; Assen: Van Gorcum, 2005), 177–90.

3. Hilarius Emonds, *Zweite Auflage im Altertum: Kulturgeschichtliche Studien zur Überlieferung der antiken Literatur* (Klassisch-Philologische Studien 14; Leipzig: Harrassowitz, 1941). Eusebius and Jerome are well-documented examples.

rect what they perceive as an error in their *Vorlage*. Editors often refuse to choose when they discover competing variants in the manuscript tradition; instead they tend to combine them to conflate readings.[4] Publishers create variants by trying to satisfy a perceived need of the marketplace; they may produce editions for lectionary purposes, which completely rearrange the text, or they may provide interlinear translations or commentaries or introductory material.

One is well advised to distinguish who caused a specific variant—author, reader, scribe, editor, or publishers—in order better to assess its value for the history of the text. If the creation of a stemma is intended, it is crucial to distinguish variants that are created during the process of production from variants that document a manuscript tradition.

The history of a literary text, therefore, is the history of its editions, and a critical edition of a literary text will want to document at least the first edition, the *editio princeps*.[5] But because the reconstruction of the *editio princeps*, like the reconstruction of the initial text, is the product of ever-changing scholarly consensus and thus ultimately elusive, a critical edition can fulfill its descriptive function only by describing the oldest documented editions as well.

For example, it has long been established that D/06, F/010, G/012, 0319, and 0320 witness a Greek edition of the Letters of Paul that was produced in antiquity, maybe even as early as the second century.[6] The decisive features of this archetype Z[7] are the colometric arrangement of the text, the absence of the Letter to the Hebrews, and a large number of shared variants that are missing from the rest of the manuscript tradition.

Some of these unique readings are the product of a deliberate editorial effort. Romans 16 contains several examples. In archetype Z the greetings to the congregation that met in the house of Prisca and Aquila is moved from the end of the sentence to the beginning (Rom 16:3–5):

Ἀσπάσασθε Πρίσκαν καὶ Ἀκύλαν τοὺς συνεργούς μου ἐν Χριστῷ Ἰησοῦ, <u>καὶ τὴν κατ' οἶκον αὐτῶν ἐκκλησίαν</u>, οἵτινες ὑπὲρ τῆς ψυχῆς μου τὸν

---

4. B. F. Westcott and F. J. A Hort, *The New Testament in the Original Greek*, vol. 2, *Introduction, Appendix* (2nd ed.; London: Macmillan, 1896), 47–52.

5. David Trobisch, "Das Neue Testament im Lichte des zweiten Jahrhunderts," in *Herkunft und Zukunft der neutestamentlichen Wissenschaft* (ed. Oda Wischmeyer; Neutestamentliche Entwürfe zur Theologie 6; Tübingen and Basel: Francke, 2003), 119–29.

6. Hermann Josef Frede, *Altlateinische Paulus-Handschriften* (AGLB 4; Freiburg: Herder, 1964).

7. Frede (*Altlateinische Paulus-Handschriften*, 94–97) proposed to refer to the archetype as Z.

ἑαυτῶν τράχηλον ὑπέθηκαν, οἷς οὐκ ἐγὼ μόνος εὐχαριστῶ ἀλλὰ καὶ πᾶσαι αἱ ἐκκλησίαι τῶν ἐθνῶν, ~~καὶ τὴν κατ' οἶκον αὐτῶν ἐκκλησίαν~~.

In 16:16b a whole sentence is removed and placed after 16:21: ἀσπάζονται ὑμᾶς αἱ ἐκκλησίαι πᾶσαι τοῦ Χριστοῦ. And the standard Pauline letter ending (cf. 2 Thess 3:18) ἡ χάρις τοῦ κυρίου ἡμῶν Ἰησοῦ Χριστοῦ μετὰ πάντων ὑμῶν ἀμήν is added after the final greetings to finish Romans.

These rearrangements are of a stylistic nature and may have been intended to increase the readability. To understand that the editors of the archetype Z tried to make the text flow better is crucial when a rearrangement at another place in this edition might invite the interpreter to speculate about a programmatic theological reason behind the change. A good example is 1Cor 14:34–35, where the famous passage "the women should be silent in churches" was removed and placed at the end of the chapter after v. 40. As standard commentaries will show, the rearrangement has sometimes been interpreted as an indication that these verses were not in the original "Pauline" text but were added later.[8] Although the point that theses sentences were not part of the letter that Paul sent to Corinth is well taken, it should not be argued on text-critical grounds citing the evidence reflected in archetype Z. The argument will have to be carried by other exegetical considerations such as structural-critical observations (the sentences interrupt the flow of thought, which is why the editors of archetype Z probably moved it) or by apparent discrepancies in the immediate context (in 1Cor 11:5 Paul has no problem with women praying and prophesying in church as long as they cover their heads).[9]

Usually new editions of familiar texts make an effort to be easily identified by their readers. One could, for example, distinguish the 26th edition of the Nestle text from the 25th edition by comparing their reconstructions of the initial text. However, one is better advised simply to look at the title sheet. Further, the extensive editorial introductions will tell us more about the intention of the editions than an analysis of the critical decisions that led to the variations in text could do. Even a casual reader could distinguish these editions by noticing the different Greek fonts used.

---

8. For example, "Here it is better to assume an interpolation in the form of an early marginal gloss. This is suggested by the positioning of vv. 34–35 at the end of the chapter in the codices D, F, and G" (Marlene Crüsemann, "Irredeemably Hostile to Women: Anti-Jewish Elements in the Exegesis of the Dispute about Women's Right to Speak (1 Cor. 14.34–35)," *JSNT* 79 [2000]: 19–36, here 22). Cf. Gordon D. Fee, *The First Epistle to the Corinthians* (NICNT; Grand Rapids: Eerdmans, 1987), 699–701; Wolfgang Schrage, *Der erste Brief an die Korinther* (4 vols.; EKKNT 7; Zurich: Benziger, 1999), 3:481-82.

9. Jerome Murphy-O'Connor ("Interpolations in 1 Corinthians," *CBQ* 48 [1986]: 81–94, esp. 90–92) puts little weight on the text-critical argument.

Apparent differences between editions apply to manuscripts as well. Different Byzantine editions in minuscule manuscripts can be distinguished by looking at the material added in the introductions, the appendixes, and in the margins.[10]

If the history of a literary text is the history of its editions, what then is the function of a critical edition of a literary work from antiquity? It is easier to say what a critical edition should not attempt to do: it should not try to reconstruct the author's text. Other methods—such as forgery criticism, or redaction criticism in combination with source and tradition criticism—aim to reconstruct the author's text before it was edited for publication.

Instead, a critical edition of an ancient text should try to provide pertinent information needed to reconstruct the text in its earliest published form, the *editio princeps*. Present editions of the New Testament are so focused on the text line, the initial text, that the larger picture is easily missed. For example, it is beyond reasonable doubt, that Acts was part of the volume containing the General Letters, serving as a sort of introduction to these letters and to the Pauline Corpus.[11] The editions of Tischendorf, Westcott and Hort, and von Soden reflected this order. But with the advent and popular success among Bible translators of the Nestle edition, which followed the Byzantine manuscripts by placing the Corpus Paulinum between Acts and General Letters, the arrangement of the *editio princeps* has been lost in almost every current edition of the New Testament.

---

10. Hermann von Soden, *Die Schriften des Neuen Testaments in ihrer ältesten erreichbaren Textgestalt hergestellt auf Grund ihrer Textgeschichte*, I, *Untersuchungen*, II, *Abteilung: Textformen* (Berlin: Arthur Glaue, 1907) 717: "Unter der grossen Zahl von Codd., die sich als Zeugen der K zu erkennen, gaben, gilt es nun Ordnung zu schaffen, die besonderen Spielarten des Textes oder der Ausstattungen herauszustellen, diese zu beschreiben und womöglich in den Gang der Entwicklung einzugliedern." Examples of characteristics used by von Soden to distinguish editions are the presence and form of Eusebius's letter concerning his canons, the titles and numbering of κεφάλαια, the numbering of sections and canons, and the notes marking the lectionary readings (pp. 719–20). Von Soden's description and transcriptions of *"Beigaben"* that define the different *"Ausstattungen"* are an invaluable resource to the student of New Testament minuscule manuscripts (pp. 292–485). Von Soden did not have the possibility of collating the text of Byzantine manuscripts extensively in order to support his assessment of differing historical editions of the Koine. Klaus Wachtel's seminal study, *Der byzantinische Text der katholischen Briefe: Eine Untersuchung zur Entstehung der Koine des Neuen Testaments* (ANTF 24; Berlin and New York: de Gruyter, 1995), which is based on the now available documented variants, strongly supports von Soden's classifications (especially K^r).

11. David Trobisch, *The First Edition of the New Testament* (Oxford: Oxford University Press, 2000), 26–28.

A critical edition of the Greek New Testament should strive to provide more than the reconstructed initial text. It should provide information about the title of the book and the titles of the individual writings, about the collection units, about nontextual features such as the *nomina sacra* and codex form, which were part of the first edition and which informed later editors and publishers as they adapted the text for their readership. In addition to describing the editorial features of the the first edition, it should document the text in the framework of its historical editions as they are reflected in the extant manuscript tradition.

4
CONCEPTUALIZING "SCRIBAL" PERFORMANCES: READER'S NOTES

Ulrich Schmid

When dealing with copies of literary texts from antiquity, the default assumption is that the physical manuscript is the work of the/a scribe.[1] Ink on papyrus or parchment confronts us with the work of scribes—the copyists of ancient literature. Hence the complete set of physical writing as found in a given manuscript can be used to describe the scribal activity that resulted in this very artifact. Or, to put it differently: every trace of writing as found in a copy of ancient literature is a scribal performance. The intention of this article is to challenge that default assumption. In contrast, I will argue that not everyone who left traces of writing on a manuscript actually performed in the role of a scribe. Or, to put it positively: there are more roles to detect in physical writing than just scribal activity. It is vital for New Testament textual critics to acknowledge, study, and describe these different roles in order to develop a better understanding of the mechanics and agents of late antique book production. This should help us to develop ideas for placing the various types of observable textual variation between the many copies of one and the same text with one or the other role.

In my article "Scribes and Variants—Sociology and Typology," I have already identified two activities that in my view transcend the normal copying activities. One is the case of editorial work on the texts, such as adding a new ending to the Gospel of Mark, or embellishing (Rom 16:24,

---

[1]. The present article is intended to further develop points that I have made in a previous article: "Scribes and Variants—Sociology and Typology," in *Textual Variation: Theological and Social Tendencies? Papers from the Fifth Birmingham Colloquium on the Textual Criticism of the New Testament* (ed. H. A. G. Houghton and D. C. Parker; Texts & Studies, Third Series 6; Piscataway, N.J.: Gorgias, 2009), 1–23.

25–27) and reordering the ending of Paul's Letter to the Romans (Rom 14:23ff.). As I have argued, using the ending of Romans as an example, these cases are best understood as conscious and deliberate efforts to improve on the text in front of the editor(s). Therefore, the resulting textual versions exhibit "comparison of different versions of texts or literary reasoning."[2] The other case I have presented is the case of reader's notes, places at which some more or less perceptive readers of the text jotted down in the margin a note to a particular passage. Some of these notes could have been copied into the text by scribes who had to copy such an "embellished" *Vorlage*. In the present article I shall apply further evidence and reflection to this issue.

In order to make my case I will start with a short review of current thinking on the issue of scribal performances. Second, I will rehearse and augment my previous discussion on reader's notes with special emphasis on the phenomenological aspects. Third, I shall discuss scribal challenges with marginal notes as perceived by the ancients. Fourth, an interpretation of some variants from the Gospel tradition as originating from marginal reader's notes will be presented. Finally, by way of conclusion, separate phases in the process of literary production/reproduction in antiquity will be phenomenologically described. This might be of service for conceptualizing not only scribal performances but even more importantly the complex mechanics of textual transmission.

1. Current Thinking about Scribal Performances

It hardly comes as a surprise that the way scholars interpret scribal products largely informs their view of scribal performances. The most obvious scribal products are the variants they produce, when compared to other copies of the same text. Thus, the study of scribal performances largely concentrates on the study of variant readings. As far as I can see, there are two angles from which approaches have been made. One angle is the study of scribal habits—the names of Ernest Cadman Colwell, James Royse, Barbara Aland, and recently Kyoung Shik Min[3] come to mind—

---

2. Schmid, "Scribes and Variants," 14.
3. E. C. Colwell, "Method in Evaluating Scribal Habits: A Study of 𝔓⁴⁶, 𝔓⁶⁶, 𝔓⁷⁵," in idem, *Studies in Methodology in Textual Criticism of the New Testament* (NTTS 9; Leiden: Brill, 1969), 106–24, originally published as "Scribal Habits in Early Papyri: A Study in the Corruption of the Text," in *The Bible in Modern Scholarship: Papers Read at the 100th Meeting of the Society of Biblical Literature, December 28–30, 1964* (ed. J. Philip Hyatt; Nashville: Abingdon, 1965), 370–89; James R. Royse, "Scribal Habits in Early New Testament Papyri" (Th.D. diss., Graduate Theological Union, 1981), later revised, augmented, and published as *Scribal Habits in Early Greek New Testament Papyri* (NTTSD 36; Leiden: Brill, 2008); Barbara Aland, "Neu-

while the other one is the study of theological/ideological intentionality behind variants; this strand of research is associated with the names of Eldon Epp, Bart Ehrman, and more recently Wayne C. Kannaday.[4] Without going into too much detail, I think it is fair to say that both approaches result in different perceptions of the work of scribes. Those who lay emphasis on scribal intentionality or even "orthodox corruption" can view scribes as taking at times great liberty while transcribing. Scribes are seen as driven by personal convictions, almost acting as agents of the correct understanding. In their efforts to reinforce the correct understanding, they did not hesitate to change their *Vorlage*. Scribes are thus seen as interpreters, editors, or even authors.

On the other hand, those who study scribal habits on the basis of the earliest manuscript evidence usually emphasize that there is little empirical evidence to that effect. The most obvious phenomena in manuscripts that they detect are mistakes, dropped words, idiosyncratic spellings, and the like. Occasional readings that appear to be conscious clarifications notwithstanding, the vast majority of readings as found in the earliest New Testament manuscripts are reflective of the one and only activity of scribes, namely, copying their *Vorlage* as faithfully as they could. Of course, some achieved a better result than others, but even those scribes who handle their *Vorlage* more freely do so within the limits of what can be perceived as an act of copying a *Vorlage*. Should scribes therefore be seen as copyists or as interpreters?

Apparently the evidence is somewhat complex and seems to support both perspectives. Even those sympathizing with the view of scribes as copyists cannot ignore the fact that the New Testament textual tradition as a whole does indeed contain phenomena that are not simply the result of copying a *Vorlage*. I take the ending of the Gospel of Mark as a case in point. On the assumption that the ending we find in the vast majority

---

testamentliche Handschriften als Interpreten des Textes? 𝔓[75] und seine Vorlagen in Joh 10," in *Jesu Rede von Gott und ihre Nachgeschichte im frühen Christentum. Beiträge zur Verkündigung Jesu und zum Kerygma der Kirche. Festschrift für Willi Marxsen zum 70. Geburtstag* (ed. Dietrich-Alex Koch, Gerhard Sellin, and Andreas Lindemann; Gütersloh: G. Mohn, 1989), 379–95; K. S. Min, *Die früheste Überlieferung des Matthäusevangeliums (bis zum 3./4. Jh.): Edition und Untersuchung* (ANTF 34; Berlin and New York: de Gruyter, 2006).

4. Bart D. Ehrman, *The Orthodox Corruption of Scripture: The Effect of Early Christological Controversies on the Text of the New Testament* (New York: Oxford University Press, 1993); Eldon Jay Epp, *The Theological Tendency of Codex Cantabrigiensis in Acts* (SNTSMS 3; Cambridge: Cambridge University Press, 1966); Wayne Kannaday, *Apologetic Discourse and the Scribal Tradition: Evidence of the Influence of Apologetic Interests on the Text of the Canonical Gospels* (SBLTCS 5; Atlanta: Society of Biblical Literature, 2004).

of manuscripts (Mark 16:9–20) is secondary, we have to conclude that a serious and conscious rewriting of the tradition at that point has taken place. This is not a scribal activity that forms part of a copying process. Furthermore, there are additional places in the tradition that are also likely the result of not just copying but some other activity. Therefore, we need to account for that type of phenomena within a concept of "scribal" activities that at the same time does justice to the normal role of scribes as copyists, which is well documented from the study of the earliest New Testament manuscripts. In what follows, the case of reader's notes is developed as part of the nonscribal activity that is evidenced by the New Testament textual tradition.

2. Reader's Notes as Nonscribal Activity

2.1 SCRIBAL AND NONSCRIBAL ACTIVITIES: A FUNCTIONAL DISTINCTION

Interpreting readings in a manuscript as the result of nonscribal activity seems counterintuitive. When reading manuscripts, however, we occasionally meet words or even entire sentences in the margins or between the lines that stand out visually as not forming part of the usual layout of the main text. This mere observation in my view serves as a reminder, even a necessary stumbling block, to start reflecting about the differing roles and objectives of those who put ink on papyrus or parchment. Whereas we are usually on the safe side to view the main body of text on a page/sheet as a scribal product in the proper sense, all the other additional materials we find in the margin or between the lines merits further examination as to what exactly their function is and why and by whom these materials might have been added. There is in my view no default assumption that we should view all of that "marginal" activity as scribal performances, at least not as functioning on the same level as the work of the person who penned the main text. This is certainly true for copies of literary texts that are distant from the autograph and in which different hands could refer to different activities. Whereas the main scribe usually acted as a copyist, hands in the margins or between lines could as well belong to people who were just reading the text and taking down notes. The reasons for such notes could range from anecdotal observations to thoroughgoing diorthosis (correction) of the main text. The intentions behind such notes might as well evidence a broader range, from memory aid or cross-reference to preparing a corrected text that is intended to serve as a *Vorlage* and be copied. Again, this next step, that is, copying such a corrected exemplar, is a different activity from the one that corrected, at times even embellished, the manuscript that is now being copied. Thus, my contention is that the mere activities/logistics behind annotating and transcribing a text should be seen as indicative of different roles that should not to be lumped together under a single category, namely, scribal activity. In other words: I propose to adopt functional distinctions between the various modes of leaving traces of writing on papyrus/parchment in order to allow for a better understanding of the mechanics of textual transmission. The label "scribal activity," at least when it comes to observing scribal activity in New Testament manuscripts, should be restricted to the process of transcribing/copying an exemplar.

To be sure, a person who annotates a text while reading it can perform the role of copyist on another occasion. While he or she is annotating, however, he or she is not engaging in transcribing that text. A good illustration of such differing roles is the famous example of a perhaps thirteenth-century reader of Codex Vaticanus, who added next to Heb 1:3 in the margin the following comment: "Fool and knave, leave the old reading, do not change it!" (ἀμαθέστατε καὶ κακέ, ἄφες τὸν παλαιόν, μὴ μεταποίει), thus referring to a correction that had been made by a previous reader and reverting to the reading of the first hand. It is rather distracting to use this example as illustrating the roles of scribes.[5] Without any doubt, this is the comment uttered by an astute reader of (that passage of) Codex Vaticanus, entering into virtual dialogue with another reader, who has changed the text in front of both. He or she used a completely different script, being centuries separated from the first hand and the correction in Codex Vaticanus and there is no indication that he or she copied any part of that manuscript.

To sum up: I take the stand that there is evidence for readers contributing comments to the margin of copies they were reading, and I consider the activity of taking down such notes to be nonscribal activity in the sense that this role is functionally distinct from copying an exemplar.

2.2. CRITERIA FOR DISTINGUISHING SCRIBAL FROM NONSCRIBAL ACTIVITIES

The first criterion for establishing potential nonscribal activities on a manuscript page is the placement of the text on that page. In order to qualify, the passage has to be found outside of the usual writing space, whether written in the margin or cramped between two regular lines.

The second criterion has to do with another empirical observation, and that is the difference in script employed by the hands we find in anci-

---

5. This is the interpretation of Kim Haines-Eitzen, *Guardians of Letters: Literacy, Power, and the Transmitters of Early Christian Literature* (Oxford: Oxford University Press, 2000), 53, 110–11. For a critical assessment of that interpretation, see my review in *TC: A Journal of Biblical Textual Criticism* 7 (2002), §§7-8 (http://rosetta.reltech.org/TC/vol07/Haines-Eitzen2002reva.html).

ent manuscripts. Let me briefly elaborate on that. In antiquity, copies of literature are often written in what is called book-hands. These are hands geared toward readability and pleasing the eye. They exhibit regular letter forms, and few of them use abbreviations. Typical book-hands use majuscule letter forms. In contrast to these book-hands, we find what are called documentary hands, that is, types of script that are geared toward speed of writing and effective use of space. Documentary hands exhibit ligatures, varying letter forms, and abbreviations. Typical documentary hands employ a cursive type of script. The reason why the scripts are distinguished like this is the empirical observation that book-hands are usually employed for transmitting literature while documentary hands are routinely used when it comes to write down "everyday" texts like contracts and letters. Generally speaking, book-hands are much slower to write than documentary hands. Moreover, book-hands also require a certain type of expert knowledge that seems not to have been available to every individual who knew how to write.[6] At the same time, it is certainly appropriate to nuance this distinction by recalling the frequent observation that literary and documentary papyri "fall somewhere along the range between a literary and a documentary hand."[7] It is also particularly important to observe the professional developments and expertise among individual scribes as they learn to write and receive advanced training. Nevertheless, even their differences are observable and can be aligned with one end of the spectrum or the other. In addition, the basic observation seems valid, namely, that it is much more likely to find documentary texts written in a documentary hand than in what is associated with a book-hand and vice versa.

Rather than applying the distinction between book-hands and documentary hands to entire manuscripts in order to discern "the function of the text itself,"[8] my current analysis is more interested in discerning different types of hands in one and the same manuscript in order to learn more about scribal versus nonscribal activities. Now, who would use what type of hand when leaving traces in one and the same manuscript? It seems obvious that a more or less contemporary reader was not bound to use a formal book-hand for his or her marginal comments. Therefore, I would expect such a reader/user to employ a more casual and informal hand when compared to the book-hand of the main text. In fact, I would make this distinction a decisive test. Reader's notes, in order to be properly so

---

6. A very helpful summary of this papyrological "commonplace" is found in Haines-Eitzen, *Guardians of Letters*, 62–63.
7. Ibid., 62.
8. Ibid., 63.

called, have to employ a distinct type of hand, distinct from the book-handish text to which they refer.

To sum up: Non-scribal activity in the form of reader's notes should meet two criteria in order to be properly identified as such. (1) The text in question should be found "outside" of the main text's layout, either in the margin or between the lines. (2) It should have been crafted in a different, decidedly more informal type of script, when compared to the main text.

2.3 NONSCRIBAL ACTIVITY IN PAPYRUS BODMER XIV[9]

In Luke 17:11–19 we read the story of the cleansing of the ten lepers. In v. 14 Jesus addresses them by saying simply, "Go, show yourselves to the priests." No sign of compassion is expressed. We do not even find a healing command. A note in the lower margin of Papyrus Bodmer XIV, better known as $\mathfrak{P}^{75}$, supplies the missing words. "I will. Be clean. And immediately they became clean" (Θέλω καθαρίσθητε καὶ εὐθέως ἐκαθαρίσθησαν). With signs in the margin and between the lines it is clearly linked to Luke 17:14. In addition, it is written in a different hand. The thicker pen strokes and the compressed letters with cursive elements clearly betray elements of a different type of script. There are groups of letters that have been written without lifting the pen.[10] Individual letter forms show semicursive traits such as very characteristically the *eta* that is written in two strokes rather than in three, and there is a cursive, almost ligatured καὶ. By contrast, the book-hand employed by the scribe of $\mathfrak{P}^{75}$ has very few cursive elements. The letters are usually separated from each other and the same letter forms are used. Although by no means inexperienced, the hand of the marginal note is clearly less formal than the book-hand used to transcribe the text of Luke. It is exactly the type of hand that one would expect to be used for jotting down a note. Therefore, in my view, this marginal note qualifies for being viewed as a reader's note.

Where does this reading come from? The very same wording—though partially expanded—occurs in the story of the healing of one leper (Mark 1:41–42; Matt 8:3; Luke 5:13). On that occasion Jesus says, "I will. Be clean. And immediately the leprosy left him and he became clean" (Mark 1:41–42: θέλω, καθαρίσθητι· καὶ εὐθὺς ἀπῆλθεν ἀπ' αὐτοῦ ἡ λέπρα, καὶ ἐκαθαρίσθη.) The parallel passages have it similarly: "I will. Be clean. And instantly his leprosy was cleansed" (Matt 8:3: θέλω, καθαρίσθητι· καὶ εὐθέως ἐκαθαρίσθη αὐτοῦ ἡ λέπρα.), "I will. Be clean. And instantly his leprosy left him" (Luke 5:13: θέλω, καθαρίσθητι· καὶ εὐθέως ἡ λέπρα ἀπῆλθεν ἀπ' αὐτοῦ.). There can

---

9. The following paragraph is taken from my "Scribes and Variants," 18–21, with the illustration from Bodmer XIV on p. 19.

10. For example, the letter combinations θαρ in καθαρίσθητε and (θ)εως in εὐθέως.

be little doubt that the reader who took down the note at Luke 17:14 was consciously using that phrasing. These are words that Jesus had used on another occasion in a very similar encounter with another leper. Our reader knew the Gospels well. Since the Matthean version as printed in NA²⁷ comes closest, one might be inclined to ascribe to the reader knowledge of that Gospel. In this case it might be interesting to note that in its current status 𝔓⁷⁵ only includes text from two Gospels, Luke and John. And since it is a single-quire codex, it is hard to imagine that 𝔓⁷⁵ ever included more than just those two Gospels. Is this proof, then, that our reader knew at least one or both of the other Gospels as well, if not from this codex, than from another one? There are two observations that leave doubts. In the first place, the Lukan version in Codex Bezae reads θέλω, καθαρίσθητι· καὶ εὐθέως ἐκαθαρίσθη, which is even closer than the Matthean version, and unfortunately Luke 5:13 is not extant in 𝔓⁷⁵. Second, ἐκαθαρίσθησαν figures prominently in Luke 17:14–17. Therefore, the marginal note could have been inspired by that phrasing. In any case, it seems sufficiently clear that our reader is intertextually well attuned. Whether he or she intended the comment to be included in the text of Luke 17:14 we do not know. It is equally possible that it served as a reminder for the reader or a pointer to the other story.

As far as I can see, this marginal note did not make it into the main text of Luke 17:14 in any of the manuscripts explored for the International Greek New Testament Project's (IGNTP) edition of Luke. However, other variants are detected at that location that betray a similar tendency. Codex Bezae adds: "Be healed" (τεθεραπευεσθε), which functions similarly from the story's point of view. It is much less sophisticated, though, because it lacks any deeper intertextual reference. Minuscule 1071, on the other hand, reads: "Jesus was moved with compassion and said: 'Go and show yourselves to the priests'" (ὁ Ἰησοῦς ἐσπλαγχνίσθη καὶ εἶπεν . . .). That, again, may recall the story of the leper in the Markan version (1:41), though the compassionate Jesus is found also in other Synoptic passages (Matt 9:36; 14:14; 15:32; 20:34; Mark 1:41; 6:34; 8:2; 9:22; Luke 7:13; 10:33; 15:20). Thus, a similar intertextual aspiration seems to be operative in the reading from 1071. Hence, other readers too sensed a certain lack in this story of the ten lepers. This marginal note in 𝔓⁷⁵, however, appears to be the most conscious effort to augment this story by referencing a similar story verbatim.

After having developed a concept of reader's notes and studied an example from a New Testament manuscript, we now turn to the perspective of the ancients on this matter. The intention is to situate marginal notes within the logistics of textual (re-)production through the eyes of ancient authors of literary texts. Special attention will be given to the depiction of the role of scribes.

3. Scribal Challenges as Reflected by the Ancients: The Problem with Marginal Notes

Scholarship on the literary world of antiquity promulgates a simple truth about ancient reading experiences that is almost completely hidden from the modern reader, namely, the experience of imperfect copies: "For critical readers, the act of reading always involved an awareness of the fallibility of the text."[11] Whereas modern readers only very occasionally encounter what is then labeled "printing errors," ancient readers had to be and were aware of a much greater frequency of errors in the handwritten copies at their disposal. Hence, we find a number of comments and complaints from authors from (late) antiquity where they hint at such lamentable situations. In a recent study, *Der Autor und sein Text*,[12] Markus Mülke collected and commented on such complaints as they were uttered by ancient authors in view of the fate of their or their fellow colleague's literary products. Apart from more formal admonitions to the reader (*admonitio lectoris*), which is a topos that extends into the Middle Ages and beyond, ancient authors occasionally commented in passing about the casualties they suspected to have befallen the text in front of them. From these comments we get the impression that the default experience with literary texts in antiquity, indeed, was that of imperfect copies. Hence, an informed reading of texts almost routinely contained the element of the reader "correcting" (*emendatio*) the text in front of him or herself. This not only pertains to simple mistakes that are easily spotted—as scribes occasionally dropped words, which resulted in nonsense readings—but also involves wrong choices made by scribes while they were copying exemplars that contained marginal readings. This especially is relevant to our focus on reader's notes.

In order to appreciate the background for marginal readings, it seems appropriate to recall James E. G. Zetzel's observation based mainly on Latin classical manuscripts from antiquity: "Our manuscripts are those of amateurs and wealthy book-lovers; and like modern readers, they wrote comments in the margins, made corrections of errors where they noticed them, and generally created a book that was of service to themselves."[13]

---

11. H. Gregory Snyder, *Teachers and Texts in the Ancient World: Philosophers, Jews, and Christians* (Religion in the First Christian Centuries; London and New York: Routledge, 2000), 52.

12. Markus Mülke, *Der Autor und sein Text: Die Verfälschung des Originals im Urteil antiker Autoren* (Untersuchungen zur antiken Literatur und Geschichte 93; Berlin and New York: de Gruyter, 2008).

13. James E. G. Zetzel, *Latin Textual Criticism in Antiquity* (Monographs in Classical Studies; New York: Arno, 1981), 238.

Readers' notes can therefore be seen as part of the personal appropriation of a supposedly imperfect copy!

Particularly illuminating for the issue of marginal notes are comments by the famous late-second-century physicist Galen. On one occasion he highlights the confusion of a copyist of one of his books that was used in teaching, where he himself had placed an alternative reading in the margin of the main text. Apparently, only the reading of the main text was intended to be accepted, whereas the marginal alternative was only meant to be discussed. The first copyist of that book, however, copied both, and then the mistake was not corrected; hence the book circulated uncorrected in public.[14] In that case we have an author adding a marginal reading apparently intended for scholarly discussion in a public setting. But there are other reasons for marginal readings given by Galen himself, and that is marginalia for the sake of a memory aid (εἰς ὑπόμνησιν).[15] This is not only interesting in that it provides more background information on such marginal notes. It also makes it unmistakably clear that ancient authors viewed such instances as particularly challenging for scribes who had to copy embellished exemplars of that kind. Moreover, the common expectation, or rather experience, was that scribes made wrong choices when confronted with marginal readings. The inclination of scribes, at least in the view of the ancients, seems to have been toward the inclusion of marginal material into the main text. The very same expectation is expressed by Jerome in view of a reading he found in a Latin Psalter manuscript at Ps 73:8 (LXX, Vulgate).[16] There he suspects that a "clueless" (*temerarius*) copyist added into the main text a reading from one of Jerome's own marginal comments, which were intended to explain the reading of the Psalm text,. Some general advice for copyists follows: "Therefore, if something for the sake of study has been added to the margin, it should not be put into the main text."[17] Instances like these, where, almost by default and rather mechanically, material from the margin has been incorporated into the main text, are often easily spotted because the resulting text includes real oddities. A nice example is the marginal note of Augustinus to his secretary/copyist exhorting the fellow to find and

---

14. Ἐνὶ γάρ, ὑπὲρ ἑνὸς πράγματος διττῶς ἡμῶν γραψάντων, εἶτα τῆς μὲν ἑτέρας γραφῆς κατὰ τὸ ὕφος οὔσης, τῆς δ' ἑτέρας ἐπὶ θάτερα τῶν μετώπων, ὅπως κρίνωμεν αὐτῶν τὴν ἑτέραν ἐπὶ σχολῆς δοκιμάσαντες, ὁ πρῶτος μεταγράφων τὸ βιβλίον ἀμφότερα ἔγραψεν, εἶτα μὴ προσχόντων ἡμῶν τοῖς γεγονόσι μηδ' ἐπανορθωσαμένων τὸ σφάλμα, διαδόθεν εἰς πολλοὺς τὸ βιβλίον ἀνεπανόρθωτον ἔμεινεν (*Corpus Medicorum Graecorum* [CMG] 5.10.1, p. 43; citation has been reproduced from Mülke, *Autor*, 48; cf. 290).

15. *CMG* 5.10.2, p. 100; see Mülke, *Autor*, 47.

16. Jerome, *Epist.* 106.46 (CSEL 55:269–70).

17. Unde, si quid pro studio e latere additum est, non debet poni in corpore (CSEL 55:270); cf. Mülke, *Autor*, 48.

insert a reference/quotation to Aulus Gellius Noctes Atticae into the text of his *Quaestiones in Heptateuchum*. The secretary/copyist, however, simply inserted that note mechanically into the main text itself.[18]

Based on comments and examples such as these, it seems even more appropriate to reexamine our New Testament material in the light of the ancients' experience with scribes who wrongly incorporated text from the margins of their exemplars. The default assumption for such a scenario is that some readers of the Gospels added comments or notes like the one presented from $\mathfrak{P}^{75}$ to the margins of the copies they were reading.

4. Gospel Variants Interpreted as Reader's Notes

From our close reading of the marginal note in $\mathfrak{P}^{75}$ and other variants in Luke 17:14, we can tentatively extrapolate criteria for identifying reader's notes among the variants in the textual tradition of the New Testament. As we have seen, our reader of $\mathfrak{P}^{75}$ sensed a gap in the story. An element was felt to be missing and was therefore supplied. Apparently others sensed that gap as well, as we learn from the other readings of Codex Bezae and 1071. A similar example of that type is found in John 20:16–17, where a gap in the narrative has been detected, as evidenced by the testimony of some Greek, Latin, and Syriac witnesses. In 20:16, the risen Lord addresses Mary by calling out her name. She replies by calling him "Rabbuni" Then we read the explanatory gloss "which is to say, 'Teacher!'" After that, v. 17 has Jesus abruptly coming back to Mary and saying: "Don't touch me, for I haven't yet ascended to my Father." A small but widespread group of witnesses of the tradition in Greek, Latin, and Syriac read: "And she ran (toward him) in order to touch him"[19] between the two parts of the dialogue, in order to account for Jesus' solemn statement that otherwise seems poorly motivated from a narrative point of view. The motivation for the addition is therefore easily detected. The parallel example from the reader's note in $\mathfrak{P}^{75}$ in Luke 17:14 illustrates how the reading was probably generated, that is, in the margin. The comments from Galen and Jerome explain the mechanics of introducing this marginal note into the main text. Apparently, gaps in the narrative are one reason for supplying additional text. The inspiration (or aspiration) as to how to fill in that gap, however, can take different forms. Whereas the supplied text in the Johannine passage does not transcend the narrative's frame, the passage at the bottom margin of $\mathfrak{P}^{75}$ is rich at evoking inter-

---

18. CCSL 33:13: sed considerandum est quemadmodum hoc dicat A. Gellius et diligenter inserendum.

19. καὶ προσέδραμεν ἅψασται αὐτοῦ, as Corrector Ca in Codex Sinaiticus. Θ, Ψ and part of family 13 have it.

textual links to similar narratives from other parts of the Gospel(s). Both passages, however, are excellent examples of good quality amendments to narratives that appear to lack something for at least some readers. Hence, the narrative flow is improved rather than hampered.

If we now turn to marginal comments oddly introduced into the main text as illustrated by the example from Augustinus, we find examples of that in the Gospel tradition as well. One that comes to mind is a singular reading of W at Mark 13:33, about which Larry Hurtado has this to say:

> W inserts εἰ μὴ ὁ πατὴρ καὶ ὁ υἱός after οὐκ οἴδατε γάρ. This addition is out of character for the text of W, which generally has a more concise account. The variant occurs in a passage which says that no man knows the time of the end. The inserted words modify this statement to make it clear that the Father and Son do know the time. This is especially curious in that W preserves the usual text in Mark 13:32, which restricts this eschatological knowledge to the Father only. The addition here in 13:33 must be an attempt to soften the statement about Jesus' limited foreknowledge. The attempt is not well thought out, it seems, for the resultant text of W creates a contradiction between 13:32 and 13:33, and the opening phrase of 13:33, as it appears in W, is somewhat awkward.[20]

Because of the syntactic and contextual oddities that come with this reading it makes most sense, in my view, to explain its genesis as a reader's comment in the margin that was intended to balance the admonition that stresses the complete ignorance of the right time (καιρός). A reader wanted to express his or her firm belief that such complete ignorance is not including the Father nor the Son. A subsequent copyist included this note even in a syntactically questionable position in the main text, which resulted in a glaring contradiction to Mark 13:32. This is a classic example of a scribe mechanically copying a reading from the margin into the main text while barely paying attention to the context.

A famous instance of variation is found in Matt 27:49. Jesus on the cross has just received the vinegar (27:48), and some have expressed their curiosity: "Wait. Let's see, if Elijah comes and rescues him." Attached to that we read in a number of very ancient and important witnesses: "But someone else took a spear and opened his side, and water and blood came out."[21] And just thereafter Jesus cried out with a loud voice and gave up his spirit (27:50). The interjection of the spear incident at that point gives way to a startling interpretation of the sequence of events, in that it appears as if the piercing of Jesus' side has effectively caused his death.

---

20. Larry W. Hurtado, *Text-Critical Methodology and the Pre-Caesarean Text: Codex W in the Gospel of Mark* (SD 43; Grand Rapids: Eerdmans, 1981), 79.

21. Ἄλλος δὲ λαβὼν λόγχην ἔνυξεν αὐτοῦ τὴν πλευράν καὶ ἐξῆλθεν ὕδωρ καὶ αἷμα.

Despite the fact that this is the reading of the most ancient witnesses to the passage,[22] modern editions usually relegate the spear incident in Matt 27:49 to the apparatus, because it stems from John 19:34 and hardly fits in at that point in Matthew. It is reasonably close—that is, it relates to the final stages of Jesus' crucifixion—but it is just not right in Matthew. Therefore, it has long been suspected that a marginal note has crept in the text at that point.[23] A reader of Matthew jotted down a story element from another parallel Gospel account, in this case John 19:34, in the margin of his or her manuscript. Notice, again, the intertextual signature of the note. Notice, too, that the version of John 19:34 embodied in the text of Matt 27:49 is a slightly rephrased version, lacking the εὐθύς and having a reversed word order for water and blood when compared to John 19:34. This reader's note was likely never intended to be inserted into the text of Matthew, certainly not at that point, because it also violates the Johannine sequence of events. It could have been a pointer to the parallel account of John or a note to aid memory for an exposition. In any case one scribe who was copying that manuscript must have got it wrong and put it into the running text of Matthew. Further, this mistake must have happened at an early stage of the transmission, because it forms part of the oldest stratum of our extant textual tradition. In addition, the interpolated text must have been revered by some, because one manuscript, 030 (ninth century), has it assimilated toward the Johannine version by including εὐθέως and adapting the word order for blood and water from John 19:34.

In both of the aforementioned cases, the oddity of the resulting text with the interpolation can be sensed. I would finally like to point to a passage, however, where the interpolation again produces a good, even theologically reflective, text. After Mark 15:27, where it says that two criminals were crucified with Jesus, one to his right and one to his left, we read in the majority of manuscripts "and the scripture has been fulfilled that says: and he has been counted among the lawless" (Isa 53:12). This reference to Isaiah in the Markan account, however, is lacking from all the ancient witnesses (Codices Sinaiticus, Alexandrinus, Vaticanus, Ephraemi rescriptus, and Bezae) of Mark, while being at the same time a firmly established part of the pericope about the two swords in Luke 22:35–38, which is Lukan *Sondergut*. In contrast to the previous example, the interpolation perfectly fits the context. The crucifixion scene, and in particular the mentioning of the two criminals in whose midst the cross of Jesus has been erected,

---

22. Codex Sinaiticus, Codex Vaticanus and Codex Ephraemi rescriptus.
23. See, e.g., A. H. McNeile (*The Gospel according to St. Matthew* [1915; repr., London: Macmillan, 1957], 422): "Its position before 'Jesus again cried with a loud voice' must have been due to the carelessness of a scribe, who carried it into his text from the margin, mechanically making ἄλλος to follow εἷς (v. 48)."

certainly is a most appropriate place to situate the reference to Isa 53:12. This time it is not a story element that has been transferred, as in the previous example or in John 20:16–17. It is a scriptural proof-text that has been relocated to a central place of Christian theological reflection: Jesus' crucifixion. Hence, this time we have to credit the person who wrote this passage in the margin of a copy of Mark 15:27 with a high level of christological reflection, and the copyist who added it into the main text was spot on regarding the exact position of this proof-text.

5. The Process of Literary Production/Reproduction in Antiquity

The material we have just looked at is intended to enhance our perception of "scribal" performances. In my view there is good evidence to see more than just scribal activities at work in the transmission of New Testament texts. Our focus, rather, was on the activity of interested readers of the Gospels who felt prompted to react to what they read by adding comments in the margin. Those comments, whether deepening a theological understanding or augmenting a narrative or just referencing a parallel passage, are born of a mind-set that reflects on the text as it is being read and engages with its understanding, even from within an intertextual perspective. In my view this is part of another stage of literary production/reproduction that should not be classified with the work of scribes. Yet the occasional and almost haphazard character of these types of embellishments and the impression that they are not easily tied to only one single part of the tradition seem to suggest that neither is this a conscious editorial interference with the text.[24] It rather fits more with occasional comments made by readers of the text that subsequently entered the tradition through being copied from a *Vorlage* that contained the comment(s).

Let me finally develop a more systematic description of how the process of literary production/reproduction in antiquity should be depicted. The intention of this exercise is to imagine the various steps in functional perspective, in order to identify different roles that individuals involved in that process could and to some extent did actually perform. It is hoped that such a description contributes to situating the evidence from our manuscripts with the appropriate roles of scribal and nonscribal activities.

The first step in the process of literary production/reproduction in antiquity is the authorial stage, during which an author produces a liter-

---

24. By contrast, the model of reader's notes is certainly not appropriate to explain the genesis of the Bezan version of Acts. That appears to be a more consciously and purposefully rewritten version of that book.

ary writing. A second and rather distinct step I see is an editorial stage that focuses on getting an authored piece of literature into the public domain. Editorial activities involve acquiring copies of texts and selecting and preparing them for publication—a stage that could include adding titles and prefaces, subdividing longer texts into books or chapters, even reworking the texts to fit the needs of a certain targeted audience. The third step is the manufacturing stage, which revolves around the physical work of creating the tangible artifacts. Activities involved are preparing the sheets, the nib, and the ink; ruling the pages; and transcribing the texts. The fourth step is the use of the artifacts. The activities involved in this stage are reading the books, using them for display, lending or exchanging them, annotating them, even reusing them or dispensing with them altogether. Using the artifacts is the most important incentive that leads to reproducing them.

This works on two levels. An object itself can become the *Vorlage* for one or more other copies. More importantly, the use of books makes their content popular and creates the demand for additional copies; that is, the business aspect of literary production/reproduction comes into play: new audiences are reached, for example, institutional use of texts in worship or education requires different editions, and so on. All of these activities are known to have taken place in antiquity and are well documented from literary and documentary sources and also from manuscripts themselves.[25]

To be sure, the stages of literary production/reproduction that I have mentioned are meant as a sketch. I do not claim that every literary text of antiquity underwent a long and complicated editorial process. I rather want to stress that these are different parts of a process from the author to the audience and back again—at least to the editorial stage—that should not be lumped together under the umbrella of scribal performances. Clearly, individuals can perform more than one role in this process; for example, it is entirely conceivable that authors were also involved

---

25. Christopher de Hamel (*The Book: A History of the Bible* [London: Phaidon, 2001]), discusses the many editorial changes (regarding format, size, selection of contents, use of illustrations, etc.) that the Bible has undergone during the last two thousand years. See also Hilarius Emonds, *Zweite Auflage im Altertum: Kulturgeschichtliche Studien zur Überlieferung der antiken Literatur* (Klassisch-Philologische Studien 14; Leipzig: Harrassowitz, 1941). Prominent examples of Christian texts with a history of multiple editions are Tertullian's books "against Marcion" (see *Aduersus Marcionem* 1.1.1–2, discussed in Harry Y. Gamble, *Books and Readers in the Early Church: A History of Early Christian Texts* [New Haven and London: Yale University Press, 1995], 118–20); Eusebius's *Ecclesiastical History* (see E. Schwartz, *Eusebius Werke*, 2.3, *Einleitung* [GCS 9.3; Leipzig: Hinrichs, 1909], esp. "Einleitung II: Die Antiken Ausgaben der KG"), and Paul's Letter to the Romans.

in editing their work, or those that selected and prepared certain texts for publication could also be readers and users of the resulting copies. I would, however, prefer to conceive of the manufacturing stage, that phase that is traditionally the domain of the scribes, as a distinct and restricted technical part of text transmission. In that part of the process I hardly see much theological/ideological creativity at work. In that regard I am clearly with those who argue for scribes as copyists. On the other hand, there are undeniably variant readings in the textual tradition of the New Testament that are hard to imagine as the result of merely copying a text. Hitherto some textual critics have used such evidence to expand on the roles of scribes. In their view scribes became at times creative rewriters of the text in front of them. From my perspective it is neither justified nor necessary to project the complex logistics of literary production/reproduction in antiquity onto just one role of scribal activity. Not only were there more roles available; some of these other roles, especially those of editors and readers/users, offer more potential to localize the creative phenomena evident in the New Testament textual tradition with them than with the traditional role of scribes as copyists.

5
WORKING WITH AN OPEN TEXTUAL TRADITION: CHALLENGES IN THEORY AND PRACTICE

Michael W. Holmes

1. INTRODUCTION

This paper explores (at the request of the conference organizers) "the problems resulting from contamination in textual theory and textcritical practice." Permit me to begin with a quotation from Paul Maas. In his justly famous and slender volume on textual criticism, he writes at the end of a chapter discussing genealogical relationships the following well-known and controversial statement: "the stemma settles the relationship of witnesses for every passage in the text—*if* we have a pure tradition. No cure has yet been discovered against contamination."[1]

This remark (1) calls to our attention the phenomenon we wish to discuss today, (2) directly raises the issue of the terminology we utilize to

---

1. Paul Maas, *Textual Criticism* (trans. Barbara Flower; Oxford: Clarendon, 1958), 49 (modified); trans. of *Textkritik* (1927; 3rd ed.; Leipzig: Teubner, 1957): "im Stemma das Abhängigkeitsverhältnis der Zeugen für jede Stelle des Textes [festgelegt ist]—wenn jungfräuliche Überlieferung vorliegt. Gegen die Kontamination ist noch kein Kraut gewachsen." (cited from the 2nd ed. Leipzig: Teubner, 1950], 31). This perspective has been echoed more recently by, e.g., Ben J. P. Salemans: "At the moment no convincing solution for contamination is known" ("Cladistics or the Resurrection of the Method of Lachmann," in *Studies in Stemmatology* [ed. Pieter van Reenen and Margot van Mulken; Amsterdam and Philadelphia: John Benjamins, 1996], 9 n. 6). Maas's successor in the Teubner series, Martin L. West, is less pessimistic regarding the difficulties of dealing with contamination (*Textual Criticism and Editorial Technique applicable to Greek and Latin Texts* [Stuttgart: Teubner, 1973]).

describe or label that phenomenon, and (3) indirectly reminds us of the larger context of intellectual history within which our discussion occurs. It therefore serves as a suitable *point de départ* for our discussion. For the sake of clarity, let us speak first about the issue of terminology.

2. Definition of Terms

We may begin by describing two different examples of manuscript transmission. In the first, each and every copy of a given document reproduces (more or less faithfully) the text of one exemplar only; that is, all lines of relationship are strictly vertical. In such a tradition, the lines of descent are clearly defined and unambiguous, and the earliest recoverable source of the tradition generally may be confidently reconstructed from the surviving witnesses. This type of manuscript tradition is typically termed a "pure" or "unmixed" or *"jungfräuliche"*[2] or "mechanical"[3] or "closed"[4] manuscript tradition. In the second example, at least one or more of the copies reproduces a text drawn from two or more exemplars. This means that, in addition to the vertical line of relationship between exemplar and copy, there are relationships that may be said to run "horizontally"—that is, they represent contact between manuscripts, rather than descent from a manuscript's exemplar. In such a tradition, at least some of the lines of descent among the surviving witnesses are blurred or indistinct or perhaps even untraceable. This type of tradition has been given many labels: it is said to suffer from "conflation" or "text bastardy"[5] or "hybridisation"[6] or "cross-fertilization," or is characterized as a "contaminated" or "cross-pollinated" or "mixed" or "nonmechanical"[7] or "open"[8] manuscript tradition.

In some respects the precise labels we use to describe these two different examples are relatively unimportant. In other respects, however, these labels do matter, for it is easy for a label such as "contaminated" or "bastardized" to convey a negative connotation, especially if it is allowed to imply that an "uncontaminated" or "pure" or "unmixed" tradition is

---

2. Maas, *Textkritik*, 2nd ed., p. 31.
3. Sebastiano Timpanaro, *The Genesis of Lachmann's Method* (ed. and trans. Glenn W. Most; Chicago and London: University of Chicago Press, 2005), 137; see esp. n. 51. Timpanaro declined to follow Giorgio Pasquali's use of "closed" and "open" recensions because Pasquali used the term in a multivalent way.
4. So Giorgio Pasquali, *Storia della tradizione e critica del testo* (2nd ed.; Florence: Felice Le Monnier, 1952), followed by West, *Textual Criticism and Editorial Technique*.
5. Salemans, "Cladistics," 9.
6. So ibid., 43.
7. Timpanaro, *Genesis*, 137 n. 51.
8. So Pasquali, *Storia della tradizione*, followed by West, *Textual Criticism*.

somehow normative or to be preferred.⁹ Preference has nothing to do with the matter: we are dealing with historical questions, and we have an obligation to accept a manuscript tradition in whatever form it has survived. For these reasons, descriptive or value-neutral labels are to be preferred to labels that suggest that one type of tradition is somehow "better" or "worse" than the other. Consequently, I will use—following the example of Pasquali and West[10]—the terms "closed" and "open" to characterize the two general types of tradition described above.

Regardless of terminology, the key point is this: a closed or restricted manuscript tradition is one in which the source of each copy of a document is restricted to a single exemplar, whereas in an open or unrestricted tradition, the contents of at least some of the copies derive from two or more sources. It is a contrast between a strictly vertical and unidirectional transmission, on the one hand, and, on the other hand, a pattern of transmission that is both vertical and horizontal, and possibly bi-directional.[11] To borrow a phrase from Sebastiano Timpanaro, in a closed tradition, all readings are inherited (from the exemplar), whereas in an open tradition, it is a matter of both inheritance and acquisition (inherited readings coming from the exemplar, and acquired readings coming from other sources).[12]

So far, we have been examining the terminology used to label the traditions. What term shall we use for the process that produces an "open" or "unrestricted" tradition? The most widely utilized term in contemporary discussion is "contamination." But here again, we encounter the issue of bias. I would prefer, therefore, to employ a more neutral label such as

---

9. The question of terminology opens a door to a consideration of the larger intellectual context in which Lachmann's method developed (the third point mentioned in the introduction above). Although space limitations preclude any extended discussion of this point, one may nonetheless suggest that one reason the idea of a closed manuscript tradition at times has been so attractive or favored is the appearance of scientific rigor, of an almost mathematical purity, that accompanies the reconstruction of its archetype. Especially if the stemma exhibits a tripartite form, reconstructing the archetype is a matter of rigorous logic, a seemingly "objective" procedure that leaves no room for subjective judgment. But this is a deceptive objectivity in that it masks all the "subjective" decisions that have been made in the course of determining the stemma—that is, deciding whether a particular reading is genetically significant or not. Nonetheless, there have been times in the intellectual climate of scholarship when this sort of seeming "objectivity" was highly valued; see Timpanaro, *Genesis*, ch. 8.

10. Cf. Pasquali, *Storia della tradizione*, 183; West, *Textual Criticism*, 14.

11. For example, it is possible that the corrector of $\mathfrak{P}^{66}$ may have incorporated a reading or two from $\mathfrak{P}^{66}$ into the second exemplar against which he was correcting $\mathfrak{P}^{66}$.

12. Cf. Timpanaro, *Genesis*, 126 (for the idea of readings as acquired by contact rather than inherited from the exemplar), 129.

"mixture" or "cross-pollination" to describe the process by which horizontal transmission of information occurs in an "open" or "unrestricted" manuscript tradition.

3. Examples of How "Mixture" Occurs

Let us now turn to the phenomenon itself: how does mixture occur in the process of textual transmission? Recent discussions have centered around three possible models.

The simplest (and least problematic) model has been labeled "successive" mixture: a copyist uses one exemplar for one part of the transcription and then a different exemplar for another part, and perhaps even a third or fourth exemplar for other sections.[13] In New Testament textual criticism, this familiar phenomenon is customarily labeled "block mixture." Well-known examples include Codex Sinaiticus (ℵ/01) in the Gospel of John (where 1:1–8:38 is "Western," while 8:39–21:25 is "primary Alexandrian"), and Codex Washingtonianus (W/032), where Matthew + Luke 8:13–24:53 is Byzantine; Mark 1:1–5:30 is Western; Mark 5:31–16:20 is similar to $\mathfrak{P}^{45}$; and Luke 1:1–8:12 and John 5:12–21:25 are Alexandrian.[14] Then there is the minuscule manuscript 574, which, according to E. C. Colwell, has eight ancestors in the first generation.[15] This sort of block mixture is one of the easiest to detect and—if this is all that is involved—the easiest to compensate for: one simply treats the resultant manuscript as if it were two (or more, as the case may be) witnesses rather than one.[16]

A second model has been termed "simultaneous" mixture: it involves, as the name implies, the simultaneous use of multiple exemplars, with the copyist first comparing the exemplars and then selecting one reading to be transcribed as the copy is executed.[17] Maas envisions "a scribe having

---

13. Evert Wattel and Margot van Mulken, "Shock Waves in Text Traditions," in *Studies in Stemmatology* (ed. Pieter van Reenen and Margot van Mulken; Amsterdam and Philadelphia: John Benjamins, 1996), 106.

14. The section containing John 1:1–5:11 is a later supplement replacing lost leaves.

15. E. C. Colwell, "Genealogical Method: Its Achievements and Its Limitations," *JBL* 66 (1947): 109–33; repr. in *Studies in Methodology in Textual Criticism of the New Testament* (NTTS 9; Leiden: Brill; Grand Rapids: Eerdmans, 1969) 63–83, here 69.

16. As did, for example, Bart D. Ehrman, Gordon D. Fee, and Michael W. Holmes with regard to Sinaiticus in their work on Origen (*The Text of the Fourth Gospel in the Writings of Origen*, vol. 1 [NTGF 3; Atlanta: Scholars Press, 1992], 30).

17. See Wattel and van Mulken ("Shock Waves," 106): "simultaneous (the copyist borrowing from several exemplars at his disposal at the same time)"; also Margot van Mulken: "the copyist used several sources simultaneously to produce

two exemplars before him and giving now the text of one, now that of the other," but he immediately observes that "this is a very exhausting and, for that reason, unlikely procedure."[18] I am inclined to agree with Maas on this point: one can imagine an Origen, perhaps, with multiple volumes open around him as he works, but the inefficiency of such a procedure suggests that it was not often employed.

A third model is that of "incidental" mixture, in which a manuscript copied from one exemplar is corrected against another.[19] Here, of course, a premier example is the well-known and much-studied Bodmer Papyrus II, $\mathfrak{P}^{66}$. In this very early (ca. 200 C.E.) manuscript, there are over one hundred scribal corrections[20] — nearly a quarter of the total such corrections in this manuscript — that are the result of the initial copy being corrected against a different *Vorlage*.[21] It seems probable (though it is not clear how one might prove it) that this was a primary means by which mixture occurred. Any time, for example, that the process of *diorthosis*,[22] or "correction," utilized an exemplar different from the one initially copied, mixture of textual traditions is to some degree an almost inevitable outcome.

One could, no doubt, extend this list of examples of how mixture occurs; the above examples, however, likely reflect the most common models of how mixture occurred.[23] Let us turn, therefore, to consider the effects and consequences of mixture on textual transmission.

---

a new text. . . . he compared readings and made choices" ("The Manuscript Tradition of the *Cligés* of Chrétien de Troyes," in *Studies in Stemmatology II* [ed. Pieter van Reenen, August den Hollander, and Margot van Mulken; Amsterdam and Philadelphia: John Benjamins, 2004] 116).

18. Maas, *Textual Criticism*, 8.

19. See Wattel and van Mulken ("Shock Waves," 106), who envision "the copyist using one exemplar to complete his transcription and other exemplars to verify or to improve it afterwards by erasing former readings or by interpolating new ones."

20. According to Gordon D. Fee (*Papyrus Bodmer II [P66]: Its Textual Relationships and Scribal Characteristics* [SD 34; Salt Lake City: University of Utah Press, 1968], 61–69), there are 112 such corrections, while James R. Royse (*Scribal Habits in Early Greek New Testament Papyri* [NTTSD 36; Leiden and Boston: Brill, 2008], 463) records 107.

21. For the most recent discussion (and bibliography of earlier discussion), see Royse, *Scribal Habits*, 461–74.

22. For a discussion of this term and its implications for textual transmission, see Michael W. Holmes, "Codex Bezae as a Recension of the Gospels," in *Codex Bezae: Studies from the Lunel Colloquium, June 1994* (ed. D. C. Parker and C.-B. Amphoux; NTTS 22; Leiden: Brill, 1996), 144–45.

23. See further Alphonse Dain, *Les Manuscrits* (Paris: Belles Lettres, 1949).

4. Effects and Consequences of Mixture

In theory, an analysis of the effects of mixture ought to include some discussion, first, of the extent of mixture, but we may dispense with this point in the current context, inasmuch as the New Testament, as Zuntz reminds us, "affords, beside Homer, the paramount example of a 'contaminated tradition,'"[24] a tradition in which (in my estimation) every surviving manuscript and every textual tradition (Alexandrian, Western, Byzantine, etc.) exhibits the presence and effects of mixture.[25]

However mixture occurs, its effect is essentially the same: to render inoperative, for the portion of the textual tradition so affected, the classical methods that have proven so effective and fruitful in dealing with closed traditions. The first step of the classical method was *recensio*, an investigative and taxonomic process that analyzes the relationships between the extant witnesses and seeks to work back from the more recent to the more ancient forms by the observation of shared significant errors (*Leitfehler*),[26] a key assumption being that shared significant errors imply a shared ancestor. As an example of *recensio* applied to a closed manuscript tradition, consider fig. 1:[27]

Assumptions:
1. ABCDEF share errors in agreement—therefore they all share a common source[28]—and each has unique errors, therefore none is the source. So we postulate a lost archetype [α].
2. BCDEF share errors in agreement not found in A—indicating a separate branch for A, and a common source for BCDEF—and each has

---

24. Günther Zuntz, *The Text of the Epistles: A Disquisition upon the* Corpus Paulinum (Schweich Lectures 1946; London: Oxford University Press for the British Academy, 1953), 9.

25. See, on this point (which appears to be a widely held consensus in the discipline), Michael W. Holmes, "The Case for Reasoned Eclecticism," in *Rethinking New Testamaent Textual Criticism* (ed. D. A. Black; Grand Rapids: Baker Academic, 2002), 77–100. In the same volume, a differing perspective is offered by M. A. Robinson, "The Case for Byzantine Priority," 125–39.

26. See Michael W. Holmes, "Reasoned Eclecticism in New Testament Textual Criticism," in *The Text of the New Testament in Contemporary Research: Essays on the* Status Quaestionis (ed. Bart D. Ehrman and Michael W. Holmes; SD 46; Grand Rapids: Eerdmans, 1995), 347; Zuntz, *Text*, 8.

27. West, *Textual Criticism*, 32 (modified).

28. An example of a manuscript tradition in which all extant Greek manuscripts share a common source: the nine Greek manuscripts of the *Letter of Polycarp to the Philippians*, all derived from the same defective source, in which 9.2 (through δι' ὑμᾶς ὑπό) is immediately followed by the similarly defective text of the *Epistle of Barnabas*, beginning in 5.7.

Figure 1: Basic Stemmatic Theory

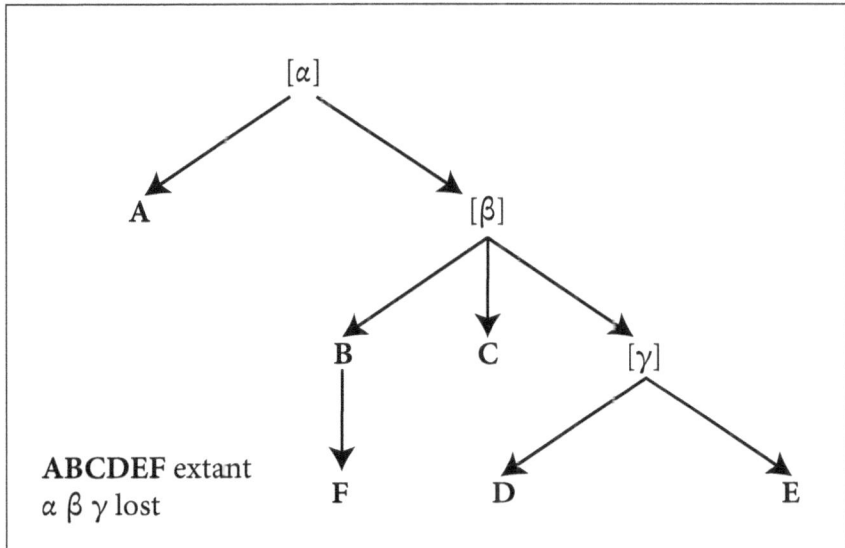

ABCDEF extant
α β γ lost

unique errors, and therefore none is the source. So we postulate a lost hypearchetype [β].
3. BF share errors in agreement not found in CDE, and F is missing a paragraph (due to homoioteleuton) found in B, so F is a descendent of B.
4. DE share errors in agreement not found in BCF—therefore DE share a common source—but each has unique errors, therefore neither is the source. So we postulate a lost hypearchetype [γ].
5. Of the three copies of [β], namely, B C [γ] (as reconstructed from DE), no two agree in error where the third has the correct reading. Thus all three are independent copies of [β].

In short, the logic of a closed tradition permits the confident reconstruction of the lost archetype of the entire tradition.[29]

Confronted with an open tradition, however, *recensio* first of all cannot reveal whether agreement in error is evidence of common descent or of mixture between lines of descent. Second, it cannot even reveal the direc-

---

29. To be more precise, it permits the confident reconstruction of the lost archetype of the entire tradition whenever A and β agree. In cases where A and β disagree, *recensio* reaches the limits of its applicability. See Holmes, "Reasoned Eclecticism," 347–48.

tion of transmission.[30] Consider, for example, this hypothetical example, in which F has been corrected against A, and A has subsequently been lost. The actual lines of transmission would look like fig. 2:[31]

Figure 2: An "Open" Tradition

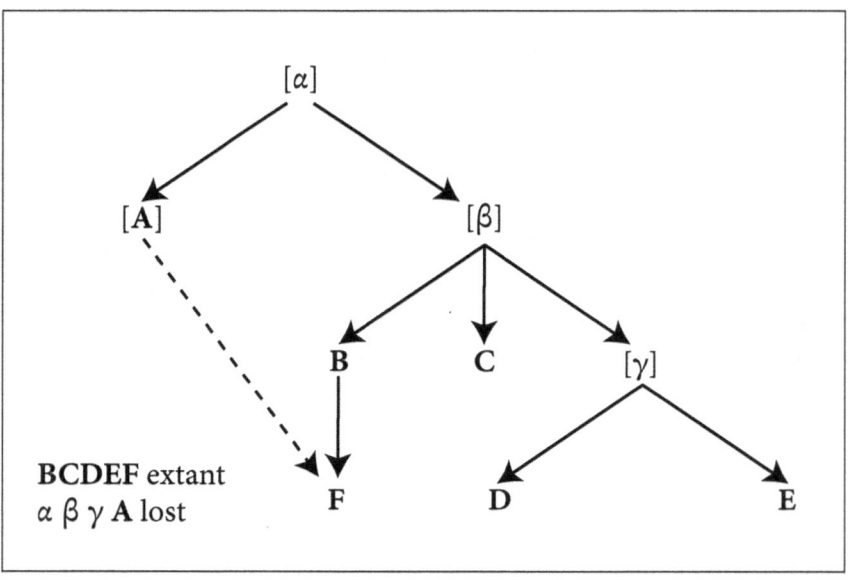

But this is not the stemma we would reconstruct on the basis the surviving manuscripts BCDEF. Following the logic of *recensio*, "we would observe that F"—because of readings it acquired from A—"sometimes avoided errors common to the rest (suggesting its independence from them), and that B sometimes sided with C and [γ], sometimes with F. We would construct this stemma,"[32] seen in fig. 3.

Owing to the effect of mixture, we would view F, in fact a descendant of B, as its ancestor. As a result, "[w]e would discard B as a contaminated manuscript offering nothing that was not to be found in the other sources, and we would treat the peculiar readings of F as being as likely as those of

---

30. See especially on the following point Gerd Mink, "Problems of a Highly Contaminated Tradition, the New Testament: Stemmata of Variants as a Source of a Genealogy for Witnesses," in *Studies in Stemmatology II* (ed. Pieter van Reenen, August den Hollander, and Margot van Mulken; Amsterdam and Philadelphia: John Benjamins, 2004), 49–51.

31. West, *Textual Criticism*, 35 (modified).

32. West, *Textual Criticism*, 35; 36 (modified).

Figure 3: The Resulting Stemma

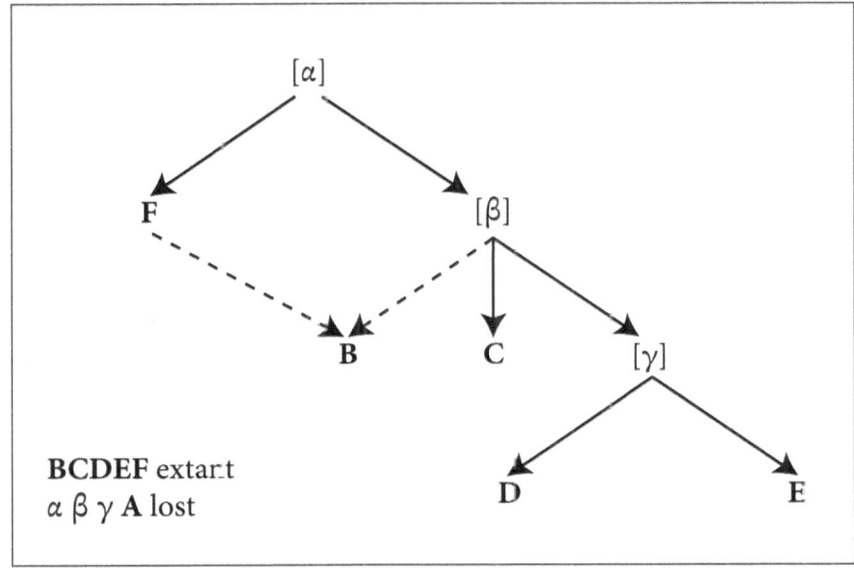

[β] to be those of the archetype. Insofar as they were drawn from A, this would be correct, but insofar as they were errors made by B, or in copying from B, it would be false."[33]

The primary point is this: as a result of mixture, *a derivative manuscript can appear instead as a source manuscript*.[34] In an open textual tradition—especially one with as many "missing links" as the New Testament apparently has[35]—the apparent direction of relationships may be the polar opposite of the actual direction of the relationships.

In short, both the lines of descent and the direction of descent are obscured in an open textual tradition. Some of the consequences of such a state of affairs include (merely to list them):

---

33. West, *Textual Criticism*, 36; see similarly Timpanaro, *Genesis*, 176–77.
34. Indeed, "[i]n so far as mixture operates, it exactly inverts the results of the simpler form of transmission, its effect being to produce convergence rather than divergence" (B. F. Westcott and F. J. A. Hort, *The New Testament in the Original Greek*, vol. 2, *Introduction, Appendix* [Cambridge: Macmillan, 1881], 48; similarly Louis Havet, *Manuel de critique verbale appliquée aux textes latins* [Paris: Librairie Hachette, 1911], 418–24, and Colwell, "Genealogical Method," 68).
35. On the effect of "missing links" in the chain of tradition, see Mink, "Problems of a Highly Contaminated Tradition," 32–33.

- *Recensio* in the traditional or classical sense of the term is not possible. Contemporary claims to have resurrected Lachmann's method,[36] whether by means of phylogenetic analysis, cladistic analysis, or similar procedures, in fact work on the basis of mathematical probability rather than the deductive logic of Lachmannian *recensio*.[37]
- Purely quantitative methods are not applicable (because the transmission of data is random, rather than regular).
- It becomes more difficult to determine whether shared errors represent genetically significant agreements or merely accidental agreements (what Timpanaro terms "polygenetic" agreements), even as it becomes more vital to be able to do so (because only the former are of any use for determining relationships between manuscripts).[38]
- It requires that we differentiate between texts, on the one hand, and the manuscripts that carry them, on the other. (A text may be much older than the manuscript that conveys it; therefore, the date of a manuscript, which can be an important point of information in the analysis of a closed tradition, is no longer of as much significance).[39]
- It means that even late or otherwise inconsequential manuscripts potentially may be carriers of original readings.
- It disallows any sort of programmatic appeal to a "best manuscript" or a "best tradition": any one witness or combination of witnesses—even those that statistically are the more reliable in general—may, at any given point, preserve a secondary reading.[40]

---

36. E.g., Salemans, "Cladistics."

37. See also the comments by Peter M. W. Robinson ("Computer-Assisted Stemmatic Analysis and 'Best-Text' Historical Editing," in *Studies in Stemmatology* [ed. Pieter van Reenen and Margot van Mulken; Amsterdam and Philadelphia: John Benjamins, 1996], 88–89) on the limits of both cladistic analysis and classical stemmatics.

38. See G. P. Farthing ("Using Probability Theory as a Key to Unlock Textual History," in *Studies in the Early Text of the Gospels and Acts: The Papers of the First Birmingham Colloquium on the Textual Criticism of the New Testament* [ed. D. G. K. Taylor; Birmingham, UK: University of Birmingham Press, 1999], 95–100, 113–17) for a discussion of the significance of genetically significant agreements (which he terms "unique irreversible changes") versus accidental agreements (which he terms "non-unique reversible changes") with regard to the analysis of manuscript relationships.

39. Mink, "Problems of a Highly Contaminated Tradition," 24.

40. For examples of major witnesses or combinations of witnesses preserving original readings (sometimes almost alone) in some instances and secondary readings in other instances, see Michael W. Holmes, "Reasoned Eclecticism and the Text of Romans," in *Romans and the People of God: Essays in Honor of Gordon D. Fee* (Grand Rapids: Eerdmans, 1999), 191–96.

5. Reconceptualizing the Role of *Recensio*

This is not to say, however, that we are without recourse in the face of mixture, even if it is very extensive. Indeed, one of the major methodological achievements of New Testament textual criticism in the twentieth century was the adaptation or redefinition of the classical method of *recensio* to deal with the realities of a mixed textual tradition. A key move was the recognition that in an "open" tradition, characterized by cross-pollination between witnesses, one cannot eliminate any textual tradition or source from consideration, at least initially, in the effort to understand the earliest stages of the transmission of the textual tradition and to determine the archetype of the text of the New Testament.

Thus, instead of creating a stemma of all *manuscripts* and then on the basis of that stemma eliminating those manuscripts that cannot (because of their subordinate position on the stemma) contribute to the recovery of the archetype, our contemporary methodological approach—it is not important whether one calls it the "local-genealogical" method or "reasoned eclecticism"—utilizes all available evidence in an effort to discern, on a variant-by-variant basis, a stemma of *readings*, which is then employed not to identify a single witness or textual tradition as closest to the archetype, but rather to identify variant by variant, the *reading(s)* closest to the archetype at any given point in the tradition. That is, whereas in a closed tradition one seeks the earliest recoverable *archetype* from which the surviving manuscripts descended, in a mixed or contaminated tradition, in which the lines of descent are thoroughly confused, one seeks instead, on a variant-by-variant basis, the earliest recoverable *reading* (or readings) from which all others derive—the *Ausgangstext*, if you will. To quote the Kurt and Barbara Aland, it is a matter of "applying to each passage individually the approach used by classical philology for a whole tradition."[41]

It will be observed that a major consequence of this methodological shift is that the role played in a closed tradition by the fixed abstraction of the stemma is filled instead, in an open tradition, by historical data and insight.[42]

Why must we rely on historical data and insight? Because the open character of the surviving textual tradition requires it. But precisely here we encounter an additional problem that we may add to the list given earlier: sometimes the surviving evidence fails to provide data or consid-

---

41. Kurt Aland and Barbara Aland, *The Text of the New Testament: An Introduction to the Critical Editions and to the Theory and Practice of Modern Textual Criticism* (2nd ed.; Grand Rapids: Eerdmans; Leiden: Brill, 1989; 1st German ed., 1981), 34; similarly Zuntz, *Text*, 9–10.

42. See Zuntz, *Text*, 10.

erations by which to choose between variants. Consider, for example, the following set of variant readings in Matt 15:30, which, in the Nestle-Aland edition, reads: καὶ προσῆλθον αὐτῷ ὄχλοι πολλοὶ ἔχοντες μεθ' ἑαυτῶν χωλούς, τυφλούς, κυλλούς, κωφούς, καὶ ἑτέρους πολλοὺς . . .):

1	2	3	4
χωλούς,	τυφλούς,	κυλλούς,	κωφούς

1 2 3 4	ℵ 157 pc a b ff² syˢ NA²⁶⁻²⁷ / UBS¹⁻⁴
1 3 2 4	B 0281 pc saᵐˢˢ mae WH† NA⁶·¹⁶·²⁵ Legg Merk¹¹ BFBS²
1 2 4 3	P U Γ Θ f¹† f¹³ 2.700.1071 pm f syᶜ·ᵖ saᵐˢˢ bo TR Tischendorf⁸ HuckGreeven Souter RobinsonPierpont¹·² Hodges-Farstad
1 4 2 3	C K M Π 565 pm
4 1 2 3	L W Δ al l q vgˢᵗ·ʷʷ syʰ
4 2 1 3	33.892.1241.ℓ844.ℓ2211 pc aur (ff¹) vgᶜˡ Origen⁴³
2 4 1 3	579
2 1 3 4	Davies & Allison⁴⁴

---

43. Origen, *Commentarium in evangelium Matthaei* 11.18.66 (see next note).

44. W. D. Davies and Dale C. Allison, Jr. (*A Critical and Exegetical Commentary on the Gospel according to Saint Matthew*, vol. 2, *VIII–XVIII* [ICC; Edinburgh: T&T Clark, 1991] 567 n. 23) stand as a notable exception among editors and commentators. They print τυφλούς, χωλούς, κυλλούς, κωφούς (i.e., 2 1 3 4), claiming Origen (probably on the basis of the apparatus in the Huck-Greeven *Synopsis*) as support for the first two words and ℵ 157 pc a b ff² syˢ as support for the last two words (their two primary arguments in favor of their text, however, rest on authorial proclivities rather than external evidence). The appeal to Origen for support for the order τυφλούς χωλούς, however, is problematic. In *Commentarium in evangelium Matthaei* 11.18.66, Origen's text reads: Ἀναβιβάζωμεν οὖν μεθ' ἑαυτῶν ἐπὶ τὸ ὄρος ἔνθα καθέζεται ὁ Ἰησοῦς, τὴν ἐκκλησίαν αὐτοῦ, τοὺς βουλομένους ἀναβαίνειν ἐπ' αὐτὸ μεθ' ἡμῶν κωφούς, τυφλούς, χωλούς, κυλλούς [4 2 1 3], καὶ ἑτέρους πολλούς, καὶ ῥίπτωμεν αὐτοὺς παρὰ τοὺς πόδας τοῦ Ἰησοῦ, ἵνα θεραπεύσῃ αὐτούς, ὥστε θαυμάσαι ἐπὶ τῇ τούτων θεραπείᾳ τοὺς ὄχλους. Here he is clearly presenting, in indirect speech, the text of Matt 15:30. The same order occurs in two allusions earlier in 11.18 (κεκωφωμένους . . . τυφλοὺς . . . χωλοὺς . . . κυλλούς; κωφότητος . . . τυφλότητος χωλότητος . . . κυλλότητος). Later in 11.19.49, in his analysis of the passage, his text reads: ἐνταῦθα δὲ τοὺς μετὰ τῶν ὄχλων οὐκ ἀρρώστους θεραπεύει [cf. Matt 14:14], ἀλλὰ τυφλοὺς καὶ χωλοὺς καὶ κωφοὺς καὶ κυλλούς· (i.e., 2 1 4 3)· διὸ καὶ ἐπὶ τούτοις μὲν θαυμάζουσιν οἱ τετρακισχίλιοι (i.e., 2 1 4 3). The thrice-repeated καί is the first clue that this text almost certainly reflects Origen's own rephrasing of the passage, and the presence of θαυμάζουσιν raises the possibility that 15:31 (θαυμάσαι) is in view rather than 15:30 (though the word order does not match that of 15:31 either). Moreover, the order here in 11.19 does not match the order of any known manuscript of 15:30. It seems probable, therefore, that the thrice-repeated order found in 11.18 reflects the text of Matt 15:30 known to Origen, and almost certain that the order in 11.19 does not.

4 2 3 1	1424
1 2 3	D pc

(‡ acc. to Swanson, 118 has the order *1 2 4 3*, while 1 and 1582 read *4 2 1 3*)

Matt. 15:31: κωφούς ... κυλλούς ... χωλούς ... τυφλούς ... [4 3 1 2]

The meaning of the text is clear enough, so it is unlikely that exegetes will spend much time pondering the textual problem in this verse. But an editor must print something here: How is one to decide between these many options? Unless one works with a history of the text that favors a particular strand of external evidence as a "default" option,[45] one lacks here determinative data on the basis of which to decide between readings. In the face of ambiguous or incomplete data, historical insight sometimes fails us.

There is one final matter I wish to mention, in this case not so much an additional problem as rather a temptation that we must constantly withstand when dealing with an open tradition: the temptation to reduce a complex and challenging situation to over-simple terms. Let me offer an example involving Hort. The concept of "textual traditions," which can be traced back to Griesbach and even Bengel before him, has done much to bring some sense of order to the mass of evidence with which New Testament textual criticism is blessed. The observation that most manuscripts, at least most of the time, tend to align with one of the three major textual traditions is a legitimate and helpful simplification of an otherwise difficult-to-navigate sea of data. But Hort took matters one step further: at a crucial point in his argument he treated the three textual traditions—each of which may be compared to a flowing stream whose character changes over time—as if they were three individual manuscripts, static and fixed, which could then be treated as if they were a closed tradition.[46] By this move he was able to eliminate, to his satisfaction at least, the Byzantine tradition from consideration as a source of original readings. But this was a false move, one that rendered his reconstruction of the history of the New Testament text false and problematic.[47] He succumbed, I suggest, to the temptation to over-simplify and thus fell off the tracks before reaching his destination.

---

45. As do, e.g., Westcott & Hort, *Appendix*, 13.
46. See Colwell, "Genealogical Method," 69–71, for this insight.
47. See further Michael W. Holmes, "Westcott and Hort at 125 (and Zuntz at 60): Their Legacies and Our Challenges," (paper presented in the New Testament Textual Criticism Section, Society of Biblical Literature annual meeting, Washington, D.C., November 19, 2006).

6. Conclusion

Maas, I suggest, was incorrect: for all the problems an open textual tradition presents, there are ways of treating it successfully. But as Zuntz so pointedly observed, no treatment

> can be carried out mechanically. At every stage the critic has to use his brains. Were it different, we could put the critical slide-rule into the hands of any fool and leave it to him to settle the problems of the New Testament text.... Textual criticism is not a branch of science. Its criteria are necessarily different from those sought by the scientist: they are not, for that reason, less exacting nor less definite.[48]

This is why the "local-genealogical" method or "reasoned eclecticism" is so central to contemporary New Testament textual criticism: it deals with each variation unit on its own terms.

But each variation unit is a piece of a larger mosaic, and each individual textual decision implies something about the history of transmission as a whole. Precisely here, however, one encounters one of the real challenges in utilizing the "local" approach: it is difficult to keep in mind, let alone integrate, the implications of each decision for the larger whole; it is easy to become so focused on each piece of the mosaic that it is difficult to see the pattern of the mosaic as a whole.

It is in this respect that the CBGM will be of value, for it offers the textual critic a means by which to assess and analyze the larger implications of individual textual decisions. By aggregating the implications of each decision, it offers hypotheses regarding the transmission of the tradition as a whole—the original mosaic, of which we now posses only scattered and fragmentary portions that have been scrambled in transmission. Any help in better reassembling the original image will be warmly welcomed.

---

48. Zuntz, *Text*, 12–13.

6
TRADITIONAL "CANONS" OF NEW TESTAMENT TEXTUAL CRITICISM: THEIR VALUE, VALIDITY, AND VIABILITY— OR LACK THEREOF

Eldon Jay Epp

1. The Emergence of External and Internal Criteria for the Priority of Readings

When scholars first employed two or more manuscripts to produce a printed text of the Greek New Testament, such as that of Desiderius Erasmus in 1516 or the Complutensian Polyglot in 1522,[1] the "critical text"

This essay is an expanded version of a paper presented at the Münster Colloquium on the Textual History of the Greek New Testament, August 3–6, 2008. It owes much to my earlier researches while a Fellow of the John Simon Guggenheim Memorial Foundation (1974/1975). At that time the results were published as "The Eclectic Method in New Testament Textual Criticism: Solution or Symptom?" *HTR* 69 (1976): 211–57; repr. in the author's *Perspectives on New Testament Textual Criticism: Collected Essays, 1962–2004* (NovTSup 116; Leiden: Brill, 2005), 125–84 [with Added Notes, 2004]). The present study is not only retrospective but assesses also the developments in these methods during the past thirty-some years.

Bibliographic resources on the criteria discussed are extensive, and no attempt is made to report them here, but a particularly insightful survey is Michael W. Holmes, "Reasoned Eclecticism in New Testament Textual Criticism," in *The Text of the New Testament in Contemporary Research: Essays on the Status Quaestionis* (ed. Bart D. Ehrman and Michael W. Holmes; SD 46; Grand Rapids: Eerdmans, 1995), 336–60.

1. See Jerry H. Bentley, *Humanists and Holy Writ: New Testament Scholarship in the Renaissance* (Princeton: Princeton University Press, 1983), 112–37, on Erasmus's

was born. Soon thereafter "critical editions" appeared—Greek texts with a display of variant readings. Among the first rudimentary examples were the 1550 edition of Robert Estienne (hereafter Stephanus), Brian Walton's *London Polyglot* of 1657, and John Fell's edition in 1675.[2] John Mill's 1707 volume,[3] however, was the first to qualify as a critical edition in the modern sense, but only in its prolegomena, apparatus, and appendix, for its text at the top of the pages was essentially that of Stephanus. Virtually all Greek editions from 1550 to the early nineteenth century printed Stephanus's text or that of the 1633 edition of the Elzevir publishers (explicitly designated as the *textus receptus*).[4] Increasingly, critical editions included modifications to the text in favor of readings found in older manuscripts. At first these alternate readings took the form of marginal notes, as in the editions of Johann Albrecht Bengel (1734), Johann Jakob Wettstein (1751–52), and Johann Jakob Griesbach (1775–1807), though their prolegomena, contradictorily, all advocate reliance on the oldest textual witnesses. This inconsistency was understandable because of the pervasive reluctance, at the time, to alter the commonly used text. Indeed, printing a New Testament text that would follow logically from these scholars' expounded principles could be ecclesiastically dangerous.[5] Therefore, the texts actually favored by these editors had to be constructed by their readers from the marginal readings offered or from the apparatus of each edition.

A basic change, though only theoretically, appeared in Richard Bentley's 1720 *Proposals for Printing* a Greek/Latin New Testament,[6] which

---

editions and the manuscripts employed; and 70–111 on the preparation of the Complutensian New Testament. See also on Erasmus the essays by Henk Jan de Jonge, "Novum testamentum a nobis versum: The Essence of Erasmus' Edition of the New Testament," *JTS* 35 (1984): 394–413; and Pierre-Yves Brandt, "Manuscrits grecs utilisés par Erasme pour son édition du *Novum Instrumentum* de 1516," *TZ* 54 (1998): 120–24.

2. On Stephanus, see J. Keith Elliott, "Manuscripts Cited by Stephanus," *NTS* 55 (2009): 390–95; on Fell, see Adam Fox, *John Mill and Richard Bentley: A Study of the Textual Criticism of the New Testament 1675–1729* (Aularian Series 3; Oxford: Blackwell, 1954), 52–55.

3. On Mill, see Fox, *John Mill and Richard Bentley*, 56–88, 142–46.

4. See H. J. de Jonge, *Daniel Heinsius and the Textus Receptus of the New Testament: A Study of His Contributions to the Editions of the Greek Testament Printed by the Elzeviers at Leiden in 1624 and 1633* (Leiden: Brill, 1971), esp. 48–66.

5. Witness the fifteen-year harassment of Wettstein for his alleged Arian/Socinian views, charges that arose out of his preference for six variant readings in Codex Alexandrinus: see C. L. Hulbert-Powell, *John James Wettstein 1693–1754: An Account of His Life, Work, and Some of His Contemporaries* (London: SPCK, 1937), 47–95.

6. For the text of his *Proposals*, see Arthur A. Ellis, *Bentleii critica sacra: Notes on the Greek and Latin Text of the New Testament, Extracted from the Bentley MSS. in*

advocated a fresh eclectic text drawn from the most ancient majuscule manuscripts. As we are all aware, he never was able to carry out his plan. That change to a newly constructed text arrived, in actuality only with Karl Lachmann's Greek New Testament of 1831,[7] whose aim was to reproduce the text of the late fourth century. Bentley and Lachmann were both preeminent classical scholars, open to creating fresh texts or revising existing texts of Greek and Latin literary works from available manuscripts and accustomed to offering numerous emendations and conjectures in the process. Although both eschewed emending the "sacred" New Testament text, they felt that it was both natural and necessary to reach for the earliest attainable text, and they approached their tasks with no intimidation from the long-dominant *textus receptus*. Both Bentley and Lachmann, though separated by more than a century, focused entirely on external criteria—that is, on the most ancient manuscripts, versions, and patristic citations.

Lachmann's decisive break with the *textus receptus* was more than three hundred years overdue. Yet many noteworthy editions that followed were based on methodologies developed and utilized over that lengthy period but further refined in more recent times. These editions included

---

Trinity College Library (Cambridge: Deighton, Bell, 1862), xvii–xix. See also Fox, *John Mill and Richard Bentley*, 112–26; C. O. Brink, *English Classical Scholarship: Historical Reflections on Bentley, Porson, and Housman* (Cambridge: James Clarke; New York: Oxford University Press, 1986), 71–83; Sebastiano Timpanaro, *The Genesis of Lachmann's Method* (ed. and trans. Glenn W. Most; Chicago and London: University of Chicago Press, 2005), 54–56, 63–64.

7. On Lachmann, see Timpanaro, *Genesis*. 75–89, 115–18; and Brink, *English Classical Scholarship*, 136–38. Note, however, that beginning a century earlier, several editions of the Greek New Testament moved, in small or major ways, toward a freshly constructed text based on the principles enunciated by Mill, or Bengel, or Wettstein. These three, as noted, did not follow through on their own canons, but Edward Wells used Mill's apparatus to publish an edition (1709–19) that departed 210 times from the Elzevir text, and he deserves credit as "the first to edit a complete New Testament that abandoned the Textus Receptus in favor of readings from more ancient manuscripts" (Bruce M. Metzger and Bart D. Ehrman, *The Text of the New Testament: Its Transmission, Corruption, and Restoration* [4th ed.; New York and Oxford: Oxford University Press, 2005], 155). Daniel Mace in 1729 did much the same in his (anonymous) Greek and English diglot, and later, after the editions of Bengel and Wettstein appeared, William Bowyer, Jr., in 1763 and Edward Harwood in 1776 issued critical editions. Harwood's Greek Testament departed from the *textus receptus* at the rate of 70 percent, and Lachmann's edition, when it appeared, agreed with Harwood in 643 passages (Metzger and Ehrman, 162–63). For more detail on Wells and Mace, see also Fox, *John Mill and Richard Bentley*, 95–102; on Mace, see H. McLachlan, "An Almost Forgotten Pioneer in New Testament Textual Criticism," *HibJ* 37 (1938–39): 617–25.

those of Constantin von Tischendorf (1869–72); Samuel Prideaux Tregelles (1857–72); Brooke Foss Westcott and Fenton John Anthony Hort (1881–82); Bernhard Weiss (1894–1900); then those of Eberhard Nestle (1898–1912); Erwin Nestle (1914–52); and Nestle-Aland (Erwin Nestle and Kurt Aland, 1956–); to be joined by the United Bible Societies' editions (1966–) and most recently by the *Editio Critica Maior* (1997–),[8] currently in process. Altogether, it has been estimated that more than one thousand editions of the Greek New Testament have been printed since the Complutensian Polyglot's first fascicle in 1514,[9] and all of the most substantive editions, in one way or another, have had to deal with the criteria employed in the selection of variants to be printed in the text (at the top of the pages), and in the apparatus for variants not in the text.

Actually, the evolution of these "criteria for the priority of readings" can be traced from fourth-century comments by Origen and Jerome.[10] More than a millennium later, somewhat clearer criteria appeared in the *Annotations* published with Erasmus's edition (1517) or found in Fell's Greek Testament (1675), followed by some more explicit principles in Mill's prolegomena of 1707.[11] The first formal, published list of "canons

---

8. The Institute for New Testament Textual Research, ed., *Novum Testamentum Graecum, Editio Critica Maior: IV, Catholic Epistles* (ed. Barbara Aland, †Kurt Aland, Gerd Mink, and Klaus Wachtel; Stuttgart: Deutsche Bibelgesellschaft, 1997–2005) [2 parts each]: 1. *James* (1997); 2. *The Letters of Peter* (2000); 3. *The First Letter of John* (2003); 4. *The Second and Third Letter of John, The Letter of Jude* (added editor: Holger Strutwolf, 2007).

9. Metzger and Ehrman, *Text of the New Testament*, 194.

10. B. M. Metzger, "The Practice of Textual Criticism among the Church Fathers," *StPatr* XII (1975), 1:340–41 (on Irenaeus, *Against Heresies* 5.30.1) and 1:342 (on Origen, *Commentary on Matthew*, 121 [GCS 38 = *Origenes Werke* 11:255, 24–31 Klostermann]). See also K. K. Hulley, "Principles of Textual Criticism Known to St. Jerome," *HSCP* 55 (1944): 87–109; B. M. Metzger, "Explicit References in the Works of Origen to Variant Readings in New Testament Manuscripts," in *Biblical and Patristic Studies in Memory of Robert Pierce Casey* (ed. J. Neville Birdsall and Robert W. Thomson; Freiburg: Herder, 1963), 78–95 (repr. in Metzger's *Historical and Literary Studies: Pagan, Jewish, and Christian* [NTTS 8; Leiden: Brill, 1968], 88–103); idem, "St Jerome's Explicit References to Variant Readings in Manuscripts of the New Testament," in *Text and Interpretation: Studies in the New Testament Presented to Matthew Black* (ed. Ernest Best and R. McL. Wilson; Cambridge: Cambridge University Press, 1979), 179–90 (repr. in Metzger's *New Testament Studies: Philological, Versional, and Patristic* [NTTS 10; Leiden: Brill, 1980], 199–210).

11. On Erasmus, see Erika Rummel, *Erasmus' Annotations on the New Testament: From Philologist to Theologian* (Erasmus Studies 8; Toronto: University of Toronto Press, 1986), 109–21; on the more difficult reading criterion, 117, 120. On Fell, see Fox, *John Mill and Richard Bentley*, 92; on Mill's prolegomena and his discussion of the more difficult reading criterion, see Fox, 147–48.

of criticism" (as they were commonly called) appeared, however, in the 1711 Greek Testament of Gerhard von Maestricht (hereafter Gerhard). His forty-three canons became a model in *form* (though certainly not in *content*), for several of his canons stated that readings from one or a few manuscripts cannot overrule readings in "a great number of manuscript codices," because, he asserted (Canons VIII–XII), "certainly no reason is compelling that will prefer a variant reading to a received reading"—a reference to the *textus receptus*. On the other hand, absurd readings, as well as those due to harmonization or to a specific scribe's or manuscripts's tendencies to add or to omit, were to be rejected. Gerhard's Canon XXIV claimed that a variant reading usually disappears when the origin of that reading is ascertained,[12] which became not only a prominent modern criterion but increasingly the principal one. By then Mill (1707) had already stated that smooth and easy readings and those due to harmonization were to be rejected and had intimated his preference for early manuscripts.[13] Very soon thereafter Bentley would defend with vigor his conviction that the text of the New Testament must be determined from the "most ancient and venerable MSS. in Greek and Roman capital letters" and from versions and patristic citations "within the first five centuries."[14]

What had emerged in little more than a decade from Mill to Bentley was a twofold set of criteria, external and internal, that, while partial and rudimentary, formed the foundation of text-critical methodology ever after. These criteria were more clearly defined over time, but basically *external evidence* assesses factors such as the age, quality, geographical distribution, and groupings of manuscripts and other witnesses, while *internal evidence* assesses what authors were most likely to write and what scribes were likely to transcribe. During the eighteenth century and through the nineteenth, virtually all notable editors stated a basic, general principle that the text should be formed from the most ancient textual witnesses, and (except for Lachmann) their editions also included a list of internal criteria. Bengel (1725 and 1742) offered twenty-seven canons, Wettstein (1730 and 1751–52) listed eighteen, Griesbach (1796–1806) fifteen, Tischendorf (1869–72, in the prolegomena by Caspar René Gregory)

---

12. Gerhard von Maestricht [editor listed on title page only as G.D.T.M.D., i.e. Gerhardus de Trajecto Mosae Doctor], 'Η ΚΑΙΝΗ ΔΙΑΘΗΚΗ (Amsterdam: Wetsteniana, 1711), criteria listed, 11-16; discussed, 48-69; Canon XXIV, 14 [cited hereafter as Gerhard]. On the name, see Ezra Abbot, "Gerhard von Mastricht," in his *The Authorship of the Fourth Gospel and Other Critical Essays* (Boston: Ellis, 1888), 184–88.
13. Fox, *John Mill and Richard Bentley*, 147–48.
14. Bentley's proposals I and IV; see Ellis, *Bentleii critica sacra*, xvii–xviii.

five, Tregelles (1857–72) nine, and Westcott and Hort (1881–82) also offered some nine, though not in a formal list.¹⁵

The shift toward valuing the more ancient witnesses was at the same time, of course, a move away from counting manuscripts, which still had been a strong emphasis in Gerhard's canons. Only fourteen years later, in 1725, Bengel asserted that textual witnesses must be weighed and not merely counted, and this fundamental principle issued from Bengel's innovative grouping of manuscripts and would lead to the eventual formation of text-types or other forms of grouping witnesses. Bengel divided textual witnesses into two "nations," an early "African" group, which he subdivided into two "tribes," and a later "Asiatic" group. Essentially that was a threefold scheme featuring an early Eastern or Alexandrian text-group and an early Western text-group, succeeded by a later Constantinopolitan or Byzantine text-type, though the name "text-type" would emerge only later. With varying terminology, Griesbach, Lachmann, and Tischendorf followed this threefold pattern (though Griesbach later combined the two early groups when new discoveries made it difficult to differentiate them). Westcott and Hort finally worked the scheme into a classical formulation, consisting *essentially* of two early and one later stream of textual tradition.¹⁶ Although this formulation of textual grouping, with subsequent refinements, is held by the majority of textual critics today, reconsideration of "text-types" has appeared in the twenty-first century (see below).

At the end of the nineteenth century, then, there were, on the one hand, two sets of criteria, external and internal, and these were joined, on the other hand, by the text-type or grouping phenomenon that assisted in explaining the historical transmission of the text. The second half of the nineteenth century also was particularly fruitful for new resources. For example, the 1850s and 1860s saw the discovery and full publication

---

15. For these lists, see Epp, "Eclectic Method in New Testament Textual Criticism," 219–44 (repr. in idem, *Perspectives*, 133–59). Kurt Aland and Barbara Aland (*The Text of the New Testament: An Introduction to the Critical Editions and to the Theory and Practice of Modern Textual Criticism* [2nd ed.; Grand Rapids: Eerdmans; Leiden: Brill, 1989], 280–81) offer "Twelve Rules," containing four on external evidence, four internal, and four others.

16. Brooke Foss Westcott, and Fenton John Anthony Hort, *The New Testament in the Original Greek* (2 vols; London: Macmillan, 1881–82), vol. 2, *Introduction, Appendix* (2nd ed., 1896), 90–148. They identify three pre-Syrian (i.e., pre–*textus receptus*) streams of tradition, Western, Alexandrian, and Neutral, but the latter two have a common ancestor and are closely similar, resulting, basically, in two early streams (usually designated "Western" or D-text and Alexandrian or B-text) and one later (usually designated Byzantine or "Syrian"). See Metzger and Ehrman, *Text of the New Testament*, 180, for a helpful diagram.

of Codex Sinaiticus (א, 01) and finally, in 1867, the full collation and first reliable publication of Codex Vaticanus (B, 03), as well as the appearance of other Greek manuscripts and editions of early versions. Also in this period, the criteria for the priority of readings blossomed and reached a broad consensus. Tregelles, for instance, published his text of the Gospels before Codex Sinaiticus was found and before Codex Vaticanus was fully known, yet he discussed, in sophisticated fashion, his various criteria in some one hundred pages (1854).[17] Tischendorf, in addition to his reliance on the most ancient witnesses, listed five internal criteria, though it is often said that he was more interested in utilizing for his text of the New Testament his latest manuscript discovery, exemplified most notably in his use of Codex Sinaiticus.[18] Therefore it remained for Westcott and Hort in 1881-82 to provide a new eclectic text with an entire second volume of rationale for their theory of text-types, their external criteria, and their internal principles.[19] The next generation brought numerous modifications and new directions in these areas of textual criticism that reverberate to this day, materially assisted by the discovery of the Oxyrhynchus New Testament papyri at the end of the nineteenth century.

The first half of the twentieth century and beyond brought to light more remarkable discoveries: the Chester Beatty papyri in the 1930s and the Bodmer papyri in the 1950s, as well as other early manuscripts and hundreds upon hundreds of later texts. The new papyri and other early manuscripts facilitated an increased understanding of how scribes and readers affected the texts they copied and used, which in turn influenced

---

17. Samuel Prideaux Tregelles, *An Account of the Printed Text of the Greek New Testament; with Remarks on Its Revision upon Critical Principles* (London: Bagster, 1854), 132-54, 174-261; he also discussed critical principles in each major edition from Erasmus to Tischendorf (pp. 1-129).

18. The Latin text of Tischendorf's criteria may be found in Caspar Renatus Gregory's *Prolegomena* to Tischendorf's *Novum Testamentum Graece* (3 vols; Leipzig: Hinrichs, 1884-94), 3:47-48, 53-54, followed by examples, 3:54-65; English translations of the criteria appear in Tregelles, *Account of the Printed Text*, 119-21. Tischendorf's basic principle was that "[t]he text is only to be sought from ancient evidence, and especially from Greek MSS., but without neglecting the testimonies of versions and fathers," and noteworthy was number 4 "In discrepant readings, that should be preferred which may have given occasion to the rest, or which appears to comprise the elements of the others." On Tischendorf's relative non-use of criteria, see Léon Vaganay, and Christian-Bernard Amphoux, *An Introduction to New Testament Textual Criticism* (2nd ed.; English ed. amplified by Amphoux and Jenny Heimerdinger; Cambridge: Cambridge University Press, 1991), 147-49.

19. Westcott and Hort, *New Testament in the Original Greek*; vol. 2 consists of an *Introduction* (pp. 1-330) and a separately numbered *Appendix* of "Notes on Select Readings" (pp. 1-180).

our criteria. The early papyri also (in the view of some) provided opportunities to rethink the formation of text-types.[20] New theories were offered, such as the Caesarean Text proposal (in the 1920s and 1930s) and Burnett Hillman Streeter's theory of Local Texts (1924), but both have withered on the vine.[21] Gaps in the history of textual transmission have been filled, for example, by $\mathfrak{P}^{75}$ for the B-textual cluster. Yet the papyri have not altered the established text as much as might have been expected, though they have offered early confirmatory evidence for numerous readings, which indeed is a methodological development of great significance.

As already noted, the age, constitution, and nature of early textual clusters remain controversial, and the term "text-type" has been rejected by some. All textual critics appear to agree that a later, Byzantine text-type (here the term is more appropriate) existed from 400 c.e., and that an early Alexandrian or B-textual cluster can be identified as early as the second century. Many of us think that a textual cluster parallel to the B-group, namely, the D-textual cluster, can be sketched out and traced back to a similarly early period, though this is deemed unlikely or impossible by some others.[22] Indeed, there has been a long-held and increasing sentiment, notably among members of the Münster Institute, that has questioned such traditional formulations of text-types, and a major purpose of the 2008 Münster Colloquium was to hear and to assess Gerd Mink's "Coherence-Based Genealogical Method" (hereafter CBGM) and other related research. A current view on "text-types" was exemplified recently by Klaus Wachtel, who concluded that "for terminological and method-

---

20. See, e.g., Eldon Jay Epp, "Issues in New Testament Textual Criticism: Moving from the Nineteenth Century to the Twenty-First Century," in *Rethinking New Testament Textual Criticism* (ed. David Alan Black; Grand Rapids: Baker Academic, 2002), 37–44 (repr., idem, *Perspectives*, 660–66).

21. On the demise of the Caesarean text-type, see Larry W. Hurtado, *Text-Critical Methodology and the Pre-Caesarean Text: Codex W in the Gospel of Mark* (SD 43; Grand Rapids: Eerdmans, 1981), passim, esp. 88–89; Eldon Jay Epp, "The Twentieth Century Interlude in New Testament Textual Criticism," *JBL* 93 (1974): 393–96 (repr., idem, *Perspectives*, 69–73). The disappearance of the Caesarean text is evident from the two editions of Bruce M. Metzger, *A Textual Commentary on the Greek New Testament: A Companion Volume to the United Bible Societies' Greek New Testament* (London: United Bible Societies, 1971; 2nd ed., Stuttgart: Deutsche Bibelgesellschaft/United Bible Societies, 1994). The 1st ed. (pp. xxviii–xxxi) listed witnesses to the four text-types, including the Caesarean, but the 2nd ed. (pp. 14*–16*) no longer has the Caesarean text. See the same in Metzger and Ehrman, *Text of the New Testament*, 276–80. Streeter's theory is treated further below.

22. On an early D-cluster, see Epp, "Issues in New Testament Textual Criticism," 38–44 and n. 63 (repr., idem, *Perspectives*, 660–65 and n. 64).

ological reasons the concept of text-types has become problematic,"[23] and a more direct and more radical stance was taken against "text-types" by David Parker in 2008. For example, Parker affirmed bluntly that "[i]t is now possible to move on, abandoning the concept of the text-type and, with the new tools and methods now available, retelling the history of the text."[24] He emphasized his further view that "the theory of two texts" in Acts should be abandoned,[25] namely, the coexistence of an Alexandrian (or B-text), and a so-called "Western" (or D-text). Parker's comments were in the context of new textual-critical methodologies, including the CBGM. The present writer, in a Society of Biblical Literature paper (Boston, November 2008), offered a defense of textual clusters (a term we shall now use often instead of the traditional "text-types"). That paper focused largely on the D-textual cluster of Acts. The argument was straightforward: the nature of the surviving witnesses (largely non-Greek) supporting this group render certain current methods, including the CBGM and others that cannot accommodate non-Greek evidence, ineffectual in proving or disproving the cluster's existence. A new method appropriate to the evidence was proposed in my paper, called the Triangulation of Witnesses.[26]

It is obvious, then, that fresh ways of defining groups constitute a current issue, even as the concept of forming groups is itself being questioned. This is welcome indeed, for, as in every generation, new approaches are essential for rethinking past methods and for moving forward to a better understanding of the myriad witnesses to the New Testament text. The present essay is not the place to pursue these matters further, yet they are important, for similar readings can be used to identify manuscript relationships that may lead to manuscript grouping, and the results assist in determining the priority of readings. When a variant in a variation unit is shared by two or preferably more members of a group that commonly share readings, that variant may gain the support of its entire group and may no longer be merely a reading of two or several individual witnesses. This is of particular interest, for example, when two competing readings

---

23. Klaus Wachtel, "Colwell Revisited: Grouping New Testament Manuscripts," in *The New Testament Text in Early Christianity: Proceedings of the Lille Colloquium, July 2000; Le texte du Nouveau Testament au début du christianisme: Actes du colloque de Lille, juillet 2000* (ed. C.-B. Amphoux and J. K. Elliott; Lausanne: Zèbre, 2003), 42.

24. David C. Parker, *An Introduction to the New Testament Manuscripts and Their Texts* (Cambridge: Cambridge University Press, 2008), 174.

25. Ibid., 298.

26. Eldon Jay Epp, "On David Parker's *An Introduction to the New Testament Manuscripts and Their Texts*." The paper itself will not be published, but the arguments presented there will be repeated in a forthcoming publication.

in a variation unit each can be identified as from a different textual group, which might indicate two or more separate streams of textual tradition within Christianity. Information of this kind assists not only in determining the earliest attainable text, but also in the task of understanding the history of the New Testament text.

SUMMARY

This brief survey reveals that two areas of exploration were and remain involved in the evolution of the criteria for the priority of readings in New Testament textual criticism. The first concerns the "canons of criticism" themselves, so named already at the outset of the eighteenth century, and variously designated since that time (see the discussion below). These are guidelines for determining which textual variants preceded others in a single variation unit, and historically they have numbered from several to more than three dozen.

Second, and concomitantly, manuscripts (and also versions and patristic citations) have been assigned various values in accordance with their consistency in supporting early or "reliable" readings, and some have emerged as "better" or "best" witnesses. Over time, certain of these textual clusters came to be identified (in the same manner as individual witnesses) as more likely than others to preserve earlier or "better" readings.

Finally, it is fair to say that after editors of critical texts and editions of the Greek New Testament had presented and discussed their critical principles over some four hundred years, a general consensus arose and lists of criteria began to look more and more alike, with discarded canons left by the wayside. A current list will be offered below, following discussion of a preliminary issue, namely, terminology

2. Terminology for the "Canons of Criticism"

One area of possible confusion during the lengthy history of the "canons of criticism" stems from the terminology employed, at least in English, for these criteria commonly have been designated individually as a "canon," "principle," "rule," "standard," or "criterion." Several of these terms in dictionary definitions tend to be defined by two or three of the other terms,[27] frustrating distinctions among them. *Canon*, for example, may be glossed in Greek and Latin usage as "rule" or "standard," and in English as "an established or basic rule or principle;" or "a standard to

---

27. Selected glosses from *Webster's New World College Dictionary* (4th ed.; Cleveland: Wiley, 2002) or *Webster's Ninth New Collegiate Dictionary* (Springfield, MA: Meriam-Webster, 1990), in loc.

judge by; a criterion." *Rule* likewise is used for "a standard of judgment: criterion" or "a regulating principle." *Principle* generally comes out as "a fundamental and comprehensive law." Finally, *criterion* is glossed as "a standard, rule, [and this is important] or test *by which something can be judged*; a measure of value."

It is clear, then, that one overlapping area of usage emphasizes something fixed, regulated, or established, while the range of usage includes also—for most of the terms—the *means for judging* something. The latter, I would say, is the core Greek usage of κριτήριον, as "criterion" is in English, namely, a *means or basis* for judging and deciding something and, therefore, would not refer to the judgment or decision itself, nor is it something already fixed or established. Understood in this way, for our purposes the term "criterion" is preferable to all the others, for, in textual criticism, a criterion is akin to a guideline, a consideration, or an argument, or to a proposition, a proposal, or a probability *utilized as a basis for making a judgment* about the priority of one reading over another. That is why Tregelles, in his extensive discussions of these criteria, several times employed the phrase "the balance of probabilities"[28] and why Westcott and Hort divided their main approach into "Intrinsic Probabilities" and "Transcriptional Probabilities."[29] Sir Frederic Kenyon also used the phrase "internal probabilities,"[30] so in my opinion we should speak of external and internal criteria, though we could very well speak of "External Probabilities" and "Internal Probabilities," and elsewhere employ "probability" as the equivalent of "criterion."

For example, one criterion is that the harder (that is, the more difficult or rougher) reading has priority over a smooth or easy reading. Yet, in a given variation unit, that criterion may be applicable to one variant, but another variant may be strongly supported by numerous early witnesses or appear to explain the rise of all the other variants, including the "harder reading." This illustrates that none of these common criteria can be simply a fixed "principle" or "rule." Rather, each criterion constitutes a means by which a decision is made, so every variant must be tested to determine its *probability* of being prior to every other variant in the unit, and more than one might appear to qualify. So the balance of probabilities comes in and the question repeats itself: Which criterion is more probable in a given case? The phrase, "in a given case," then opens further discussion, because the criteria as fixed or authoritative "rules" are no

---

28. Tregelles, *Account of the Printed Text*, 149–50.
29. Westcott and Hort, *New Testament in the Original Greek*, 2:19–39.
30. Frederic G. Kenyon, *Handbook to the Textual Criticism of the New Testament* (2nd ed.; London: Macmillan, 1926), 288, referring to Lachmann's refusal to employ "internal probabilities," that is, internal criteria.

longer relevant (if they ever were), nor can they be applied mechanically. Rather, each individual situation must be examined from all angles. Then new probabilities arise: Is one variant supported by geographically distributed witnesses? Does one variant evince harmonization with parallel passages, or show conformity to standard liturgical formulations, or to orthodox theological viewpoints, and so on. The critic must employ all applicable criteria, place the results on the balance scale, and make a decision in the direction that the scale tips. So the final question actually is this: Which probability is more probable or more plausible in view of these immediate and larger contexts of the passage and other additional factors in the "local" situation of a variation unit?

It will be obvious from these generalized though not atypical examples that textual criticism is rarely if ever mechanistic or a "science" (though it has its scientific elements), but far more it is an "art." With my students, therefore, I insist that, in reality, the exegete becomes the final arbiter in text-critical decisions, since the whole literary and sociocultural universe surrounding a variation unit theoretically comes into play in reaching a text-critical decision. Quite naturally, however, exegetes on occasion express the wish that textual critics produce a handy manual giving solutions to several hundred problematic variation units in the New Testament in accordance with established rules or principles. But there are no shortcuts—no simplistic ways to circumvent the interactive and often conflicting criteria with their layers of probability. Nor can textual critics escape their obligation to initiate exegetes into these mysteries by insisting that the whole sophisticated discipline be understood better.

Perhaps due in part to complexities of these kinds, Lachmann rejected the internal criteria because, he said, "by their nature almost all cancel each other out,"[31] and Frederic G. Kenyon characterized Lachmann's action as an attempt to "eliminate altogether the 'personal equation.'"[32] More than once Henry Alford has been quoted as sharing this skeptical view of "canons of subjective criticism," as he called the internal criteria, for he said:

> In very many cases they may be made to tell with equal force either way. One critic adopts a reading because it is in accord with the usage of the sacred writer; another holds it, for this very reason, to have been a subsequent conformation of the text. One believes a particle to have been inserted to give completeness; another to have been omitted as appearing superfluous.[33]

---

31. Timpanaro, *Genesis*, 88.
32. Kenyon, *Handbook*, 288.
33. Henry Alford, *The Greek Testament, with a Critically Revised Text* (4 vols.; 6th ed.; Boston, 1868; repr., Chicago: Moody, 1958), 1:87–88. Quoted in part by S. P.

But to quote only this much from Alford is a disservice to him, for in the immediately following context he refused to "cast contempt" on the use of these criteria. He stated forthrightly that "where the probabilities appear to be balanced, we are bound . . . to give the ancient witnesses the benefit of the doubt," but "where the preponderance appears to us to be clear, we ought . . . to reject them [the ancient witnesses] in this case, as we boldly follow them in others."[34]

To us, of course, this is nothing less than an accurate characterization of how external and internal criteria function, but—in contrast to Lachmann—we choose to view this process positively, as affording an opportunity to assess all aspects of a set of variants and then move toward a decision. Therefore, treated properly as "criteria" and recognizing that "probabilities" are involved at virtually every stage, we welcome all credible criteria and employ them as appropriate in each given situation.

The relevance of all or most of the criteria for determining the priority of readings (as in the list to follow) is widely recognized by New Testament textual critics, though the usefulness of a few has been questioned in recent decades. To the contrary, however, the advocates of "Thoroughgoing Eclecticism," notably the late George Kilpatrick and currently and prominently J. Keith Elliott, limit their validity almost exclusively to internal criteria.[35] This is understandable because adherents of this viewpoint are concerned almost entirely with individual readings and much less with manuscripts as a whole, and even less with groups of manuscripts, that is, textual clusters. As Elliott put it, "In the eyes of the thoroughgoing eclectic textual critics there is in fact no such thing as a <<good>> manuscript or a <<bad>> manuscript, only good readings or secondary readings,"[36] and the aim of textual criticism for them is "to try to establish . . . the original words of the New Testament authors." This kind of eclecticism, says Elliott, "produces reasons how the secondary readings

---

Tregelles, in T. H. Horne, *An Introduction to the Critical Study and Knowledge of the Holy Scriptures* (4 vols.; 11th ed.; London: Longman, Green, Longman, and Roberts, 1860), 4:755; Philip Schaff, *A Companion to the Greek Testament and the English Version* (New York and London: Harper, 1903), 268; and by Marvin R. Vincent, *A History of the Textual Criticism of the New Testament* (New York: Macmillan, 1903), 138.

34. Alford, *Greek Testament*, 88.

35. George D. Kilpatrick, *The Principles and Practice of New Testament Textual Criticism: Collected Essays of G. D. Kilpatrick* (ed. J. K. Elliott; BETL 96; Leuven: Peeters, 1990), will illustrate his views; J. Keith Elliott,"Can We Recover the Original Text of the New Testament? An Examination of the Rôle of Thoroughgoing Eclecticism," in his *Essays and Studies in New Testament Textual Criticism* (Estudios de filología neotestamentaria 3; Cordova: Ediciones el Almendro, 1992), 39 et passim (This was a new essay written for his volume of previously published articles).

36. Elliott, "Can We Recover the Original Text," 38; see also 27–28.

arose," so "it tends to be a history of textual variation" and not a "history of documents which tries to explain the rise of alleged major recensions" nor "an attempt to trace the genealogical pedigree of manuscripts." Indeed, for him "the extent to which a reconstruction of [a history of the text] becomes significant in selecting readings is dubious."[37] For this and other reasons, external criteria are largely dismissed.

For very different reasons, proponents variously of the *textus receptus*, the majority text, or the Byzantine text, who assert that the authoritative text has been preserved in the manuscripts that survive in the greatest numbers, naturally march to a different drummer than the one who taps out the rhythm of seeking the most ancient witnesses.[38]

It is appropriate here to present, one by one, the traditional external and internal criteria as currently modified and widely accepted (though the formulations remain my own), and to discuss or comment on several, particularly those recently in dispute.

3. A Listing of Current External and Internal Criteria/Probabilities

Obviously our sketch of how the criteria for the priority of readings developed could be expanded much further.[39] My views on criteria, both external and internal, also have evolved over time,[40] yet most textual critics may find the following list helpful, if only as a basis for discussion. Naturally, such a list remains provisional and subject to modification both in substance and in phraseology—and perhaps also in arrangement. It will be observed that the criteria below are biased toward the view that

---

37. Ibid., 37.

38. For a recent explanation by the leading scholar defending this view, see Maurice A. Robinson, "The Case for Byzantine Priority," in Black, *Rethinking New Testament Textual Criticism*, 125–39.

39. For an extensive history of the development of the criteria, see my forthcoming chapters in *The New Cambridge History of the Bible* (4 vols; Cambridge: Cambridge University Press, 2010): "Critical Editions and the Development of Text-Critical Methods," two parts (in vols. 3 and 4).

40. Earlier lists appeared in 1976 (rudimentary) and 1997 (expanded and refined): see Epp, *Perspectives*, 157–58, 480–82; and 492. The present list supersedes both previous versions. In addition to lists of criteria referred to in the preceding discussions, see C. E. Hammond, *Outlines of Textual Criticism Applied to the New Testament* (Clarendon Press Series; Oxford: Clarendon, 1880), 93–99; these, as well as the criteria of Allen P. Wikgren, are summarized in Edward Hobbs, "An Introduction to Methods of Textual Criticism," in *The Critical Study of Sacred Texts* (ed. Wendy Doniger O'Flaherty; Berkeley Religious Studies Series 2; Berkeley: Graduate Theological Union, , 1979), 24–26.

the goal of New Testament textual criticism is, in the first instance but only partially, to establish the earliest attainable text, since it has become problematic to speak of establishing the "original text."[41] A more nuanced statement of textual criticism's goal will follow. It is assumed also that the criteria below are not concerned with nonsense readings, though all must be scrutinized to be certain that that they do not make sense.

I have chosen to form three divisions of criteria rather than the traditional two, for reasons that will be explained in attendant comments. Also, I have retained the somewhat awkward expression "criteria/probability" in view of the earlier discussion of terminology for the criteria. Please note that the criteria in each of the three sections have been phrased in such a way that if a variant meets a given criterion, that variant gains in its priority over the other variants in its variation unit. Each criterion is followed by a rationale (and on occasion by qualifications), and all are numbered sequentially for a total of sixteen.

A. The Preeminent Criterion/Probability: Local Genealogical Priority

If this criterion accurately describes one textual variant within a variation unit, that variant has a highly increased probability of belonging to the earliest attainable text:

1. *The variant is able to account for the origin, development, or presence of all other readings in its variation-unit.*

{Because such a variant logically must have preceded all others that can be shown to have evolved from it. (Kurt Aland calls this the "local genealogical method." It is considered by most to be the preeminent criterion, and all other criteria, external and internal, can be considered its subsidiaries.)}

This criterion—that the variant explaining all other variant readings in its variation unit has priority—commonly is considered preeminent among all criteria, external and internal, and decisive in those cases where it is applicable. Moreover, it is among the oldest known criteria, since it was Canon XXIV in Gerhard's 1711 list: "When the origin of variant readings is known, for the most part a varying reading disappears," and he offered harmonizations among the Gospels as examples.[42] The criterion appeared in several subsequent canon lists, though apparently no list assigned it to the first position, but comments on it over time often give it predominance. It has been said that Bengel's overall urgent question was, Which reading (in each case) is likely to have given rise to the others? His answer appears

---

41. Eldon Jay Epp, "The Multivalence of the Term 'Original Text' in New Testament Textual Criticism," *HTR* 92 (1999): 245–81.

42. Gerhard, Ἡ ΚΑΙΝΗ ΔΙΑΘΗΚΗ, 14; examples, 64.

to have been the harder-reading criterion—the more difficult reading is to be preferred to the easy. This was likely his premier criterion,[43] though subsidiary to the larger question raised. Griesbach's opening principle in his list asserted that the shorter reading is to be preferred to the longer, and this is explained and qualified by numerous familiar but subsidiary criteria, of which the eleventh affirmed that the reading explaining all others has priority.[44] Tischendorf placed this criterion of the explanatory variant as number 4 among five but noted, "Taken broadly, this is the foremost among all rules."[45] Tregelles asserted that "the rule is good, but the application is often very difficult,"[46] but Westcott and Hort employed it as the very definition of Transcriptional Probability, which, along with Intrinsic Probability, constituted their two categories of internal evidence. Intrinsic Probability referred to "what an author is likely to have written," and Transcriptional Probability to "what copyists are likely to have made him [the author] seem to write"; hence, Transcriptional Probability is concerned with "the relative fitness of each [reading] for explaining the existence of the others."[47] Kurt and Barbara Aland listed this criterion as number 8 in a list of twelve "rules," noting, however, that it is "an extremely important device, because the reading which can most easily explain the derivation of the other forms is itself the most likely original."[48] Hence, they named it the "local genealogical method," which earlier was characterized as "the only [method] which meets the requirements of the New Testament textual tradition"[49] (though one wonders, then, why it was not placed higher in their list). The Alands made it clear, however, that this "local" method was to be distinguished from genealogical method in the study of classical literature, where it meant establishing a stemma of all manuscripts preserving a writing. Rather, the complex nature of the transmission of the New Testament, including numerous manuscripts with a mixed text, requires a variant-by-variant approach, that is, establishing a stemma of readings for each variation unit, thereby "reflecting the lines of development among

---

43. Werner Georg Kümmel, *The New Testament: The History of the Investigation of Its Problems* (Nashville and New York: Abingdon, 1972), 48, 414 n. 45.

44. Johann Jakob Griesbach, *Novum Testamentum Graece: Textum ad fidem codicum versionum et patrum* (2nd ed.; 2 vols.; London: Elmsly; Halle: Haeredes, 1796-1806), 1:lxiii–lxiv = 'Prolegomena,' §III, ¶11.

45. For Tischendorf's criteria, and esp. number 4, see n. 18, above.

46. Tregelles, *Account of the Printed Text*, 222; for examples, 191–92, 230.

47. Westcott and Hort, *New Testament in the Original Greek*, 2:22; see 23.

48. Aland and Aland, *Text of the New Testament*, 281, 291.

49. Kurt Aland et al., eds., *Novum Testamentum Graece* (26th ed.; 4th rev. printing; Stuttgart: Deutsche Bibelstiftung, 1981), 43*. "Determining the 'source-variant'" is better than the other criteria for Vaganay and Amphoux, *Introduction to New Testament Textual Criticism*, 81–83.

the readings, demonstrating which reading must be original because it best explains the rise of the other readings."⁵⁰ All things considered, this criterion is the preeminent one, and for that reason we place it in its own category and at the head of our list.

The assertion that all other criteria, external and internal, can be subsumed under this preeminent criterion is justified because the other criteria at times play a role in discerning the genealogical path taken by variants within a single variation unit. To be specific, the first external criterion (no. 2 below), emphasizing the support of the earliest witnesses (manuscripts, versions, patristic citations), provides approximate dates for those witnesses, and on occasion more exact dates at which specific readings were known. Readings, to be sure, can be much earlier than the documents in which they appear, but those in the first hand cannot have originated later than the date of copying.⁵¹ Naturally, complications arise. For example, correctors of manuscripts must be clearly identified chronologically; second, patristic citations may have been altered in the course of transmission and, therefore, they themselves must submit to text-critical scrutiny; and, third, the earliest versional manuscripts generally are later, and often much later, than the version's time of origin, so that they are not as helpful as might have been expected.

The second external criterion (no. 3), involving the "best quality" witnesses, has its problematic side, not least the slipperiness of the term "best," but also the long experience required to make such judgments and the continuing differences of opinion that will persist. Yet such quality judgments have been found useful. In using the third external criterion (no. 4), on geographical diversity, ideally distinctive variants in each locale should be shown to have independent origins, without possible linking during their transmission. The same caveats apply to the use of criterion no. 5, involving groups of manuscripts (and other witnesses linked to them) that support a given reading: an assured group reading must belong to a group that is sufficiently separated from other groups to ensure an independent tradition or transmission. If so, obviously the antiquity, "best" quality, and geographical location of a group can assist in identifying a given variant's place in a local genealogical stemma. Finally, the last external criterion (no. 6), involving multiple support by

---

50. Aland and Aland, *Text of the New Testament*, 291; see also 34, 281. It is mentioned in Metzger and Ehrman, *Text of the New Testament*, 235 n. 66, where Gerd Mink is credited as the developer of the method: G. Mink, "Eine umfassende Genealogie der neutestamentlichen Überlieferung," *NTS* 39 (1993): 481–99.

51. Naturally, the same variant, earlier or later, may arise independently in another manuscript or witness—with no interconnection and permitting no easy determination of a variant's ultimate *terminus a quo*.

two or more criteria (external or internal) provides "strength in numbers" in favor of a given variant reading over against readings with less support in the local genealogy of a variation unit.

It is not necessary to review all the internal criteria to see how they contribute to the preeminent criterion. In sum, the probability of a variant having priority increases to the extent that it is the harder reading, or is in conformity with the author's style and theology, or with common Semitic expressions of the day, or if it lacks conformity to parallel passages or other items in the immediate context, or to Old Testament passages, liturgical forms, or other theological or ideological contexts of the scribe's time. The complications here, however, are legion compared with the external criteria, for, as everyone knows, few variants will meet all such tests: some criteria will not apply, and others will be in conflict—one criterion favoring a given variant's priority, but others detracting from it. So, once again the textual critic must resort to balancing the probabilities, that is, assessing how strong the arguments are on each side, and, using the skills of the art, make a reasonable decision.

Our preeminent criterion, then, becomes something of a "super criterion" that embraces the other various criteria and employs them as appropriate. In one case, for instance, a variant heavily supported by early witnesses (manuscripts, versions, patristic quotations) against readings with clearly later attestation would be sufficient evidence for many of us that the earliest attainable reading has been identified. Yet the textual critic will insist that the priority of that chosen variant must be demonstrated in every possible way. For example, the reading identified as earliest by external criteria actually might be an alteration of a still earlier reading no longer readily visible. In some such cases, the hidden underlying variant might have been preserved and can be found in a later extant witness— and the local genealogical technique might reveal that such a reading in a later witness takes priority over the one in the older source. Rarely, of course, are situations as simple and clear as in this theoretical example. But it illustrates the functionality of the preeminent criterion.

B. Criteria/Probabilities related to External Evidence
If a criterion accurately describes one textual variant within a variation unit, that variant has an increased probability of belonging to the earliest attainable text.
2. *A variant supported by the earliest manuscripts, patristic citations, or versions, or by manuscripts (or other witnesses) assuredly preserving early texts.*[52]

---

52. Johann Salomo Semler (1765) differentiated "external age" (the antiquity of a manuscript) from "internal age" (the antiquity of the readings attested by it), though Nicolaas Heinsius (1661) earlier had recognized that "very correct read-

{Because historians of the text conclude that ancient manuscripts have been less likely subject to conflation, conformity to ecclesiastical texts or traditions, and other scribal alterations. (A difficulty, of course, is that scribal alterations intrude from the earliest time.)}

Normally this criterion, emphasizing the antiquity of witnesses, would be placed first because virtually the entire history of critical editions of the Greek New Testament, and the accompanying development of criteria for the priority of readings, is the story of how the relatively few ancient manuscripts triumphed over the exceedingly numerous later manuscripts. However, since manuscripts and other witnesses of comparable antiquity not infrequently disagree with one another (for example, $\mathfrak{P}^{45}$ and $\mathfrak{P}^{75}$, Codices ℵ and B, Codices D [05] and W [032], etc.), some other procedure usually is necessary to determine the prior reading. Ancient manuscripts are not, by any means, denigrated thereby, for most textual critics begin the analysis of a variation unit by identifying the earliest witnesses and the readings they support. Should one reading be supported by third- and fourth-century papyri, majuscules, and patristic evidence, for instance, it would attract immediate attention, but then the support of other readings will be explored, thereby invoking the local genealogical procedure that operates until a text-critical decision is reached.

Although Erasmus (1516), under pressure from his publisher, showed little interest in finding ancient manuscripts, Mill (as reported by Bentley) had intended to publish, along with his edition of 1707, texts of ancient manuscripts then known, such as Codices Alexandrinus (A, 02), Bezae (D, 05), and Claromontanus (D^p, 06), thus indicating his preference for these early manuscripts, but his plan never came to fruition.[53] Bentley himself, however, was explicit and emphatic about the importance and use of ancient manuscripts in his 1720 *Proposals for Printing* a Greek and Latin New Testament. Its text would follow that "represented in the most ancient and venerable MSS. in Greek and Roman capital letters" (Proposal I), and readings selected for the text must be confirmed by the use of "the old versions, Syriac, Coptic, Gothic, and Aethiopic, and of all the fathers, Greeks and Latins, within the first five centuries" (Proposal IV).[54] Alas, circumstances prevented the completion of his edition, but this emphasis on ancient textual witnesses was continued by Bengel (1742), who stated that *"most important of all, ancient witnesses* [are to be preferred] to modern

---

ings" could occur in a recent manuscript, as reported by Timpanaro, *Genesis of Lachmann's Method*, 69–70 and n. 33

53. Tregelles, *Account of the Printed Text*, 45–46; 45[note] provides the Latin text of the relevant portion of Bentley's *Epistola ad Joannem Millium* (1691).

54. For Bentley's "Proposals," see Ellis, *Bentleii critica sacra*, xvii–xix.

ones";[55] by Wettstein (1751–52) in three or four maxims;[56] by Griesbach (1796–1806), for whom the "old and weighty witnesses" were crucial, and these were to be found in the two oldest of his three "recensions"—the Alexandrian and Western, with the Constantinopolitan coming later;[57] by Lachmann (1831, 1842–50), who sought the text of the late fourth century—the date of the oldest known manuscripts at that time—and who relied "nowhere on his own judgment, but the usage of the most ancient eastern churches";[58] and finally, with rare exceptions, by all textual critics who followed.

As noted earlier, two very different viewpoints currently are the most prominent exceptions to the otherwise unanimous preference for the most ancient witnesses. First, those arguing for the priority of the *textus receptus*, the majority text, or the Byzantine obviously will not regard the oldest manuscripts as major transmitters of the original text.[59] Second (but with no relation to the view above), proponents of Thoroughgoing Eclecticism would appear to pay much less attention to external evidence generally than the history of New Testament textual criticism commends. Nonetheless, they and we share the same goal, to discover the earliest attainable text, by separating, as Elliott stated it, the "good" or "original" reading from the secondary reading(s) in each variation unit. He affirmed, however, that this can be done by the use of internal criteria with little

---

55. Johann Albrecht Bengel, *Gnomon Novi Testamenti* (3rd ed., ed. J. Steudel; Tübingen, 1855), xiii [= Latin ed.], his canon 12); idem, *New Testament Word Studies* (2 vols.; Grand Rapids: Kregel, 1971), 1:xviii [= English ed.]. Also, in his summary of five principles (canon 15), first comes "The antiquity of witnesses" (Latin ed., xiii; English ed., 1:xviii).

56. Johann Jakob Wettstein, Ἡ ΚΑΙΝΗ ΔΙΑΘΗΚΗ: *Novum Testamentum Graecum* Amsterdam: Dommeriana, 1751–52), 2:869 (his maxim 17; see also 2:867–68 for maxims 13 and 14, on the great weight placed on the witness of ancient versions and the Fathers); also in Wettstein, *Libelli ad crisin* (Halle: Trampe, 1766), 96–99, 86–90; and in Francis Wrangham, *Briani Waltoni S.T.P. in biblia polyglotta prolegomena* (Cambridge: Deighton; Oxford: Parker, 1828), 1:511–12. For translation, see Hulbert-Powell, *John James Wettstein*, 119–20; Tregelles, *Account of the Printed Text*, 79–80.

57. Griesbach, *Novum Testamentum Graece*, 1:lix–lxxxi = 'Prolegomena,' §III; on the phrase, "ancient and weighty witnesses," lx, ¶1; on the oldest groups, lxxix–lxxx, ¶e, ¶f, ¶g. See Tregelles, in Horne, *Introduction*, 4:71–76.

58. Lachmann's basic principles were given in ninety-two words at the end of his small 1831 edition. The Latin text is provided in Caspar René Gregory, *Textkritik des Neuen Testamentes* (Leipzig: Hinrichs, 1909), 966–67, and in Tregelles, *Account of the Printed Text*, 98 n.*. He altered his approach for the text in his larger, two-volume edition of 1842–50 by adopting the combined evidence of eastern *and western* witnesses (as he understood those terms): Tregelles, 100.

59. See n. 38 above.

attention to age of manuscript(s) or to any other external criteria, allowing, for instance, a late minority reading to be judged original.[60] All of us are open, theoretically and practically, to such a possibility, but we see no reason to ignore readily available ancient evidence or to avoid forming value judgments about our ancient witnesses based on extensive observation and long collective experience. It is fair to say, therefore, that most of us affirm the overriding significance of the oldest manuscripts, versions, and patristic citations. After all, in addition to our technical arguments, in the quest for the earliest attainable text, do we not have "common sense" on our side, which suggests that the logical starting point is the earliest extant material, even though it is recognized that antiquity of witnesses is not in itself sufficient for the text-critical task.

> 3. *A variant's support by the "best quality" manuscripts (or other witnesses).*
> {Because manuscripts evidencing careful copying and transmission are less likely to have been subject to textual corruption or contamination, and because manuscripts that frequently and consistently offer readings accredited as the earliest attainable text thereby acquire a reputation of general high quality. (Note, however, that internal criteria are utilized to reach the conclusion that certain manuscripts are consistently "best." Naturally, all manuscripts are open to scribal alterations.)}

"Best quality" in this criterion is placed in quotation marks because it is ambiguous and relative. "Best" in what sense? "Best" in whose judgment? "Best" by what standards? Westcott- and Hort also placed the term in quotation marks, but for them "best" was neither ambiguous nor relative, for it referred to the purity of a text—its lack of corruption or contamination—and such manuscripts were designated "neutral," led by Codices ℵ and B.[51] At the same time, experience, that is, observing the manuscripts and other witnesses that time and time again were found in support of the earliest attainable readings in their respective variation units, has brought about a broad consensus that certain witnesses are "better" representatives of that earliest reachable text than most others.

A caveat is essential here: obviously bias can enter these judgments, and a prominent though complex example might be the numerous cases in which readings in the B- or Alexandrian textual cluster stand in contrast to those in the D- (or so-called "Western") textual cluster. This long-standing B-/D-text controversy really has not been resolved, and a defensible

---

60. Elliott, "Can We Recover the Original Text," 40; see also 37–39.
61. Westcott and Hort, *New Testament in the Original Greek*, 2:35, for "best"; on the "purity" of B and ℵ, 2:251; see also, e.g., 150, 210, 220, 224, 239, 271.

argument can still be made for their comparable age. Yet, when the D-text cluster was judged as very ancient but also as corrupt (except for a small number of "Western non-interpolations"), as in Westcott and Hort's view, it easily could be disregarded in a rather consistent fashion.[62] Similarly, when the D-text manuscripts were placed in a separate category, as by the Alands (apparently three steps removed from manuscripts "with a very high proportion of early text. . . , presumably the original text"[63]), the impression given was that already they had been pre-judged and, in a sense, had been sent into exile.

Advocates of Thoroughgoing Eclecticism have been most vociferous in rejecting the notion of any "best" manuscript, describing, with some justice, Westcott and Hort's veneration of Codices ℵ and B as the "cult of the 'best' manuscripts" and similarly characterizing others' preference for these two manuscripts. As quoted earlier, Elliott affirms that there are no "good" manuscripts or texts or "bad" manuscripts or texts, "only good readings or secondary readings," and he calls for a shift, "in which the cult of the best manuscripts gives way to the cult of the best readings."[64] In the final analysis, however, textual critics will continue to make reasoned judgments about the relative quality of individual witnesses and also of their groups.

> 4. *A variant supported by manuscripts (or other witnesses) with wide geographical distribution.*
> {Because readings attested in more than one locality are less likely to be accidental or idiosyncratic. (However, the provenance of relatively few manuscripts is certain, though the general locale of versions and patristic citations is more frequently known. A difficulty is determining whether witnesses from different locales represent genuinely separate traditions.)}

This geographical distribution criterion has a long history. It appeared first in Bentley's 1713 *Remarks upon a Late Discourse of Free-Thinking*, where he effectively justified John Mill's thirty thousand variant readings in his much maligned Greek New Testament. In this connection, Bentley spoke of manuscripts from Egypt, Asia, and the Western churches, stating that "the very distances of places, as well as the numbers of the books, demonstrate that there could be no collusion, no altering nor interpolating

---

62. Ibid., 2:178; also 122–23, 131, 172–73; on the early date of the "Western" or D-text, 2:120, 149.
63. Aland and Aland, *Text of the New Testament*, 335–36; see also 64 and 95.
64. See, e.g., Elliott, "Can We Recover the Original Text," 27–28, 38.

one copy by another, nor all by any of them."[65] Soon thereafter, in 1725, Bengel divided his witnesses into two "nations," African (the oldest manuscripts and versions) and Asiatic (witnesses from the area of Constantinople), but, as already noted, he subdivided the earlier African "nation" into two "tribes," resulting in a configuration of two early groups and a later one. On this basis, Bengel asserted "explicitly that it is the consensus of manuscripts *belonging to different families* that guarantees the antiquity of a reading."[66] This pattern, with some modifications, was followed by Johannes Salomo Semler in 1764 with an Eastern group and a Western or Egypto-Palestinian group (where the term Western was already geographically inexact, for it included the Syriac). Later, in 1767, he separated the Egyptian witnesses to form an additional Alexandrian group.[67] Griesbach, in his second edition of 1796–1806, held to the Alexandrian, Western, and Constantinopolitan scheme, though a year before his death he merged the two early groups because he was unable to differentiate them due to the discovery of new readings.[68] In 1331, Lachmann's Italian (Eastern) and African (Western), plus the ever-present *textus receptus*, followed the same pattern, and he states the geographical criterion in simple terms: ancient witnesses that "derive from the most widely separated places" carry great weight. Moreover, "Where manuscripts from distant regions agree with one another, this is likely to have been propagated from very ancient sources into the various places."[69] Tischendorf proposed two pairs of witnesses: (1) Alexandrian and Latin, and (2) Asiatic and Byzantine, though he did little with this classification, and Tregelles thought it "impossible" to be definite about manuscript classifications, although he acknowledged two large families, the more ancient Alexandrian and a later Constantinopolitan group, but allowing that a Western branch might be drawn from the Alexandrian, forming a two-branched family.[70]

This brings us to Westcott and Hort and their 1881–82 edition of *The New Testament in the Original Greek*. The development of their configuration of text-types is more easily and better understood when the hypotheses of

---

65. An eighty-five page letter to Francis Hare from Bentley (who wrote under the pseudonym Phileleutherus Lipsiensis) published in London. It went through eight editions, the latest in 1825. See Fox, *John Mill and Richard Bentley*, 114 and 161 n. 20.

66. Timpanaro, *Genesis*, 66; see n. 20 for three quotations from Bengel.

67. On Semler, see Metzger and Ehrman, *Text of the New Testament*, 161–62.

68. See Tregelles, in Horne, *Introduction*, 4:71–75; idem, *Account of the Printed Text*, 90–91.

69. Timpanaro, *Genesis*, 85–86 and n. 8. See Tregelles, in Horne, *Introduction*, 4:134–36.

70. On Tischendorf, see Tregelles, *Account of the Printed Text*, 127–28; for Tregelles' own views, ibid., 104–7, esp. 106.

the preceding two centuries have been reviewed. The evolving terminology began with Bentley's Egypt, the Western churches, and Asia. In Bengel Egypt/Egyptian becomes African and then, with Semler and Griesbach, turned into Alexandrian; Western carried through as such; and Asia/Asiatic became Constantinopolitan or Byzantine in Semler, Griesbach, and Tischendorf. Lachmann, however stayed with Eastern and Western. Yet, as early as Griesbach at the end of the eighteenth century three groups of witnesses emerged: Alexandrian, Western, and Constantinopolitan.

Westcott and Hort's meticulously elaborated theory identified its text-types largely by locale, namely, a Western, an Alexandrian, and a Syrian or Eastern text. They judged the Western as probably the earliest, with the Alexandrian (which shared a common ancestor with their "Neutral" text and therefore part of the same textual line) a close contemporary, and these two early textual streams evolved, by conflation and other scribal or editorial alterations and additions, into the later Syrian or Byzantine text-type.[71] Their "Western text" soon was judged, however, to contain strong Eastern witnesses and thus was incorrect geographically, though the name has persisted over time and rather widely.

Kirsopp Lake in 1904 emphasized "local texts," though he used the phrase in a broad sense to refer to New Testament texts in use by early churches, for example, in Africa, in Alexandria, in the East, or by various church writers in their specific times and places.[72] Then, in 1924, Streeter developed his "theory of local texts," an attempt to demonstrate that by about 200 C.E. distinguishable text-types had developed in the great centers of Christianity, namely, Alexandria; the East at Caesarea and Antioch; and the West at Italy-Gaul and Carthage.[73] To be sure, appropriate witnesses—Greek manuscripts, versions, and patristic citations—can be identified with Alexandria, but beyond that the theory did not stand the test of time, for the Caesarean text has all but disappeared, and distinctive groups of textual witnesses cannot assuredly be identified with the remaining centers.[74] Naturally, as time went on, new manuscript discoveries also played havoc with Streeter's tidy proposal.

The outcome of this extensive concern with localities was twofold.

---

71. Westcott and Hort, *New Testament in the Original Greek*, 2:90–179; see summaries on 145–46, 178–79. See Metzger and Ehrman, *Text of the New Testament*, 174–83, and their diagram, 180.

72. Kirsopp Lake, *The Influence of Textual Criticism on the Exegesis of the New Testament: An Inaugural Lecture Delivered before the University of Leiden, on January 27, 1904* (Oxford: Parker, 1904), 6–7, 10–12 [a 27-page pamphlet].

73. Burnett Hillman Streeter, *The Four Gospels: A Study of Origins* (1925; rev. 4th impression, 1930; repr., London: Macmillan, 1951), 26–76; see Metzger and Ehrman, *Text of the New Testament*, 214-18, for a summary.

74. Metzger and Ehrman, *Text of the New Testament*, 218, 310–11.

First, witnesses from one locality—whether a large area or one more restricted—rarely show uniformity of text, especially in the earlier periods. An obvious example is Egypt, where virtually all the Greek papyri have been discovered, but they represent, from the earliest time and beyond, a wide variety of texts. Second, as a result, clear distinctions among textual witnesses or groups of witnesses cannot be drawn solely on the basis of localities.

Yet certain useful judgments can be made. For example, the geographical origin or use of some Greek manuscripts can be discerned, though the number is relatively small. More obviously, patristic citations almost automatically can be located, and versions likewise more readily can be identified with the general locations in which a given language was used, for example, Latin in the West, Coptic in Egypt, Syriac with Syriac-speaking Christians in the East and later in the West as well, and so forth.

The current criterion, however, differs in emphasis from what might have been expected from a review of geographical considerations involving the New Testament text. No longer will a simple geographical scheme work, such as an "African" group (with the oldest manuscripts and versions), and an "Asiatic" group (with later Constantinopolitan manuscripts). Rather, the current criterion favors an *individual* variant that has wide geographical support—a variant, namely, that occurs in several witnesses of varying geographical locations. The assumption is that such a variant is unlikely to have arisen accidentally but (as described by Bengel) more likely to have found its way, through the process of transmission, to a variety of locations. Such a variant is reckoned thereby as a more stable element in the textual tradition than variants not so widely distributed.

> 5. *A variant supported by one or more established **groups** of manuscripts (or other witnesses) of recognized antiquity, character, and perhaps location, i.e., of recognized "best quality."*
> {Because, not only individual manuscripts (and other witnesses), but families and textual clusters can be judged as to age, quality, and (sometimes) location. (Again, internal criteria contribute to these judgments.)}

This criterion, which assumes that a variant found in a witness that is a member of a recognized textual group, such as a family or larger textual cluster, has a claim to the characteristics of that group. If a group qualifies as more ancient or consistently carries "better" readings than other groups, the variant in question gains support simply by its association with that group. This subject, as all will recognize, is not only vastly complicated but also controversial, and the criterion, therefore, will be accepted or rejected in accordance with one's views on the nature of textual groups, their times of origin, but also one's convictions about their very existence. The issues cannot be pursued anew at this juncture. I wish only to point to a paper presented in Münster at the 1993 International Meeting of the Society of Biblical Literature and published in 1994, namely, Jacobus Petzer's "The History of the New Testament Text—Its Reconstruction, Significance and Use in New Testament Textual Criticism."[75] In Petzer's insightful and instructive essay, which gently—or not so gently—skewers many of us, he deftly outlines the difficulties presented by the text-type issue and by some of our basic methodologies. Current and future studies will clarify the issue.[76]

> 6. *A variant with multiple attestation, that is, support by two or more of the preceding or following criteria.*
> {Because multiplied support by the earliest witnesses or groups of witnesses, by witnesses shown to be most reliable in quality, or most diverse in location, and/or by multiple internal criteria, has a cumulative weight in decision making.}

This criterion on multiple attestation is not found, I think, in any list, but is a "commonsense" extension of the criteria phenomenon. In one sense the results from the application of the criteria are not cumulative—that is, if one criterion works in ten instances, there is no guarantee that it will be applicable in the eleventh case, for each variation unit requires a fresh and independent investigation. In another sense, however, if in a given case two or more criteria support a variant as having priority over the others in its variation unit, there is a cumulative effect. For example, a variant accredited as best explaining all others that is also supported by early witnesses and is a harder reading would gain credibility with the addition of each supportive probability.

So much for the external criteria, and attention turns now to the list of internal criteria—concerning what an author most likely wrote and what a scribe was likely to transcribe or a reader was likely to understand. The list is longer than the external probabilities, and several are quite self-evident. Comments will accompany most, but especially those requiring further qualification or in active dispute.

---

75. Jacobus H. Petzer, "The History of the New Testament Text—Its Reconstruction, Significance and Use in New Testament Textual Criticism," in *New Testament Textual Criticism, Exegesis, and Early Church History: A Discussion of Methods* (ed. Barbara Aland and Joël Delobel; Contributions to Biblical Exegesis and Theology 7; Kampen: Kok Pharos, 1994), 11–36.

76. My own view is summarized in "Issues in New Testament Textual Criticism," 34–44.

> C. Criteria/Probabilities related to Internal Evidence
> *If a criterion accurately describes one textual variant within a variation unit, that variant has an increased probability of belonging to the earliest attainable text.*
> 7. A variant that is the harder/hardest reading in its variation-unit.
>   {Because scribes tend to smooth or otherwise remedy rough or difficult readings rather than create them. (Obvious scribal errors and nonsense readings do not qualify, nor can preference be given to readings difficult to the extent of absurdity.)}

The preference for the "harder" or more difficult reading in New Testament criticism was first expressed by Erasmus (1516),[77] but more precisely formulated by Jean Le Clerc in his *Ars critica* (1697). Referring to readings, Le Clerc stated, "If one of them is more obscure and the others clearer, then the more obscure one is likely to be true, the others glosses."[78] Mill (1707) stated it more verbosely: Discussing Colinaeus's Greek Testament (1534) and his most frequent motivation for diverging from earlier editions, Mill asserts:

> For this editor seems to have determined in his own mind that that is the best reading and to be preferred to the rest which would be clearer and more lucid than the remainder. Now nothing is more misleading than this rule, in these sacred books particularly. In them, in proportion as a thing is more obscure, it is generally speaking more authentic, and out of the various readings that occur, those which seem clearer are justly suspected of falsification on the ground that they have crept in from the margin of the manuscripts in the room of other obscurer ones.[79]

Bengel (1725) provided an abiding name for this criterion, *proclivi scriptioni praestat ardua*[80] ("the difficult [reading] is superior to the easy reading"), later expressed as *difficilior lectio potior* ("the more difficult reading is preferable [to the easier reading]," or simply as *lectio difficilior*.[81] For

---

77. Bentley, *Humanists and Holy Writ*, 153–54, with examples from Matt 5:22 and John 7:1; see his explicit use regarding 1 Cor 15:51 (pp. 155–58).

78. Timpanaro, *Genesis*, 68 and n. 29; see n. 28 for earlier formulations, as far back as Galen. Le Clerc's contemporary Richard Simon preferred the "simpler" reading: ibid., 61 n. 9; cf. 68 n. 28.

79. See Fox, *John Mill and Richard Bentley*, 147, for the Latin text and translation.

80. Johann Albrecht Bengel, *Apparatus criticus ad Novum Testamentum* (ed. Philip David Burk; Tübingen, 1763 [1st ed., 1734], 69 (§XXXIV). See his further explanation, 17 (§XXI) = Latin text; translation from Timpanaro, *Genesis*, 69 n. 30.

81. Timpanaro, *Genesis*, 58 n. 29; also 61 n. 9 refers to the clarification of the more difficult reading as "banalization."

Wettstein (1751–52), the variant in clearer or better Greek is not necessarily preferable; more often the contrary and unusual readings are preferable.[82] This criterion also is affirmed by Griesbach, Tregelles, Westcott and Hort, Metzger and Ehrman, Kurt and Barbara Aland, and the UBS *Textual Commentary*.[83] Handbooks on textual criticism generally include it also. The status of this criterion appears to be firm, with little criticism, except that the Alands remind us that it "must not be taken too mechanically, with the most difficult reading (*lectio difficilima*) adopted as original simply because of its degree of difficulty."[84] Pertinent to that sensible caution is the following quotation from Edward Hobbs, who, wishing to emphasize that our criteria have limitations, carried the point to the extreme of absurdity, stating [in reverse order]:

> If you follow the harder readings, you will end up with an unintelligible text; if you follow the shorter readings, you will end up with no text at all.[85]

This leads to the next criterion and to a lengthy discussion.

---

8. *A variant—depending on circumstances—that is the shorter/shortest reading or that is the longer/longest reading in its variation-unit.*
   {Because (a) scribes tend to shorten readings by omission due to parablepsis, especially as a result of homoioteleuton, in which case the longer reading is preferable. But (b) scribes also tend to add material through interpretation, harmonization, and grammatical or stylistic improvement, in which case the shorter reading is preferable. In all cases, both readings must be tested also by the other criteria. (*This criterion currently is debated, but the compromise formulation given here accommodates the range of known textual phenomena, which were recognized already by Griesbach.*)}

---

82. Wettstein, Ἡ ΚΑΙΝΗ ΔΙΑΘΗΚΗ, 2:859-62 (his maxims VII–VIII); also in Wettstein, *Libelli ad crisin*, 48–62; Wrangham, *Briani Waltoni*, 511-12. English trans., Hulbert-Powell, *John James Wettstein*, 117; Tregelles, *Account of the Printed Text*, 80.

83. Griesbach, *Novum Testamentum Graece*, 1:lxi = 'Prolegomena,' §III, ¶2; Tregelles, *Account of the Printed Text*, 201–2, 221–22; Westcott and Hort, *New Testament in the Original Greek*, 2:27–28; Metzger and Ehrman, *Text of the New Testament*, 302–3; Metzger, *Textual Commentary* (2nd ed., 1994), 12*–13*. See also Eugene A. Nida, "The 'Harder Reading' in Textual Criticism: An Application of the Second Law of Thermodynamics," BT 32 (1981): 101–7, esp. 106.

84. Aland and Aland, *Text of the New Testament*, 281; similarly, Metzger and Ehrman, *Text of the New Testament*, 303.

85. Hobbs, "Introduction to Methods," 19.

The so-called shorter reading criterion without question is the most seriously debated of all, and not least at the present time. Le Clerc, in the late seventeenth century, discussed such matters (see below), and Bengel alluded to this criterion in 1734 when, in speaking of readings, he asserted:

> Where the one is more easy, the other less so, the one that is old, weighty, *brief*, is preferred; the one that charms us by its greater perspicacity and *fullness*, as though it had been introduced deliberately, is generally set aside."[86]

In his Admonition 14, Bengel added that "the recurrence of the same words suggests an *omission*."[87] Wettstein invoked the principle in 1730 and repeated it in his edition of the Greek New Testament (1751–52).[88] It was Griesbach, however, who brought the shorter reading criterion to prominence by making it his first canon and discussing it at length—in 212 words (in Latin). As part of this discussion, he invoked a half-dozen additional criteria in subsidiary fashion (before offering a list of fourteen others). Later Tregelles endorsed the criterion, though it did not appear in Tischendorf's list or in Westcott and Hort's discussion. The Alands affirmed that it is "certainly right in many instances" but cannot be used mechanically;[89] and it is found in the Metzger/Ehrman handbook, the UBS *Textual Commentary*,[90] and most other modern manuals, not infrequently with qualifications.

Indeed, some relevant cautions and qualifications were noted already by Le Clerc in his noteworthy *Epistola de editione Milliana* (inserted into Ludolf Küster's unauthorized reprint of Mill's Greek New Testament, 1710), when he referred to ὀπίσω μου in Matt 3:11 (". . .he who is coming *after me* is mightier than I"). These words are present in some witnesses

---

86. Bengel, *Apparatus criticus*, 17 (§XXI).
87. Bengel, *Gnomon*, xiii [= Latin ed.] (his canon 14); idem, *New Testament Word Studies*, xviii [= English ed.].
88. Wettstein, Ἡ ΚΑΙΝΗ ΔΙΑΘΗΚΗ, 2:862–63 (his maxim IX); or Wettstein, *Libelli ad crisin*, 62–66; Wrangham, *Briani Waltoni*, 511–12. English trans., Hulbert-Powell, *John James Wettstein*, 117; Tregelles, *Account of the Printed Text*, 80.
89. Aland and Aland, *Text of the New Testament*, 281.
90. With qualifications in Metzger and Ehrman, *Text of the New Testament*, 166–67, 303; Metzger, *Textual Commentary*, 13*. The numerous qualifications lead J. David Miller ("The Long and Short of *lectio brevior potior*," *BT* [Technical Papers] [2006]: 11–16) to advocate abandoning the criterion because preference for the shorter or longer reading is "always for reasons other than its length" (p. 16). For a recent defense of the shorter reading criterion, see Wim M. A. Hendriks, "Brevior lectio praeferenda est verbosiori," *RB* 112 (2005): 567–95, who seeks its more objective application; his example is Matt 6:33, including a chronological ordering of forty-four patristic citations to assess its two variant clauses (esp. pp. 576–81).

and absent in others, and later were listed in the Nestle-Aland[27] apparatus as omitted in 𝔓[101] a d sa[mss] Cyprian. Le Clerc at first took these words to be authentic: "For there was no reason why these words should have been added, for they are obscure and add nothing to clarify the meaning of the passage. . . ." Seen in this light, ὀπίσω μου, the longer reading, represented the harder reading, whereas the witnesses omitting them would have the clearer reading—and the shorter reading. But Le Clerc's statement continued: "On the contrary, for these very reasons they [the two words] could have been eliminated as obscure and useless." In that case, the shorter text would be secondary, and the longer would have priority. Timpanaro summarizes: "Le Clerc speaks of an intentional alteration . . . and demonstrates that the *lectio longier* can even be the *lectio difficilior.*"[91]

Griesbach's formulation of the shorter reading criterion contained its own cautions, and it is striking that one-third of his description referred to occasions when the *longer* reading is preferable. He began as follows: "The shorter reading (unless it lacks entirely the authority of the ancient and weighty authorities) is to be preferred to the more verbose, for scribes were much more prone to add than to omit."[92] This portion has been quoted frequently ever since, often in a shorter and more simple form of Griesbach's opening statement, such as, "The shorter reading is preferable, for scribes were more prone to add than to omit." But this is to overlook Griesbach's careful qualifications that followed and is a disservice to him. Surely he emphasized the shorter reading and its priority, but his full criterion should be in view—as in the following paraphrase:

> The *shorter reading* was to be preferred (a) if it was also a "more difficult, more obscure, ambiguous, elliptical, hebraizing, or solecistic" reading, (b) if the same matter was expressed differently in various manuscripts, (c) if the word order was inconsistent and unstable, (d) if a short reading began a pericope, or (e) if the longer reading evidenced a gloss or interpretation, or agreed with the wording of parallel passages, or appeared to have come from a lectionary.

> The *longer reading*, however, was preferable to the shorter (unless the latter was supported by many notable witnesses), (1) if the omission from the longer reading (a) could be attributed to homoioteleuton, (b) would have appeared to scribes as obscure, rough, superfluous, unusual, paradoxical, offensive to pious ears, erroneous, or inconsistent with parallels, or (c) did not, by its omission, damage the sense or word structure, or (2) if the shorter reading (a) was less in accord with the author's character,

---

91. Timpanaro, *Genesis*, 69 n. 30.
92. Griesbach, *Novum Testamentum Graece*, 1:lx–lxi = 'Prolegomena,' §III, ¶1.

style, or goal, (b) absolutely made no sense, or (c) might be an intrusion from parallel passages or lectionaries.[93]

So other criteria came into play, including priority of the more difficult reading or of a reading in accord with the author's style. Note that harmonization was listed on both sides of the issue—alerting one either to addition or to omission. Griesbach's qualifications and exceptions far exceeded those in any other criterion and thereby indicated that this shorter reading canon was highly complex and ambiguous. At the same time, however, the qualifications also illustrated how all the criteria function—through a balancing of probabilities. In Griesbach's formulation, therefore, this criterion was seen already as not merely the "shorter reading criterion," but also a guideline for judging both "shorter" and "longer" readings.

In the last forty-five years, critiques of the shorter reading principle have quickened in pace, beginning in 1965 with Ernest Colwell's implication that, among the variants in the singular readings[94] of three early and extensive papyri ($\mathfrak{P}^{45}$, $\mathfrak{P}^{66}$, $\mathfrak{P}^{75}$), the scribes more frequently omitted material than added it.[95] James Royse made this the subject of a dissertation, doubling the size of the sample by adding $\mathfrak{P}^{46}$, $\mathfrak{P}^{47}$, and $\mathfrak{P}^{72}$ and tightening the methodology. His result, again referring to singular readings, was stronger than Colwell's: "The general tendency during the early period of textual transmission was to omit" and, therefore, "other things being equal, one should prefer the longer reading."[96] Keith Elliott in 1992 stated his view succinctly:

> The thoroughgoing eclectic critic is inclined to the maxim that the longer text is likely to be original, other things being equal. To shorten a text is often accidental, and is a fault which a careless scribe can be prone

---

93. The paraphrase largely follows the translation in Metzger and Ehrman, *Text of the New Testament*, 166–67.

94. A "singular reading" (as defined in this kind of research) is a reading not found, to date, in any other Greek manuscript.

95. Ernest C. Colwell, "Scribal Habits in Early Papyri: A Study in the Corruption of the Text," in *The Bible in Modern Scholarship: Papers Read at the 100th Meeting of the Society of Biblical Literature, December 28-30, 1964* (ed. J. Philip Hyatt; Nashville: Abingdon, 1965), 376–77; repr. as "Method in Evaluating Scribal Habits: A Study of P^{45}, P^{66}, P^{75}," in Colwell, *Studies in Methodology in Textual Criticism of the New Testament* (NTTS 9; Leiden: Brill, 1969), 112.

96. James R. Royse, "Scribal Tendencies in the Transmission of the Text of the New Testament," in *The Text of the New Testament in Contemporary Research: Essays on the* Status Quaestionis (ed. Bart D. Ehrman and Michael W. Holmes; SD 46; Grand Rapids: Eerdmans, 1995), 246.

to. To add to a text involves a conscious mental effort. Thus the former is more likely to have happened, even though the latter also occurred.[97]

Later he added a qualification: "In general, the longer text is more likely to be original providing that that text is consistent with the language, style, and theology of the context."[98] This formulation is reminiscent of one of Griesbach's qualifications: "The longer reading is to be preferred to the shorter (unless the latter appears in many good witnesses) . . . if the shorter reading is less in accord with the character, style, or scope of the author."[99] The parenthetical statement may not be as readily acceptable to Elliott.

Very recently, Royse published his 1,080-page volume assessing *Scribal Habits in Early New Testament Papyri*,[100] where his massive data and meticulous analysis of scribal habits in singular readings of six early and extensive papyri ($\mathfrak{P}^{45}$, $\mathfrak{P}^{46}$, $\mathfrak{P}^{47}$, $\mathfrak{P}^{66}$, $\mathfrak{P}^{72}$, and $\mathfrak{P}^{75}$) produced a briefly worded conclusion: the scribes of these six papyri "omit more often than they add," and, "as long as the competing readings are all early, the preference must lie with the longer reading."[101] He was pleased to report that other studies, previous and recent, supported that conclusion. Peter Head, for example, followed a methodology similar to Royse's but treated singular readings in fourteen smaller papyrus fragments of the Synoptic Gospels and then, in a second study, in papyri of John from the fourth century and earlier (though including only newly published portions of $\mathfrak{P}^{45}$ and $\mathfrak{P}^{66}$).[102] Head concluded, "Once again it seems that the evidence suggests that most early scribes are more likely to omit than to add material."[103] Most recently of all, Juan Hernández published the results of his research on the singular readings of א, A, and C (04) in Revelation, again following the methodology of Royse and with similar results: in all three of these early majuscules, "each of the three omits far more *often* than they add,

---

97. Elliott, "Can We Recover the Original Text," 33; see also 39–40.
98. Ibid., 39.
99. Griesbach, *Novum Testamentum Graece*, 1:lxi = 'Prolegomena,' §III, ¶1, as translated in Metzger and Ehrman, *Text of the New Testament*, 166–67.
100. James R. Royse, *Scribal Habits in Early New Testament Papyri* (NTTSD 36; Leiden: Brill, 2008), esp. ch. 10, "The Shorter Reading?" 705–36.
101. Ibid., 705 and 734; see also 197 (on $\mathfrak{P}^{45}$); 358 (on $\mathfrak{P}^{46}$); 397 (on $\mathfrak{P}^{47}$); 544 (on $\mathfrak{P}^{66}$); 614 (on $\mathfrak{P}^{72}$); 704 (on $\mathfrak{P}^{75}$); 717–19, 735.
102. Peter Head, "Observations on Early Papyri of the Synoptic Gospels, Especially on the Scribal Habits," *Bib* 71 (1990): 240–47; idem, "The Habits of New Testament Copyists: Singular Readings in the Early Fragmentary Papyri of John," *Bib* 85 (2004): 399–408.
103. Head, "Habits of New Testament Copyists," 407–8.

and each omits *more of the text* [than they add] while doing so."[104] Hernández, however, adds another feature by recording the number of words in the omissions and additions, which again show a tendency to omit.[105] It is clear from the consensus of these several studies that when *singular readings* in *early* manuscripts are analyzed, scribes tend to omit rather than add as they copy.

Then, in 2007, Dirk Jongkind published his *Scribal Habits of Codex Sinaiticus*, a meticulously researched and carefully nuanced investigation. Our interest is primarily in two scribes, scribe A, who wrote the entire New Testament except for six folios, and scribe D, the main corrector of the text, who wrote the other six. We focus also on singular readings, which occupy 40 percent of Jongkind's study and invite comparison with the work of Royse and others discussed earlier, though Jongkind worked with a major majuscule and not papyri. More precisely, we focus on four classes of his singular readings: (1) leaps from the same to same; (2) addition/omission of *verba minora* (Jongkind's term for short readings, which include conjunctions, pronouns, articles, particles, and ἐν before dative constructions); (3) addition/omission of words and clauses; and (4) major rewritings.[106]

To be as brief as possible, Jongkind's conclusions on singular readings of scribes A and D include the following: In general, "the scribal tendency to omit rather than to add is in *Sinaiticus* similar to that found by Royse in the papyri."[107] This is based on findings that the two scribes (in the selected New Testament portions, namely, Luke 1–12, Romans, Colossians, 1–2 Thessalonians, Hebrews) added nineteen times and omitted sixty-seven times. If one adds Jongkind's analyses of singular readings in the selected Greek Old Testament sections (1 Chr 9:27–19:17, and the

---

104. Juan Hernández, Jr., *Scribal Habits and Theological Influences in the Apocalypse: The Singular Readings of Sinaiticus, Alexandrinus, and Ephraemi* (WUNT 218; Tübingen: Mohr Siebeck, 2006), 195 (italics in original); see also 194, 74–75, 113–14, 149, 153–54.

105. Ibid., 74–75 (on ℵ), 113–14 (on A), 148–49 (on Codex Ephraemi, 04). Again, only singular readings are employed in the analysis.

106. Dirk Jongkind, *Scribal Habits of Codex Sinaiticus* (Texts and Studies 3.5; Piscataway, N.J.: Gorgias, 2007), 9 (on scribes A and D), 131–246 (on singular readings), 142–43 (on Jongkind's categories of singular readings, including *verba minora*). I am uncertain whether it is fair to separate these categories from his others: orthography, nonsense readings, harmonization, editorial readings, substitutions, and transpositions, but the four I selected appeared to be the most relevant to the shorter reading criterion.

107. Ibid., 246.

Psalms), scribes created thirty-five additions and 121 omissions in the four categories selected above.¹⁰⁸

Jongkind's investigation of scribal habits in Sinaiticus is not restricted to singular readings, but those readings are recognized generally as a reliable path to understanding individual scribal behavior, and their subdivisions selected above are perhaps those most relevant to the shorter reading criterion. This brings us back to Royse's studies and those of other scholars.

As a conclusion to his thirty-one page discussion of the shorter reading issue, Royse thoughtfully provided for us his own formulation of a fresh criterion. He named it a "canon of transcriptional probability," though it might very well have been called a "criterion of the longer reading." He eschewed the latter designation apparently to avoid "an uncritical application of the principle *lectio longior potior* ('the longer reading is to be preferred'),"¹⁰⁹ and suggested rather, that now "the burden of proof should be shifted from the proponents of the longer text to the defenders of the shorter text."¹¹⁰ His criterion follows:

> In general the longer reading is to be preferred, except where:
> a) the longer reading appears, on external grounds, to be late; or
> b) the longer reading may have arisen from harmonization to the immediate context, to parallels, or to general usage; or
> c) the longer reading may have arisen from an attempt at grammatical improvement.
>
> The frequency of omissions by scribal leaps and of omissions of certain inessential words such as pronouns must be kept in mind, and when such omissions may have occurred the longer reading should be viewed as even more likely.¹¹¹

At this point the question arises: Is this the appropriate resolution of the debated "shorter reading" criterion? Hernández, as noted, provided data on the average number of words in the omissions/additions in his sample of singular readings from Revelation. He found that the average number of words added was 1.3, and in omissions 1.9. This finding prompts us to look at some earlier studies.

Moisés Silva, already thirteen years ago in two smaller-scale inquiries, assessed omissions/additions in $\mathfrak{P}^{46}$, ℵ, B, and A in Galatians and

---

108. Ibid., extracted from his extensive tables throughout ch. 4: On Paul, 202–21; on Luke, 221–40; on 1 Chronicles, 144–64; on Psalms, 164–201. My figures may differ from Jongkind's due to a few ambiguous cases.

109. Royse, *Scribal Habits*, 734–35.

110. Ibid., 735.

111. Ibid.

Philippians.[112] He employed readings in these manuscripts that differed from Nestle-Aland[26] and UBSGNT[3], but with no focus on singular readings. Thereby he made a relevant point, that understanding scribal behavior requires that all variants be taken into account. What he found was that in Galatians, $\mathfrak{P}^{46}$, ℵ, and B showed significantly more omissions than additions, though A went the other direction. The further study in Philippians brought a similar result. In these two articles, Silva referred to Royse's earlier studies, and it appeared that non-singular readings yielded results generally in line with those of Royse.

Then, however, Silva carried his research a step farther by asking about the nature of these omission/addition variants. For example, Do they involve homoioteleuton? Are they very brief, such as single words, short phrases? Are they "function words," such as conjunctions, articles, prepositions, and pronouns, and, if so, do they affect the sense of the passage? After categorizing the omissions/additions, Silva focused on items other than the function words and, upon revising his figures, found that additions equaled or exceeded omissions in all manuscripts tested except $\mathfrak{P}^{46}$ (notably a careless scribe). Silva, while admitting that his sample was small, concluded: "It appears that when we deal with what some grammarians call 'full words'—as opposed to those 'empty words' that function primarily as grammatical markers—scribes were indeed more likely to add than to omit."[113] Royse acknowledged that such discrimination can be helpful, but suggested that Silva's procedure "is tantamount to holding that scribes tend to add, assuming that one ignores most of the places where they tend to omit."[114] At the same time, Silva acknowledged that Royse's method—the use of singular readings only—dealt with the least contaminated data, for it focused on the individual scribe's own foibles inasmuch as the previous scribal errors in the manuscript being copied do not come into the picture.[115]

So, the process of clarification goes on, and the point here is to bring these continuing discussions to the forefront and thereby to raise certain questions: Are scribal practices of omission/addition in New Testament

---

112. Moisés Silva, "Internal Evidence in the Text-Critical Use of the LXX," in *La Septuaginta en la investigación contemporánea (V Congreso de la IOSCS)* (ed. N. Fernández Marcos; Madrid: Instituto Arias Montano, 1985), 154-64, esp. 157-61; idem, "The Text of Galatians: Evidence from the Earliest Greek Manuscripts," in *Scribes and Scripture: New Testament Essays in Honor of J. Harold Greenlee* (ed. D. A. Black; Winona Lake, IN.: Eisenbrauns, 1992), 23-24.

113. Silva, "Internal Evidence," 159; on his "small" sample, see idem, "Text of Galatians," 23.

114. Royse, *Scribal Habits*, 725, 735–36 n. 127.

115. Silva, "Text of Galatians," 23. Jongkind (*Scribal Habits of Codex Sinaiticus*, 137) reminds us that "not all singular readings are created by the scribe."

manuscripts adequately addressed by examining singular readings only? Should variants involving omission/addition be sorted and categorized, rejecting some as inconsequential—such as Silva's "function words" or Jongkind's *verba minora*? And finally, a recurring theme obviously requiring clarification: Which omissions/additions were unconscious or unintentional and which were conscious or intentional? Griesbach, in the text of his famous canon, not only affirmed that scribes were "much more prone to add than to omit," but added that "they scarcely ever deliberately omitted anything, but they added many things," thereby asserting that omission primarily occurred unintentionally and implying that additions were intentional. Yet it was at this juncture that he inserted his half-dozen exceptions to his canon, including several kinds of deliberate omissions, where the longer reading should be preferred.[116] The *Textual Commentary* and Metzger and Ehrman's volume, reflecting Griesbach, allowed for the longer reading where "the scribe may have omitted material that he [sic] deemed to be superfluous, harsh, or contrary to pious belief, liturgical usage, or ascetical practice," actions that inevitably would be intentional.[117] Keith Elliott stated, partly to the contrary:

> To omit from a text is a frequent and easily demonstrable scribal activity, but to add to a text demanded conscious mental effort. Obviously such activity expanding a text did occur but, in general, manuscripts tended to be accidentally shortened rather than deliberately lengthened in the process of copying.[118]

David Parker offers two helpful comments: the margins of א, "where the frequent omissions of Scribe A have been repaired, will show that the users of a text did not often suffer significant omissions to remain for long," and "The canon *'lectio brevior potior'* is in any case a rule to be applied in a certain type of circumstance, namely in a place where one suspects either an expansion which is intended to clarify the text, or a conflation of several older forms of text."[119]

So we have mixed judgments on the intentionality of omissions and the frequency of intentional additions, resulting in more qualifications and exceptions than in other criteria. Unintentional omissions would include nonsense readings and obvious scribal errors, such as homoioteleuton (a leap from the same to the same), where the longer reading would

---

116. See Griesbach's canon in Metzger and Ehrman, *Text of the New Testament*, 166.

117. Metzger, *Textual Commentary* (2nd ed., 1994), 13*; Metzger and Ehrman, *Text of the New Testament*, 303.

118. Elliott, "Can We Recover the Original Text," 39–40; see 33.

119. Parker, *Introduction to the New Testament Manuscripts*, 296.

be preferred. Also, dittography (copying something twice) would be an obvious and unintended addition. But various intentional omissions also are recognized, and one could argue that many additions would have been made virtually unintentionally through harmonization with parallel passages and by unconscious influence from a scribe's familiarity with parallel Septuagintal or lectionary passages.[120]

Is there a way to sort this out, and, even if there is, how would a criterion be formulated? Throughout its long tradition, the shorter reading criterion has accumulated numerous exceptions, which need to be retained and not overlooked, so as to ensure the proper use of the criterion. Radical abbreviation of the criterion, such as references to Griesbach's canon as "Prefer the shorter reading," both misrepresented Griesbach and led to the criterion's misunderstanding and misuse.[121] In 1995 Michael Holmes concluded, "In the light of Royse's study the venerable canon of *lectio brevior potior* is now seen as relatively useless, at least for the early papyri."[122] I would agree with that statement *if* the criterion is viewed in a simplistic fashion. My own judgment, however, is that at this juncture the discipline is not fully prepared either to drop the shorter reading criterion in favor of a longer reading canon, nor is there sufficient confidence to maintain the shorter reading option without clear accompanying recognition of the longer reading criterion. It is not an either/or situation but one requiring adjudication case by case. A compromise formulation is necessary, I think, to avoid a stalemate, and such an attempt is what stands above at the head of this section as criterion number 8. It both accurately describes

---

120. See discussion of "intentionality" in scribal activity, e.g., in David C. Parker, *The Living Text of the Gospels* (Cambridge: Cambridge University Press, 1997), 36–38; idem, *Introduction to the New Testament Manuscripts*, 151–54, 296; Royse, *Scribal Habits*, 96–97 and notes; Hernández, *Scribal Habits and Theological Influences*, 194 n. 5. J. Harold Greenlee (*Introduction to New Testament Textual Criticism* [rev. ed.; Peabody, MA: Hendrickson,1995], 112) attempted to draw a distinction between unintentional and intentional alterations. as follows: "The *shorter* reading is generally preferable if an *intentional change* has been made. The reason is that scribes at times made intentional additions to clarify a passage, but rarely made an intentional omission. . . . The longer reading is often preferable if an *unintentional change* has been made. The reason is that scribes were more likely to omit a word or a phrase accidentally than to add accidentally." But difficulties abound: notice the words "generally," "at times," and "rarely," and, in the second statement, "often" and "more likely." Also, both omissions and additions were each, at times, made consciously and unconsciously, so drawing a clean distinction between the two is difficult even if intentionality were clearly identifiable.

121. See Jongkind, *Scribal Habits of Codex Sinaiticus*, 138–39, for a critique of quoting Griesbach's canon only partially, with special reference to Royse's treatment.

122. Holmes, "Reasoned Eclecticism," 343.

our text-critical situation and retains the usefulness of the criterion—or, better, of both criteria!

> 9. *A variant that conforms to the author's recognizable style and vocabulary.*
> {Because the earliest reading is likely to follow the author's style as observed in the bulk of the writing. (To the contrary, scribes may conform aberrant stylistic features to the dominant style in a writing, thus changing what would have been a "harder" reading into a smoother reading.) (*This criterion has been questioned.*)}

This criterion was well known to ancient grammarians, such as Aristarchus, as *usus scribendi* (the author's habitual style) and was employed, for example, by Le Clerc as a criterion for conjectural emendation. For the New Testament, it was discussed by Wettstein;[123] thereafter it appeared in the criteria lists of Griesbach, Tischendorf, Tregelles, Westcott and Hort, and most that followed.[124] Naturally, the ambiguity mentioned in parentheses above was recognized, but it appears that otherwise the criterion was not challenged seriously over the years until 1990, when J. H. Petzer published an article entitled "Author's Style and the Textual Criticism of the New Testament." Here Petzer asserted that "the whole criterion is based upon the presumption that one can expect to find consistency in the use of language in a text," and then stated his contrary thesis:

> It cannot be expected or presupposed that the language employed in the New Testament documents will of necessity be consistent, or, to put it differently, the stylistic patterns identified in those documents cannot be employed as a means of determining what was written in them originally and what not.[125]

Though his argument was more elaborate and sophisticated than can be reported here, he demonstrated, through a range of examples, that consistency of language and style in the New Testament writings has been severely undermined by an author's "interfacing" with other texts. This interfacing, which can be detectable or undetectable, concerns an author's

---

123. See Timpanaro, *Genesis*, 68 nn. 26–27, 69 n. 30. Wettstein, Ἡ ΚΑΙΝΗ ΔΙΑΘΗΚΗ, 2:864 (his maxim XI); idem, *Libelli ad crisin*, 68–69.

124. For example, it is found in Metzger, *Textual Commentary* (2nd ed., 1994), 14*; Metzger and Ehrman, *Text of the New Testament*, 303, but not in Aland and Aland, *Text of the New Testament*, 280–81.

125. J. H. Petzer, "Author's Style and the Textual Criticism of the New Testament," *Neotestamentica* 24, no. 2 (1990): 187–97; quotations from 186.

use of sources and parallel passages and the involvement of redactors and scribes, who have influenced the texts during their development and transmission. But Petzer goes farther by pursuing the nature of "author" and "text," claiming that past and current practice

> presupposes a problematic view of a text, a view which completely dissociates the text from the interpreter and puts it upon a pedestal as a fixed and closed entity, with rounded-off and closed structures and patterns waiting to be "discovered" by the critic, who is able to approach the text *tabula rasa* and in fact "discover" those patterns.[126]

In reality, however, the New Testament writings evince "linguistic and stylistic fluidity" that must be explained. First, if consistency is not present in their authors' language, the criterion is "useless" without careful argumentation:

> The only way in which the criterion can possibly function under these circumstances is if a detailed analysis of the influences upon the author's style can reveal when, why and how far he was prepared to deviate from his general linguistic and stylistic pattern.[127]

As Petzer explains, he is calling for an analysis that can disclose the "'true' linguistic abilities of the original author only," something "very difficult if not impossible."[128]

Second, if interfacing with other "authors," namely, other sources or redactional and scribal influences on the text, are involved, the criterion is likewise useless, though with an exception:

> The only chance of it having any kind of success under these circumstances is if it can be accurately determined which parts of the text originated from the original author and which from redactors, in order to once again base the analysis on only those parts of text that originated from the original author of the original text.[129]

Once again Petzer judged this to be "very difficult if not impossible." His final conclusion is only slightly softened: While not denying that consistency in language and style can be found in a document, he carefully stated: "The point is that it cannot be presupposed and used as a criterion for determining textual integrity."[130]

Petzer's second article, "Style and Text in the Lucan Narrative of the

---

126. Ibid., 194.
127. Ibid.
128. Ibid., 194–95.
129. Ibid.
130. Ibid., 195.

Institution of the Lord's Supper (Luke 22. 19b-20)," constitutes a detailed example of the kind of analysis required by his earlier essay if the criterion of the author's style is to be applied:

> To conclude: there are more aspects to style than only vocabulary and grammar, and if this criticism is to yield firm and reliable results in New Testament textual criticism, its application ought to be based upon a total approach to style, which goes beyond vocabulary and grammar and which involves all the relevant aspects of this complex entity which is called the style of an author.[131]

Petzer's skepticism about the usefulness of the criterion involving an author's style is balanced to some extent by his cautious optimism that a highly sophisticated analysis of a text—including acknowledgment of an author's sources and subsequent alterations by scribes and editors—conceivably could isolate those portions of a text that originated from the original author. Assuredly, Petzer has called textual critics to a higher standard than existed previously.

This critique of a long-standing criterion will deter some from employing it in the traditional fashion, fearing that they may apply it somewhat simplistically. Others will continue to use it whether or not they are aware of or acknowledge the cautions raised by Petzer. Two years after Petzer's first article was published, Keith Elliott, in an informative description and defense of his Thoroughgoing Eclecticism, outlined his own primary criteria for the priority of readings. At the head of the list was this: "I would accept as original a variant that could be proved to agree with the language, style, or theology of the author over against a variant that disagrees."[132] The key term here is "proved," and that is what Petzer was requiring.

---

10. *A variant that conforms to the author's recognized theology or ideology.*
{Because the earliest reading is likely to display the same convictions or beliefs found in the bulk of the work. (To the contrary, a scribe may conform apparently aberrant theological statements to an author's theology—as perceived by that scribe—thus changing what would have been a "harder" reading into a smoother reading.)}

---

131. Kobus Petzer, "Style and Text in the Lucan Narrative of the Institution of the Lord's Supper (Luke 22. 19b-20)," *NTS* 37 (1991): 113–29; quotation from 129.

132. Elliott, "Can We Recover the Original Text," 39. Since Elliott's article had no footnotes, it is unclear whether he was aware of Petzer's articles.

This criterion and the preceding one are similar in nature and, therefore, similar cautions will apply. Petzer does not broach this criterion, but—without attributing the following paraphrase to him—I think it is fair to say this: Consistency in an author's theology is unlikely to be found in a New Testament writing because any author will have "interfaced" with other "authors" (in Petzer's phraseology), namely, other sources or redactional and scribal influences on the text, thereby undermining the usefulness of the criterion. Yet there may be a chance for it to work (again using Petzer's words from the discussion of criterion 10 above) "if it can be accurately determined which parts of the text originated from the original author and which from redactors," so that a determination of an author's theology can be based "on only those parts of text that originated from the original author of the original text." Though Petzer judged such an analysis to be "very difficult if not impossible" for matters of language and style, I would suggest that consistency in theology is perhaps more easily traced in a writing, as are earlier influences or later impositions upon it. The reason would be that descriptions or intimations of one's theology involve matters of content and substance that move beyond one's language or style in which the content is enshrined. That is, language and style are more subtle, while theology or ideology, by nature, requires more overt expression.

---

11. *A variant that conforms to Semitic forms of expression.*
   {Because the New Testament authors, being either Jewish or familiar with Septuagint/Greek Old Testament style, are likely to reflect such Semitic expressions in their writings. (To the contrary, scribes also could conform extraneous readings to Semitic forms.)}

---

12. *A variant—depending on circumstances—that conforms to Koine (rather than Attic) Greek, or vice versa.*
   {Because (a) scribes were thought to show a tendency to shape the text being copied to the more elegant Attic Greek style. But (b) scribes also may tend to alter Attic words and phrases to the more contemporary and popular Koine. (*This criterion currently is being debated, but the compromise formulation given here accommodates the range of known textual phenomena.*)}

George D. Kilpatrick in 1963 affirmed that scribes in the second century were inclined to alter Koine Greek toward Attic Greek style and, therefore, that a reading should be considered secondary if it showed

Atticist tendencies.¹³³ This new criterion was welcomed by many, though a few scholars raised questions about its efficacy. Colwell insisted that sure knowledge of scribal intentions in some of the examples cannot be assumed. For instance, altering the Koine ἀποκριθεὶς εἶπεν to the Attic ἔφη appears in several cases in Mark as due to harmonization with Matthew and Luke rather than to Atticizing, and ἀποκριθεὶς εἶπεν occurs 139 times in the Gospels, but ἔφη only 35 (counting in the Westcott-Hort text), leading Colwell to remark that "the scribes were not Atticizing very well."¹³⁴ Carlo Martini pointed out that some examples offered are not true Atticisms and that, in any case, it is difficult to assess Atticism before 400 C.E.¹³⁵ Finally, Gordon Fee suggested that the scribal tendency rather may have been to alter Attic Greek style to biblical (i.e., Septuagint) Greek rather than the other way around, that is, "that scribes may have preferred Koine and especially septuagintal idioms to classical ones."¹³⁶ Kilpatrick and Elliott defended the Atticizing principle against its detractors, with Kilpatrick countering Martini's attempt to show that two of Kilpatrick's examples were not salient by offering additional data and arguments to buttress his original evidence. Elliott responded to Fee's reversal of the direction in which such changes moved by reaffirming that surviving grammars and manuals of style demonstrated a return by first-century Hellenistic Greek to the classical standards, offering numerous examples.¹³⁷ The niceties of Attic and Hellenistic Greek grammar and style will not be familiar to all, but Elliott has maintained the validity of the Atticizing criterion: "I would accept as original a variant that conforms to our known standard of first

---

133. George D. Kilpatrick, "Atticism and the Text of the Greek New Testament," in *Neutestamentliche Aufsätze: Festschrift für Prof. Josef Schmid zum 70. Geburtstag* (ed. J. Blinzler, O. Kuss, and F. Mussner; Regensburg: Pustet, 1963), 125–37; repr. in idem, *Principles and Practice*, 15–32.

134. Ernest C. Colwell, "Hort Redivivus: A Plea and a Program," in *Transitions in Biblical Scholarship* (ed. J. Coert Rylaarsdam; Essays in Divinity 6; Chicago: University of Chicago Press, 1968), 137–38; repr. in idem, *Studies in Methodology*, 154–55.

135. Carlo M. Martini, "Eclecticism and Atticism in the Textual Criticism of the Greek New Testament," in *On Language, Culture, and Religion: In Honor of Eugene A. Nida* (ed. Matthew Black and William A. Smalley; Approaches to Semiotics 56; The Hague and Paris: Mouton, 1974), 151–55.

136. Gordon D. Fee, "Rigorous or Reasoned Eclecticism–Which?" in *Studies in New Testament Language and Text: Essays in Honour of George D. Kilpatrick on the Occasion of his Sixty-fifth Birthday* (ed. J. K. Elliott; NovTSup 44; Leiden: Brill, 1976), 184–91; repr. in Eldon Jay Epp and Gordon D. Fee, *Studies in the Theory and Method of New Testament Textual Criticism* (SD 45; Grand Rapids: Eerdmans, 1993), 131–36.

137. G. D. Kilpatrick, "Eclecticism and Atticism," *ETL* 53 (1977): 107–12; repr. in idem, *Principles and Practice*, 73–79 (response to Martini); Elliott, "Can We Recover the Original Text," 30–32 (response to Fee).

century Hellenistic Greek against a variant that conforms to later literary and linguistic standards."[138] In a brief 1996 summary of the Atticism issue, however, Charles Landon concluded that "a situation of stalemate still persists."[139]

The Atticistic movement in the first two centuries sought to remedy the perceived deterioration of Attic diction as Koine Greek spread and increased in popularity. Earlier Elliott had studied NT textual variants with respect to their conformity or not to Attic style, based on works of Atticist grammarians, notably Phrynichus Arabius (latter second century) and Moeris (somewhat later).[140] In 2004, Chrys Caragounis offered an array of Attic forms with their corresponding (rejected) non-Attic or Koine forms as treated in Phrynichus's *Ekloge* and in Moeris's alphabetic glossary. Caragounis listed all 500 such words and phrases discussed in Phrynichus and thirty-six examples from Moeris. Out of the 500, 204, according to his count,[141] were extant New Testament terms, and of these, 111 (54.4%) were non-Attic words rejected by Phrynichus, while sixty-five (31.9%) followed the Attic form and meaning (with the remaining words and phrases being peculiar to the New Testament).[142] In his brief comments directly on the Atticism criterion in New Testament textual criticism, Caragounis remarked:

---

138. Elliott, "Can We Recover the Original Text," 39; see also 30–32.

139. Charles Landon, *A Text-Critical Study of the Epistle of Jude* (JSNTSup 135; Sheffield: Sheffield Academic Press, 1996), 38.

140. J. Keith Elliott, "Phrynicus' Influence on the Textual Tradition of the New Testament," ZNW 63 (1972): 133–38; idem, "Moeris and the Textual Tradition of the Greek New Testament," in Elliott, *Studies in New Testament Language and Text*, 144–52. These two articles formed a single chapter in idem, *Essays and Studies in New Testament Textual Criticism* (Estudios de filología neotestamentaria 3; Cordova: Ediciones el Almendro, 1992), 65–77; see five other relevant studies, 79–111, 121–23.

141. Chrys C. Caragounis, *The Development of Greek and the New Testament: Morphology, Syntax, Phonology, and Textual Transmission* (WUNT 167; Tübingen: Mohr Siebeck, 2004), 124–40, summary on 570–71. See pp. 138–39 for thirty-six examples from Moeris, obviously selected to show that the New Testament followed the rejected forms. A main burden of Caragounis's book is the study of pronunciation of Greek by the first Christians, and in some ninety pages he treats New Testament manuscripts and textual criticism, including orthographical errors in $\mathfrak{P}^{66}$ (pp. 502–17) and text-critical analyses of thirty-six New Testament variation units (pp. 517–64).

142. Timo Flink (*Textual Dilemma: Studies in the Second-Century Text of the New Testament* [University of Joensuu Publications in Theology 21; Joensuu, Finland: University of Joensuu, 2009], 129 n. 401) has reservations about these figures, suggesting that Caragounis appears to ignore textual variations.

> The part played by Atticism is a much larger question than merely looking for a reading that exhibits a more acknowledged Greek style over against a more Koine one and choosing always the Koine form.... The possibility, too, must be considered, that the author wrote down the Attic form and that a scribe altered it to the popular form to bring it in line with popular feeling.[143]

More recently, Timo Flink examined 712 New Testament variation units involving "both the Koine and the Attic forms as variant readings," and he argued that "at times scribes acted like Atticist correctors" and replaced Koine readings with their Attic equivalents, while "at other times scribes were influenced by the natural development of Greek" and replaced Attic forms with more contemporary Koine ones.[144] His conclusion on the New Testament Atticism criterion was this:

> An internal criterion that favours the Koine over the Attic, other things being equal, is too simplistic, unless the "other things being equal" includes the information from Greek usage of the first two centuries. This requires a perennial restudy of Greek usage, when more evidence becomes available.[145]

In the final analysis (at least to date), it would appear that the Atticism criterion should be treated in a manner similar to the shorter/longer reading criterion (number 8 above), namely, that what we have in the Atticism phenomenon is not an either/or situation, for scribes and readers could and did move in both directions. Again, decisions must be made case by case, depending on, among other factors, the characteristic or predominant style in a writing, which may help to determine in which direction Attic/Koine scribal alterations moved in that writing, or perhaps the dates of scribes or correctors, to the extent that they can be known, offer clues to the direction of change—in accordance with the development of the Greek language and in view of the Atticistic movement. In the case of the shorter/longer reading dilemma, some reasons can be offered for the priority of one and other reasons for preference of the other. That is more difficult with respect to Attic/Koine alterations, but further analyses may clarify the issue. Whether the compromise statement of the criterion (above) is helpful, if only to keep the Atticism issue in view, remains to be determined, and the discipline may have to live and work with a fair measure of ambiguity as scholarship proceeds.

---

143. Caragounis, *Development of Greek and the New Testament*, 480 n. 39.
144. Flink, *Textual Dilemma*, 129.
145. Ibid., 213.

13. *A variant that **does not** conform to parallel passages or to extraneous items in the context generally.*
   {Because scribes tend, consciously or unconsciously, to shape the text being copied to familiar parallel passages, especially in the Synoptic Gospels, or to words or phrases just copied.}

14. *A variant that **does not** conform to Old Testament passages.*
   {Because scribes, who were likely to be familiar with the Jewish Bible, tend to shape their copying to the content of familiar passages (as in the preceding criterion).}

15. *A variant that **does not** conform to liturgical forms and usages.*
   {Because scribes tend to shape the text being copied to phraseology of familiar liturgical expressions used in devotion and worship.}

16. *A variant that **does not** conform to extrinsic theological, ideological, or other socio-historical contexts contemporary with and congenial to a text's scribe.*
   {Because scribes unconsciously, but more likely consciously, could bring a text into conformity with their own or their group's doctrinal beliefs or with accepted socio-cultural conventions. (Naturally, difficulties exist in identifying both the contemporary context and the copyist's time frame and provenance.)}

Erasmus offered two examples where variants had been created to support orthodox views. In Matt 24:36, he argued that "nor the son" had been erased by opponents of the Arians, and, in 1 John 4:3, he suspected that "came in the flesh" was inserted against Docetic views.[146] C. M. Pfaff in 1709 published a small book on sorting genuine from spurious readings in the New Testament with assistance from critical canons. He referred to alterations introduced in the copying process and spoke specifically of the harm done to the text by such impositions in the interests of orthodoxy.[147] Other early scholars similarly devalued variants with tendencies to support orthodoxy, including Wettstein in his canon 12, "The more orthodox reading is not necessarily preferable," and Griesbach in canon 6 is suspicious of "the reading, compared with others, that produces a meaning suited to the support of piety (especially monastic piety)," and in canon 8 finds suspect the reading "that clearly suits the opinions of

---

146. Bentley, *Humanists and Holy Writ*, 154–55; see 158.
147. Fox, *John Mill and Richard Bentley*, 91–92.

the orthodox better than other readings."[148] Such views appear to have hardened thereafter, when Tregelles, for example, admitted three variants inserted to promote ascetic (in 1 Cor 7:5) and other "corrupt customs" (in Rom 12:13) and in MS. 2816 (in Rom 14:17), where the "kingdom of God is righteousness *and asceticism*," while assuring his readers that, with these rare exceptions, there is no "evidence of doctrinal corruption of the sacred records."[149] Westcott and Hort's similar and celebrated statement extended the life of that viewpoint for the greater part of the next century: ". . . even among the numerous unquestionably spurious readings of the New Testament there are no signs of deliberate falsification of the text for dogmatic purposes."[150]

As a result, this suspicion of orthodox variations appears to have diminished considerably until a contemporary, broad-scale exploration of alterations for theological reasons was published in 1993, Bart Ehrman's *The Orthodox Corruption of Scripture*.[151] Cases are legion, such as Luke 2:33, where a variant to "his [Jesus'] father and mother" is "Joseph and his mother." The latter is surely secondary because it fits the orthodox miraculous birth theology, which the former reading does not, and the former is clearly the more difficult reading over against the latter. Plausibly the secondary variant was inserted as early as the adoptionist controversies.[152] Textual critics before and after Ehrman's influential book, largely in North America and the United Kingdom, have explored impositions upon a text of various biases, whether theological or ideological.[153]

---

148. Wettstein, Ἡ ΚΑΙΝΗ ΔΙΑΘΗΚΗ, 2:864–67 (his maxim XII); idem, *Libelli ad crisin*, 69–78; Griesbach, *Novum Testamentum Graece*, 1:lxii–lxiii = 'Prolegomena,' §III, ¶1, ¶6, ¶8.

149. Tregelles, *Account of the Printed Text*, 222–23; see 224–25. On Rom 14:17, see Metzger and Ehrman, *Text of the New Testament*, 268.

150. Westcott and Hort, *New Testament in the Original Greek*, 2:282; see 283: "The one known exception is . . . Marcion's dogmatic mutilation of the books accepted by him."

151. Bart D. Ehrman, *The Orthodox Corruption of Scripture: The Effect of Early Christological Controversies on the Text of the New Testament* (New York: Oxford University Press, 1993). For recognition of theological tendencies in textual variants in the intervening period, esp. the 1950s and 1960s, see Eldon Jay Epp, *The Theological Tendency of Codex Bezae Cantabrigiensis in Acts* (SNTSMS 3; Cambridge: Cambridge University Press, 1966), 1–4, 12–24; idem, "Anti-Judaic Tendencies in the D-Text of Acts: Forty Years of Conversation," in *The Book of Acts as Church History: Text, Textual Traditions and Ancient Interpretations/Apostelgeschichte als Kirchengeschichte: Text, Texttraditionen und antike Auslegungen* (ed. Tobias Nicklas and Michael Tilly; BZNW 120; Berlin: de Gruyter, 2003), 111–16 (repr. in Epp, *Perspectives*, 699–705).

152. Ehrman, *Orthodox Corruption of Scripture*, 55–56.

153. Examples are (1) on *theological/Christological issues*: Mikeal C. Parsons, "A Christological Tendency in P^{75}," *JBL* 105 (1986): 463–79; Peter M. Head, "Chris-

Notable is the insightful and forward-looking volume by David Parker, *The Living Text of the Gospels*,[154] which emphasized cases of multiple variants that defy the isolation of a single "original" text, but expose salient issues in the early churches. This, however, is not the forum for further pursuing these matters.

SUMMARY

Given the cautions expressed and the qualifications offered in the preceding discussions, the emphasis falls, once again, on these criteria as probabilities—on the necessity for textual critics to utilize their "art" more than their "science." Paramount is the need for extensive knowledge of and experience with both the immediate textual contexts of a variation unit and the broader contexts of the writing in which a variant reading is found, such as the rest of the New Testament, other early Christian writings, the socio-cultural environment of Christianity, and even the Roman world more broadly. In the final analysis, therefore, the exegete is the arbiter in textual-critical decisions. The process also rules out "rules" as normally understood—principles that can be applied simplistically or mechanically—and renders the text-critical task more difficult than often

---

tology and Textual Transmission: Reverential Alterations in the Synoptic Gospels," NovT 35 (1993): 105–29; (2) on *anti-Judaic bias in the D-text*: Epp, *Theological Tendency*, passim; idem, "Anti-Judaic Tendencies in the D-Text of Acts," 111–16; (3) on *anti-woman bias*: Ben Witherington, "The Anti-Feminist Tendencies of the 'Western' Text of Acts," *JBL* 103 (1984): 82–84; Richard I. Pervo, "Social and Religious Aspects of the 'Western Text'," in *The Living Text: Essays in Honor of Ernest W. Saunders* (ed. Dennis E. Groh and Robert Jewett; Lanham, Md.: University Press of America, 1985), 235–40; Michael W. Holmes, "Women and the 'Western' Text of Acts," in Nicklas and Tilly, *Book of Acts as Church History*, 183–203; in the same volume Ann Graham Brock, "Appeasement, Authority, and the Role of Women in the D-Text of Acts," 215–19; Wayne C. Kannaday, *Apologetic Discourse and the Scribal Tradition: Evidence of the Influence of Apologetic Interests on the Text of the Canonical Gospels* (SBLTCS 5; Atlanta: Society of Biblical Literature, 2004), 176–89; Eldon Jay Epp, *Junia—The First Woman Apostle* (Minneapolis: Fortress, 2005); Dominika A. Kurek-Chomycz, "Is There an 'Anti-Priscan' Tendency in the Manuscripts? Some Textual Problems with Prisca and Aquila," *JBL* 125 (2006): 107–28; David E. Malik, "The Contributions of Codex Bezae Cantabrigiensis to an Understanding of Women in the Book of Acts," *JGRChJ* 4 (2007): 158–83; (4) on *apologetic interests*: Heike Omerzu, "Die Darstellung der Römer in der Textüberlieferung der Apostelgeschichte," in Nicklas and Tilly, *Book of Acts as Church History*, 147–81; Brock [as above] 205–10; Kannaday [as above], passim; and Justin R. Howell, "The Characterization of Jesus in Codex W," *JECS* 14 (2006): 47–75.

154. David C. Parker, *The Living Text of the Gospels* (Cambridge: Cambridge University Press, 1997).

imagined, but also more rewarding, as a judicious use of the criteria leads to reasonable and satisfying decisions among variants in a given variation unit.

4. Tasks and Goal(s) of New Testament Textual Criticism

When is the task of textual criticism complete? When the relevant criteria have been applied and the earliest attainable text has been established (or, the most likely "original text," or the "initial text," as others may prefer)? Some will respond by saying, yes, that is the only task. Others may say it is the first task, with additional tasks remaining, thereby acknowledging that the variants not accredited for the earliest attainable text may have something to tell us about additional viewpoints, discussions, or events in the history of the churches. I would not quibble with Keith Elliott's assertion that there are only "good readings" or "secondary readings," for I would understand the good readings to be those of the earliest attainable text and secondary readings to be subsequent to them logically and temporally. However, I would not wish to retain the term "secondary" because it implies a subsidiary status rather than merely a later chronological position, and secondary readings so often are treated as second-class, rejected entities—mere chaff, to use Bart Ehrman's term.[155] Instead, I would lean toward considering all meaningful variants as equals, but then view the variant selected for the text as "the first among equals."

My own view, therefore, is that there is a unitary goal in New Testament textual criticism and that the criteria both facilitate the search for the earliest attainable text and, at the same time, highlight meaningful variants that spring forth from that earliest text and present to us a more complete picture of real-life church issues that reside in our extant textual materials. Textual criticism, on this view, documents for us Christian interactions with one another as well as with aspects of their cultural and societal milieu, offering enriching insights into the thought, values, and practices in the various Christianities that employed and transmitted the manuscripts containing their writings. Meaningful variants emerged as the communities shaped their faith and way of life by interpreting and reinterpreting the literature for different audiences and for varying purposes. Reading and copying manuscripts was no staid or merely mechanical exercise but a dynamic meaning-making process.

Just over a century ago, Kirsopp Lake in 1904 devoted the inaugural lecture for his professorship at Leiden University to "The Influence

---

155. Metzger and Ehrman, *Text of the New Testament*, 281.

of Textual Criticism on the Exegesis of the New Testament," pleading for attention to "doctrinal modifications of the text": "We need to know what the early Church thought [a passage] meant and how it altered its wording in order to emphasize its meaning."[156] This was Lake's way of alerting textual critics (a century ago and today) that a significant body of variants was to be found in an array of "local texts" (as he called them) throughout Christianity, and he viewed the assessment of these doctrinal and other alterations as a task prior to establishing the original text.[157] As noted, I would suggest that both aspects of the unitary task can be accomplished at the same time—and should be—so that the variants not accredited for the earliest baseline text do not immediately drop out of sight as they are relegated to the netherworld of the apparatus at the foot of the pages. In this process the criteria are found to have an important function beyond merely identifying the earliest attainable text, for they become the means for highlighting additional meaningful variants that have their own individual stories to tell, often placing them in some rough chronological sequence and thereby permitting alignment with more specific circumstances or issues in the churches.

I would offer, therefore, the following formulation of the goal of New Testament textual criticism:

> New Testament textual criticism, employing aspects of both science and art, studies the transmission of the New Testament text and the manuscripts that facilitate its transmission, with the unitary goal of establishing the earliest attainable text (which serves as a baseline) and, at the same time, of assessing the textual variants that emerge from the baseline text so as to hear the narratives of early Christian thought and life that inhere in the array of meaningful variants.

Our discipline functions somewhat like a kaleidoscope—the numerous texts with their many variants are translucent gems. With each turn of the kaleidoscope, the light shining through it reveals differing but ever-vivid images of some aspect of early Christianity. But a single view, as through a telescope or a microscope—analogous to seeking only the original or the earliest attainable text—provides merely a partial vision of the whole.

So, there is a real sense in which our criteria themselves, by their very existence, become a critique of the notion that we need focus only or predominantly on a single original or on the earliest attainable text. The ubiquitous ambiguity in the criteria is a wake-up call to see the larger picture.

---

156. Kirsopp Lake, *Influence of Textual Criticism*, 10, 12.
157. Ibid., 11.

7
WHAT SHOULD BE IN AN *APPARATUS CRITICUS?* DESIDERATA TO SUPPORT A THOROUGHGOING ECLECTIC APPROACH TO TEXTUAL CRITICISM

J. K. Elliott

Text critics are greedy people. For our work on the Greek New Testament we require and demand access to the distinctive readings of all known manuscript witnesses as well as all early versional evidence plus patristic and other support with everything displayed unambiguously in an *apparatus criticus*. We need to have access to variants of exegetical and theological significance as well as to grammatical and orthographical variation.

That is our ideal. In reality, even the greediest know that such a comprehensive and exhaustive apparatus can be achieved only slowly, resulting in a patient resignation that selectivity is bound to exist into the foreseeable future: but progress toward that ideal is still desired.

Hesitation about the practicalities of presenting an exhaustive range of variants evaporates in this electronic age. The likelihood of such material ever needing to be committed to paper reproduction in its entirety is remote. Electronic publishing is ideally suited to collecting and displaying an increasing number of manuscripts and other witnesses and an infinite number of variants in an ongoing and developing way, as more collations are made and more sources are scoured. Scholars' greed can be satisfied electronically.

"Popular" editions of the Greek New Testament inevitably must make selections both in the range of witnesses quoted and types of variants included, and that is right and proper, as long as the reasons for those selections are clearly set out. The two most popular printed editions of the Greek New Testament on the market today are NA[27] and

UBS⁴ (revised), with a new, fifth edition in prospect. These are hand editions—at one time quaintly called pocket editions!—and obviously these contain in their footnotes only a limited apparatus, in the case of UBS only about fifteen hundred readings deemed significant for translators. Eldon Jay Epp favors the highlighting of significant variants in the hand editions.[1] Such a "variation-conscious edition" could favor horizontal line displays below a constructed baseline. That makes good sense, although the construction and presentation of the material present challenges for the compositor.

But my concern in this article is for a major, scholarly research tool. Such a resource expects its readers to be able to make their own selections from the evidence on display. Those consulting an exhaustive apparatus can readily dispense with vast swathes of evidence if they so wish, rather as those consulting the material in the *Teststellen* can identify the majority, Byzantine text-type and put that to one side, if they so wish. Similarly, it is likely that any exhaustive apparatus—especially one that includes lectionary texts—will contain large numbers of, generally, identical witnesses for each variation unit.

Among publications that already provide relatively full apparatus are four, all printed in quarto format:

(a) The Wordsworth and White Latin Vulgate
(b) *Vetus Latina* (= VL). The *Vetus Latina* project claims to have an exhaustive display of Latin patristic citations that may support readings that predate or are independent of Jerome's translation, the Latin Vulgate; typically many of the pages in these fascicules contain a mere half verse of the text as the running lines, the rest of the pages being filled with densely packed citations and variants.
(c) The *Editio Critica Maior* (= ECM) of the Greek text has a generous apparatus of variants and manuscripts culled from a sifting process published in a companion series.
(d) The International Greek New Testament Project (= IGNTP) edition of Luke is another example of a fuller apparatus. Comparable work on the Gospel of John continues.

But ECM and VL and IGNTP, however worthy, do not cover the whole of the New Testament, nor are they likely to do so for decades. Biblical scholars are therefore still obliged to use the full but not always reliable

---

1. Eldon Jay Epp, "It's All about Variants: A Variant-Conscious Approach to New Testament Textual Criticism," *HTR* 100 (2007): 275–308.

apparatus in von Soden's edition of 1902–13 or in Tischendorf's eighth edition of 1869–72.

For most New Testament scholars and theologians the *Handausgaben* are perfectly adequate and serviceable. But the evidence they display is inevitably partial, and for many academic purposes their very restrictiveness can be misleading:

1. For some scholars there is a need to compare a favored manuscript with others throughout the entire run of text. The *full* text of only very few manuscripts may be reconstructed from an apparatus in the currently available editions.
2. For other scholars, assessing scribal habits and proclivities, a limited apparatus that typically excludes orthographical variants is of no use.
3. Those critics like myself who pursue what is dubbed thoroughgoing eclecticism—about which more below—need as full an apparatus as possible. With this methodology, the age, notoriety, or textual complexion of the manuscripts are less important than internal criteria when we assess how variants arose and which reading seems to have given rise to change. We take into account matters such as an author's style, first-century Greek usage, Semitic influences, and the like—but we are not working in a vacuum. We need to see not just variants but the manuscript witnesses that support each reading. We are not, as is sometimes erroneously said, disposed to accept enthusiastically conjectural emendations, as we shall state below. Our variants are verifiable in the manuscripts: thus we need to know and reveal each witness so that its evidence can be consulted.

All of us—thoroughgoing critics, followers of particular manuscripts, and investigators into scribal habits—ask for ever-fuller information about more and more variants.

Thoroughgoing eclectic critics claim that in theory the original text may have survived in any manuscript, whatever the date of that witness and however isolated the reading appears to be. If that claim is justified then we must see the readings of each and every extant witness in a search for that elusive original reading. Thus, we look to electronic editions to provide for us all the readings of every newly collated manuscript.

In a moment I shall explain further why such exhaustive evidence is needed. But first a digression on this term "original text." I know that in these allegedly postmodern days there are some who claim that such an enterprise is useless and that one cannot always expect to recover an authorial archetype or even an *Ausgangstext* (to use the Münster Institut's preferred term, indicating a text from which subsequent rewritings emerged). Nevertheless, it is often possible to be reasonably confident that one can plot the direction of changes when confronted with a number of variants. As one can readily do while applying Gert Mink's Coherence-Based methodology, one is encouraged to argue that reading x gave rise to readings y and z. It would then be the father behind the subsequent changes that would be dubbed the original reading, whether or not that necessarily went back to the author in every instance, and it should be that primitive reading which would appear in the running text in a scholarly edition.

Let us look at some examples from my earlier researches, where the need for an exhaustive apparatus is of paramount importance:

1. Our printed texts of Mark have two differing forms of John the Baptist's name, one a coined noun, "the baptist," the other a verbal (participial) form "the baptizing one." There are *v.ll.* at four of the five places where the name occurs. My argument is that for Mark "the baptizing man" was the likeliest way for him to describe John prior to the coining of the new noun.[2] Scribes later introduced this new and distinctively Christian noun into manuscript copies of Mark. Thus, I would print "baptizing one" in 6:14 and 6:24, where it is found in our printed editions but also in 6:25 and 8:28, where it is *not* found in our editions—but only because the editors deemed the manuscript support for this verb in those two places to be "weak."

2. Another example I have regularly used from Mark is the word "crowd," *ochlos*.[3] Even though there may not be much difference in meaning between "crowd" and "crowds," Mark in around forty places uses always and only the singular. In these places the manuscript tradition is firm: all known manuscripts read the singular. Then we come to Mark 10:1. Here our printed editions have the plural. One looks in vain for commentators to ask why that should be so. Some manuscripts, however, have the singular, and I would argue that these carry the correct (original) text here too. Mark would obviously have known and could have used the plural, but is he likely to have done so just once where there is no meaning obviously different from the forty other places where he wrote the singular *ochlos*? I would go against our printed editions in 10:1 and would prefer to print as "original" the singular yet again. It is consistent with Markan usage. In addition, there is a motive here for scribes to make a deliberate

---

2. J. K. Elliott, "Ho Baptizōn and Mark 1:4," *TZ* 31 (1975): 14-15.

3. J. K. Elliott, "Thoroughgoing Eclecticism in New Testament Textual Criticism." in *The Text of the New Testament in Contemporary Research: Essays on the Status Quaestionis* (ed. Bart D. Ehrman and Michael W. Holmes; SD 46; Grand Rapids: Eerdmans, 1995), 321–35, here 328.

change and have Mark agree with the parallel verse in Matthew, where the plural is found. In Matthew's Gospel both singular and plural occur throughout. But in Mark 10:1 to read the singular is to do so on the basis of (so far) only a handful of manuscripts.

3. Jerusalem. In New Testament Greek there are two different forms of that name, one a transliteration of the Hebrew in Greek characters, the other a "proper" Greek form. Both occur in the New Testament. In Acts there are firm examples of both, but also many places where our manuscripts are divided. Some have *hierosolyma;* others *hierousalēm.* Is there any logic in the way in which each was used? I, as well as others, have written on these *v.ll.* For my part I have detected a pattern where I can say that the Semitic form is original in this or that verse and where the Greek form is to be printed as the original in certain other places.[4] Those arguments take into account the context, and, if it occurs in a speech, the audience said to be addressed. To apply such reasoning we need to be sure that the rules for both forms of the name are established from firm, undisputed examples. Then we may apply our findings to disputed verses and, again, it may well be that the text form to be printed has allegedly weak attestation. But we all need to work from an apparatus that displays throughout the variant forms for both nouns.

4. In Acts 7:56 our editions have Stephen the martyr use the term "Son of Man"—and that is the only occurrence of this title outside the Gospels and the only occurrence not used on Jesus' lips. The exception here has caused commentators on that chapter in Acts to go to great lengths to explain why "Son of Man" is found here. However, it may be argued on stylistic and indeed on theological grounds that "Son of Man" should not be in the text here. There is a variant "Son of God" which is likely to be original: it fits the context well and does not present the problems caused by the alternative "Son of Man." But "Son of Man" is in the overwhelming number of witnesses; "Son of God" is poorly attested. New collations, however, may bolster the attestation for the latter.[5]

5. Many variants are found concerning nouns that have diminutive endings, or the two forms of the third declension comparative adjectives, or the augment in verbs with initial diphthong.[6] Investigations into those and many other comparable topics demand an apparatus that includes such ostensibly recherché changes. The same is true if one is pronouncing on the likelihood that Semitisms belong to the earliest stratum of New

---

4. J. K. Elliott, "Jerusalem in Acts and the Gospels," *NTS* 23 (1977): 462–69.

5. G. D. Kilpatrick, "Acts vii. 56: Son of Man?" *TZ* 21 (1965): 209; cf. idem, "Again Acts vii.56: Son of Man?" *TZ* 34 (1978): 232.

6. I have written on these topics respectively in *NovT* 12 (1970): 391–98; *NovT* 19 (1977): 234–39; *ZNW* 69 (1978): 247–52 (and *NovT* 32 [1980]: 1–11).

Testament writings and that scribes sometimes expunged these un-Greek features. Once again, one needs to be sure that in one's search into language, style, and vocabulary one has left no stone unturned in an investigation into what was written down when—and what was liable to be altered later.

A Brief excursus on conjectural emendation. We have just raised the question about authors' consistency—their fingerprints, which make the writing distinctive, whatever its literary sources and borrowings. Another question to be raised in this context by editors at work in a range of ancient literatures is the justification for modern academic editors to correct an author in places where no known textual variant has been uncovered/recovered/discovered in order to restore the author's alleged consistency of usage. To put it in other words: Should we try to restore to a totally corrupted textual tradition what we think was written? Are such conjectures valid? In the field of the New Testament there has been no shortage of inspired guesswork (for that is often what conjectural emendation has been). In antiquity one may describe some deliberate changes introduced by scribes into the manuscripts as conjectural emendations, and many such alterations have of course stood the test of time. Conjectures have continued to be put forward in modern times to solve many difficult verses and readings; very few of these conjectures have gained support. (Obviously we are concerned here with scholarly conjectures proposed since Beza's day. Many of those nineteenth- and twentieth-century conjectures are *still* reappearing in the apparatus of the Nestle edition.) I wait to be convinced that New Testament textual criticism has a place for conjectural emendation. *En passant* it remains to be seen how acceptable the ECM edition's suggested conjecture for restoring the *Ausgangstext* at 2 Pet 3:10 (namely, οὐχ εὑρεθήσεται) proves to be.

It will be clear that, when assessing textual variation, my usual methodology is to look for the author's established practice on the basis of firm examples. I then seek to argue that, whenever variation occurs, the reading that agrees with that established practice is likely to be the original, other things being equal. Such an argument may be strengthened if one can explain at the same time (as one often can) how or why the variant occurred. It may be that harmonization to a parallel was the reason for a change, especially in the Gospels; and we saw how I applied that argument to the change to "crowds" in Mark 10:1 from the Matthean parallel. Or one may be able to point to a possible paleographical reason behind a change, for example, an accidental shortening of a text through parablepsis, homoeoteleuton, and the like. Such supplementary arguments are satisfying and complete the exercise—one is not merely establishing the "original" text but explaining how the variant or variants occurred. All such arguments, of course, depend on our ability to check in an exhaustive apparatus the firmness, or otherwise, of each occurrence of the topic under our microscope.

Firm examples may cease to be firm if an exhaustive apparatus reveals newly collated variants that destroy what had previously been thought to be unchanging and undisputed. Obviously that result has to be expected, although in practice very few new "genuine," that is, meaningful variants (as opposed to orthographical errors or sheer mistakes) have come to light in recent decades. What is more likely is that readings already known but with little manuscript support are strengthened by the addition of further witnesses. And that is important. Thoroughgoing criticism is often objected to for promoting as original readings that have little or weak manuscript support. G. D. Kilpatrick prepared a diglot (Greek–English) edition of most of the New Testament between 1958 and 1964, based on the principles of thoroughgoing eclecticism; this was circulated privately. Bruce Metzger of Princeton, the former doyen of our discipline, in the standard primer on textual criticism, took Kilpatrick to task for printing readings with little support and he itemized some of them.[7] Kilpatrick's text was too radical for the British and Foreign Bible Society, for whom it was commissioned; it was too different from what had previously been printed.

What Metzger failed to note is that the Nestle-Aland text for which he was one of the co-editors is equally guilty of such a practice! At Rev 18:3 the Nestle text prints a reading with very little manuscript support (1006^c 2329 *pc*); at Acts 16:12 this edition promotes a text ("a city of the first district of Macedonia") that is found in no manuscript of the Greek New Testament at all—it is a mere conjectural reading. But with an increased, or (ideally) an exhaustive apparatus, Kilpatrick's edition and indeed the Nestle-Aland edition may find that previously weak attestation is strengthened.

Be that as may be, it is obviously always more satisfying if one can point to a chosen original text that is supported by a range of witnesses. Otherwise one may be wrong-footed, having to defend why and how the preferred reading has fortunately chanced to survive in merely a late minuscule or two. The publication of many new papyri manuscripts in the twentieth century did indeed sometimes provide early additional support for readings hitherto known only in a few, late witnesses. Many more readings may become better supported with an increasing number of newly collated manuscripts.

---

7. Repeated in Bruce M. Metzger and Bart D. Ehrman, *The Text of the New Testament: Its Transmission, Corruption, and Restoration* (4th ed.; New York and Oxford: Oxford University Press, 2005), 224–25.

The manuscripts that have chanced to survive and whose texts have been studied and collated may of course not be representative of all those hundreds of thousands ever written. Certainly the church fathers Origen and Jerome reported on readings then supported by the majority of witnesses in their days but which are now known to have little support.[8] Thus we should not be *too* mesmerized by arguments based on the current weight of support.

So, to repeat, I am prepared to continue to accept and print as the original text readings that may have few manuscripts as witnesses, just as the editors of our major editions have always done. But it is desirable to seek to have as full a representation of manuscripts in our apparatus as possible, and for that to be available, electronic storage, assembling, and publication are needed.

Manuscripts to Be Included in an Apparatus

Which witnesses should be included in an apparatus to a full Greek New Testament edition? Obviously continuous-text manuscripts and lectionaries, early versions and citations from the New Testament culled from patristic sources up to an agreed cutoff date. But there are compelling arguments that even more sources should be tapped.

Already we are accepting into existing apparatus readings from Greek manuscripts that may never have been continuous text witnesses or even lectionaries. I am thinking particularly of the many tiny scraps of papyrus that were allocated a number in the official list. Even Kurt and Barbara Aland in their *Text of the New Testament* admit that not all these witnesses should ever have been included in the *Liste*.[9] For instance, they note that papyri 43, 62, and 99 contain mere selections; papyrus 7 is a patristic fragment; papyri 55, 59, 60, 63, and 80 are commentaries; papyrus 10 a writing exercise; and so on. Among majuscules, 0152 and 0153 were

---

8. See Bruce M. Metzger's investigations into those variants in his articles „Explicit References in the Works of Origen to Variant Readings in New Testament Manuscripts," in *Biblical and Patristic Studies in Memory of Robert Pierce Casey* (ed. J. Neville Birdsall and Robert W. Thomson; Freiburg: Herder, 1968, 78–95); repr. in his *Historical and Literary Studies: Pagan, Jewish, and Christian* [NTTS 8; Leiden: Brill, 1968], 88–103); and idem, "St. Jerome's Explicit References to Variant Readings in Manuscripts of the New Testament," in *Text and Interpretation: Studies in the New Testament Presented to Matthew Black* (ed. Ernest Best and R. McL. Wilson; Cambridge: Cambridge University Press, 1979), 179–90; repr. in his *New Testament Studies: Philological, Versional, and Patristic* [NTTS 10; Leiden: Brill, 1980], 199–210).

9. Kurt Aland and Barbara Aland, *The Text of the New Testament* (2nd ed.; Grand Rapids: Eerdmans, 1989), 85.

respectively sigla for talismans and ostraca, and they were included by von Dobschütz when he controlled the Gregory list. The precedent has thus already been well established for including such witnesses.

Stuart Pickering advocates the inclusion of further noncontinuous text manuscripts such as those containing only the Lord's Prayer, say. Other possible contenders are *P. Oxyrhynchus* 1077, containing some New Testament verses written out as a series of crosses on a single page of parchment; *P. Vindob* G 29831, an amulet from a miniature codex; *P.Vindob* G 2312 with portions of Psalms, Romans, and John; *P. Palau Ribes* inv 68 and 207, an amulet containing verses from Ephesians, Colossians, and John.[10]

If we accept that proposal, then of course we could reinstate manuscripts such as 055, 0147, 0250, 0314, excluded from the IGNTP majuscule volume on John. There would then be no hesitation in including those manuscripts of John with *hermeneiai* (papyri 55, 59, 60, 63, 76, 80; also 0210 and 0302, as well as the now lost 0145 [not included in Parker's piece on this topic[11] but for which Münster has transcripts]). All such witnesses should indeed be included and carefully controlled, possibly even set out in different, separate sections of the apparatus.

Lectionary texts may best be included also in a separated apparatus. Likewise the versional evidence could stand apart, especially if the case is made for citing such evidence in its original languages. Patristic material needs to have its context revealed by means of a reference to the title of the work, as well as its chapter and verses in a modern edition, as ECM and IGNTP *Luke* do. Tjitze Baarda has even argued that readings from manuscripts now lost but included in earlier printed editions should be

---

10. Stanley E. Porter and Wendy J. Porter (in eidem, eds., *New Testament Greek Papyri and Parchments: New Editions: Texts* [Mitteilungen aus der Papyrussammlung der Österreichischen Nationalbibliothek XXIX Folge; Berlin and New York: de Gruyter, 2008], xiv) also indicate that *P. Vindob* G 348 (including four lines from the Gospels), *P. Vindob* G 8032 (with two verses from Romans and John), or *P. Vindob* G 30453 and G 26034 (a Pauline miscellany) could qualify for inclusion. See also S. E. Porter, "Why So Many Holes in the Papyrological Evidence for the Greek New Testament?" in *The Bible as Book: The Transmission of the Greek Text* (ed. Scot McKendrick and Orlaith O'Sullivan; London: British Library; New Castle, Del.: Oak Knoll Press, 2003), 167-86; and idem, "Textual Criticism in the Light of Diverse Textual Evidence for the Greek New Testament: An Expanded Proposal," in *New Testament Manuscripts: Their Texts and Their World* (ed. Thomas J. Kraus and Tobias Nicklas; Texts and Editions for New Testament Study 2; Leiden: Brill, 2006), 305-37.

11. David C. Parker, "Manuscripts of John's Gospel with *Hermeneiai*," in *Transmission and Reception: New Testament Text-critical and Exegetical Studies* (ed. J. W. Childers and D. C. Parker; TS 3rd series 4; Piscataway, N.J.: Gorgias, 2006), 48-68.

added to current apparatuses. Thereby some readings from, say, Stephanus's 1550 edition taken from manuscripts not nowadays identifiable can be re-presented.

Then there is the relevance of including New Testament references found in the Apostolic Fathers. I made a case for their inclusion in the apparatus to a Greek New Testament in a recent volume on the Apostolic Fathers.[12] Polycarp is included in the apparatus to NA^{27} at Rom 14:10 and the *Didache* appears there in the apparatus to Matthew's *Paternoster* passage (6:9–13). Again, a precedent has been set.

Inevitably, I have been concerned with the New Testament citations and allusions in the apocryphal New Testament. May these be included too? Are they not comparable to the patristic citations? If 0212, now understood to be a fragment of a Diatessaronic text, is in the *Liste* and included in the apparatus of a Greek New Testament, why not the *Gospel of Peter*? The *Gospel of Thomas* in particular, with its many *logia* that match Synoptic sayings, is surely another record of how words paralleled in the New Testament were repeated and reported.[13] The sayings collection in the *Gospel of Thomas* may well be more relevant to source or literary criticism than to textual criticism, but nonetheless this material has a relevance for our understanding the way in which Jesus' sayings were reproduced.

One obvious difficulty in using variants found in the *logia* in the *Gospel of Thomas* is the canonical Gospel to which each saying can be assigned. (The same is of course often the case when allocating the source of a saying found in a patristic source.) Perhaps one solution could be to deal with these alongside all three Synoptic Gospels together. Such an approach would permit readers to view the issues synoptically. Or, if that is not practicable or feasible, then at least copious cross-references need to be assigned to each ambiguous saying in all the potential parallels.

Another so-called apocryphal Gospel fragment, *Papyrus Egerton* 2, is found in the Nestle apparatus at John 5:39; once more the precedent has been established that such witnesses are acceptable and appropriate. So, although one must pity an editor assembling an apparatus, confronted with a seemingly endless array of potential witnesses to include, the argument that no witnesses should be jettisoned and that all possible sources should be tapped is compelling.

---

12. J. K. Elliott, "Absent Witnesses? The Critical Apparatus to the Greek New Testament and the Apostolic Fathers," in *The Reception of the New Testament in the Greek Fathers* (ed. Andrew Gregory and Christopher Tuckett; Oxford: Oxford University Press, 2005), 47–58. (The paperback reprint [2007] should not include the two queries on p. 48 lines 7–8.)

13. Some modern synopsis texts, like Aland and Huck-Greeven, print the sayings from the *Gospel of Thomas* and other apocryphal Gospels on the same page as a parallel canonical source.

To conclude: for those of us practicing that form of textual criticism which takes seriously authors' style, first-century usage, and so on, it is not the *quantity* of witnesses displayed for each variant that is paramount (although such evidence must play its part) but the *types* of variants. We need as full a range as possible, including those variants often overlooked as "merely" orthographical.

These desiderata are indeed demanding and challenging proposals, but I draw attention to them, conscious that I, like the sower in the parable, am aware that some of my seeds could fall on fertile and receptive soil. As a greedy scholar, I await a bumper harvest from those seeds.

8
CONTAMINATION, COHERENCE, AND COINCIDENCE IN TEXTUAL TRANSMISSION: THE COHERENCE-BASED GENEALOGICAL METHOD (CBGM) AS A COMPLEMENT AND CORRECTIVE TO EXISTING APPROACHES

Gerd Mink

It is indisputable that the New Testament manuscript tradition was subject to contamination. I use this term in purely a technical sense, without any pejorative connotation. On the contrary, when a copyist was confronted with conflicting data, it may have been his striving for textual fidelity that led to contamination. Contamination as a factor of textual development, is genealogically relevant. Likewise it is clear that coherence is a basic feature of the entire transmission. The questions remain though: How can coherence be described and interpreted genealogically in the context of contamination? How can text-critical decisions about the priority or posteriority of readings be made and tested, taking into account the entirety of the material? How can we gain an overview of all of our text-critical decisions as a whole?

Contamination is possible only if the contaminated witness and the sources of contamination are genealogically coherent. However, are agreements between witnesses sufficient evidence for coherence? The combinations of witnesses agreeing at variant passages change, a fact typical of contaminated traditions. Yet how can we distinguish between

---

My sincere gratitude is due to Klaus Wachtel, who translated this essay into English.

clear cases of contamination and simple coincidence? Finally, is it possible to formulate genealogical statements about the relationship between witnesses that are valid at each variant passage?

1. CBGM and Other Methods

Every editor reconstructing a text transmitted from antiquity formulates a genealogical hypothesis. He or she claims that at every passage with variants one of them is older than all the others. The editor applies internal and external criteria and weighs them according to the methodology he or she prefers, such as reasoned or thoroughgoing eclecticism, Byzantine Priority method, and so on.

The CBGM presupposes that genealogical relationships between witnesses are evidenced by genealogical relationships between variants. Therefore it strives to assess the genealogical relationships between variants and, if possible, to construct a local stemma of the variants. Whoever reconstructs a text from manuscript evidence automatically claims such a local stemma at all the passages where only two variants are extant by prioritizing one of them. Most editors are interested only in the reconstruction of the text, not in the genealogical relationships between all the variants in a passage. It is that very relationship, however, for which the scholar must formulate a hypothesis if he or she wants to arrive at a local stemma that is as complete as possible. In this process the very same methods will be applied that are used for the reconstruction of a text.

Being a meta-method, CBGM can be used by textual critics working with different basic methodologies. It just presupposes that these basic methodologies formulate hypotheses about the priority or posteriority of variants, and that is what all text-critical methods will do. CBGM will show the overall picture emerging from assessing variants as prior or posterior. In traditional textual criticism, especially if based on eclecticism, such an overall picture will hardly result from all the particular decisions made, because the critic's work is much too complex. As a rule, he or she will have a rather sketchy view of text-types or groups that cannot provide a comprehensive picture of the entire transmission.

This also means that CBGM is not identical with the local-genealogical method; it is not simply a new name for the same procedures.[1] The local-genealogical method is just one possible basic method, a variation of reasoned eclecticism. To be sure, the editors of the *Editio Critica Maior*

---

1. As understood by Maurice A. Robinson, "Rule 9, Isolated Variants, and the "Test-Tube" Nature of the NA/UBS Text: A Byzantine Priority Perspective," in *Translating the New Testament: Text, Translation, Theology* (ed. Stanley E. Porter and Mark J. Boda; Grand Rapids: Eerdmans, 2009), 27–60, esp. 54 n. 73.

(ECM)[2] are committed to the principles of reasoned eclecticism and use the CBGM to arrive at a comprehensive overview of their editorial decisions.

2. A Brief Explanation of Basic Terms

Variants and readings—The generic term "reading" comprises variants, incorrect renderings of variants, orthographical and certain morphological deviations. A witness containing a false rendering of a variant will be listed as a witness of the variant.[3] Likewise, orthographical deviations will not be treated as separate variants in the genealogical analysis. The same applies to morphological renderings that were regarded as interchangeable by many scribes.[4]

Connectivity—Variants are connective if they connect their witnesses genealogically. This will be the case (i) if the witnesses generally agree to such a degree that a coincidental match can be excluded or (ii) if the variant is too extraordinary to have emerged repeatedly.

Initial text—The reconstructed form of text from which the manuscript transmission started. Different objectives of reconstruction are possible: authorial text, redactor's text, or the archetype of the tradition as preserved.

Witness—The text of a manuscript, not the manuscript itself. The witness can be older than the manuscript.

Ancestor-descendant—Hypothetical relation between witnesses (= texts), not between manuscripts.

Local stemma—A stemma of variants at a passage (see figs. 1–4). The local stemma hypothesizes how the variants of a passage developed and which of them is the likely source of the others, that is, the initial text at that passage.

---

2. The Institute for New Testament Textual Research, ed., *Novum Testamentum Graecum, Editio Critica Maior: IV, Catholic Epistles* (ed. Barbara Aland, †Kurt Aland, Gerd Mink, and Klaus Wachtel; Stuttgart: Deutsche Bibelgesellschaft, 1997–2005) 1: *James*, Pt. 1, *Text*; Pt. 2, *Supplementary Material* (1997; 2nd rev. impr., 1998); 2: *The Letters of Peter*, Pt. 1, *Text*; Pt. 2, *Supplementary Material* (2000); 3: *The First Letter of John*, Pt. 1, *Text*; Pt. 2, *Supplementary Material* (2003); 4: *The Second and Third Letter of John, The Letter of Jude*, Pt. 1, *Text*; Pt. 2, *Supplementary Material* (2005).

3. In theory it is possible that a new variant arises from an obvious error. But in practice this possibility can be disregarded. The closest relatives of a witness containing a false reading almost always attest the reading without error. If an obvious error cannot be assigned to an existing variant, it will be listed as a separate falsely rendered variant (see ECM IV, 16*).

4. See ECM IV, 16*-17*.

Global stemma—A stemma of witnesses. The global stemma hypothesizes how the witnesses (= states of text) developed. The global stemma consists of optimal substemmata.

Optimal substemma—A substemma consists of a descendant and the ancestors from which its text can be derived at all the variant passages it contains. It is optimal if the number of ancestors is reduced to the minimum. Ancestors needed for an optimal substemma are termed *stemmatic ancestors*.

Potential ancestor—A witness is a potential ancestor of another witness if it features a higher number of variants prior to the compared witness.

Stemmatic ancestor—See *optimal substemma*.

Pre-genealogical coherence—Coherence as based just on agreements between witnesses, leaving aside genealogical statements. Strong pre-genealogical coherence (= a high degree of agreement) indicates a close relationship.

Genealogical coherence—Coherence as based on agreements and genealogical assessment of differences. Strong genealogical coherence arises between witnesses with strong pre-genealogical coherence if the text of one witness can be explained as deriving from the other at points where they differ.

Stemmatic coherence—Coherence between descendant and stemmatic ancestors according to the optimal substemma (see *optimal substemma*).

Textual flow—Textual flow leads from prior variants in witness x to posterior variants in witness y and, vice versa, from prior variants in y to posterior variants in x. Flow in both directions can be demonstrated for almost every pair of witnesses. *Predominant textual flow* means the prevalent tendency coming from the witness with the higher share of priority variants. These relationships can be expressed by directed edges (arrows) in a textual flow diagram. They can be used to display the relationship between witnesses within an attestation and between witnesses in different attestations at a given variant passage.

3. References

An extensive step-by-step introduction by the present author is available online.[5] In the following I shall refer to it as *"Introductory Presentation"* and page number. An extensive explanation of the terminology and discussions of theoretical problems of stemmatological analyses of contaminated traditions is given in my "Problems of a Highly Contam-

---

5. See http://www.uni-muenster.de/INTF/cbgm_presentation/download.html.

inated Tradition—Stemmata of Variants as a Source of a Genealogy for Witnesses."[6]

Many of the things discussed here, such as textual flow diagrams, can be tested and tried out by using *"Genealogical Queries,"* a suite of programs also available online.[7] It is accompanied by a guide, which includes many examples, and directions for the evaluation of results. The application presupposes that the user has a copy of the ECM at hand, because word and variant addresses according to this edition are required.[8] The data used in this article are in accordance with those on which *"Genealogical Queries"* (version 1.0) and the *"Introductory Presentation"* (release 1.0) are based.[9]

4. The New Material

The genealogical correlation of a manuscript text should be explored on the basis of *all* of its variants.[10] For a scribe, there were no "significant" or "insignificant" variants in terms of the textual history as studied by modern text critics. A scribe did not have a critical apparatus at hand, but he may have known some variants, from either a different *Vorlage* or some other source. In this case he had to opt for one of the variants, but apart from such cases he would just follow his main *Vorlage*. As a rule, most changes that were not caused by knowledge of variants were introduced without intention.

All the evidence must be taken into account. The study of contamination, coherence, and coincidental agreement must be based on a full collation of our primary sources. Neither a concise edition like NA^{27},[11] nor the collation of all manuscripts at test passages as in *Text und Textwert*,[12]

---

6. Gerd Mink, "Problems of a Highly Contaminated Tradition, the New Testament: Stemmata of Variants as a Source of a Genealogy for Witnesses," in *Studies in Stemmatology II* (ed. Pieter van Reenen, August den Hollander, and Margot van Mulken; Amsterdam and Philadelphia: John Benjamins, 2004), 13–85.

7. See http://intf.uni-muenster.de/cbgm/GenQ.html.

8. In a full reference to a variant passage in the ECM the word and variant addresses are included. E.g., "Jas 1:3/10-14b" means James 1, verse 3, words 10–14, variant b. With additions, an odd word address indicates a space. "Jas 1:12/31b" means James 1, verse 12, space after word 30, variant b.

9. A revision of local stemmata is currently under way and may result in diverging values in some cases.

10. For the definition of the term "variant" versus "reading" see "2. A Brief Explanation of Basic Terms" above.

11. *Nestle-Aland Novum Testamentum Graece* (ed. Barbara Aland, Kurt Aland, Johannes Karavidopoulos, Carlo M. Martini, and Bruce M. Metzger; 27th ed.; 8th rev. and exp. printing; Stuttgart: Deutsche Bibelgesellschaft, 2001).

12. The volumes relevant in this context are the following: *Text und Textwert*

provides a sufficient basis for such purposes, because they show only relatively small samples of the full evidence.

Since 1997 the ECM has been published in installments. The aim of this edition is to illuminate the textual history of the first millennium, a span of time from which relatively few documents have survived. The large number of papyrus and parchment fragments can be misleading here. We have to search for traces of earlier phases of the textual history in the manuscripts of later centuries. Such evidence is likely to be found in documents deviating from the main stream of transmission. On the other hand, it must not be excluded that the Byzantine tradition itself preserves such elements. Therefore, the textual epoch from the ninth century on is well represented in the selection of manuscripts for the ECM.

At any rate, we have to face the fact that a large part of the transmission has been lost, and so a genealogy of preserved manuscripts cannot be achieved. The high number of lost manuscripts, that is, the links missing between preserved documents, renders this impossible. We may try, however, to detect genealogical structures to which preserved documents can be assigned. Research in this field necessitates that we set aside for now the study of manuscripts as physical artifacts and focus instead on the texts they carry, whose sequences of variants can be compared with DNA chains. That is, the witnesses in terms of genealogical research are the texts, not the manuscripts. Whenever we use the term "witnesses," specified by Gregory-Aland numbers, in the following, we are solely referring to texts. Moreover, it should be borne in mind that these texts, apart from changes introduced by the respective copyists, are much older than the manuscripts carrying them. Thus, one should not wonder why most manuscripts included in the ECM are from the second millennium, although the focus is on the textual history of the first. Nearly all manuscripts from the first millennium are lost. What we have from the early phases of transmission is not likely to be representative of the text in those times; therefore, we have to rely on later sources to trace older variants.

Again, the study of coherence and contamination requires full collation of relevant witnesses. For fragments this means that they can hardly be adequately assigned to established genealogical structures, simply because we cannot assess what is not extant. With larger pieces we may still be able to recognize trends, but the smaller the fragment the less precise its genealogical classification.

Considering that the entirety of the evidence should be taken into account and that so many witnesses from the first millennium are lost, one

---

der griechischen Handschriften des Neuen Testaments, I. Die Katholischen Briefe, Band I-III (ed. Kurt Aland in association with Annette Benduhn-Mertz and Gerd Mink; ANTF 9–11; Berlin: de Gruyter, 1987).

may ask whether this means that genealogical research should be based on full collation of *all* extant manuscripts. In principle, this would be preferable. It can be shown, on the other hand, that such effort would not be justified by a gain of knowledge about the textual history of the first millennium. One hundred twenty-three continuous text witnesses were included consistently in the ECM apparatus of the Catholic Letters. For the Letter of James, however, the number is 164, because the editors wanted to make sure not to miss relevant variants that might be preserved in witnesses coming close to the majority text.[13] It turned out that the gain achieved by taking forty-one more manuscripts into account was very small.[14] Restricting the selection of manuscripts to those that show some distance to the majority text does not lead to a considerable loss of variants.[15]

For *Text und Textwert*, Catholic Letters, 552 manuscripts were collated at 98 test passages. The ECM apparatus lists 3,046 variant passages for

---

13. The selection was carried out on the basis of *Text und Textwert* (vol. I) and Klaus Wachtel, *Der byzantinische Text der katholischen Briefe: Eine Untersuchung zur Entstehung der Koine des Neuen Testaments* (ANTF 24; Berlin and New York: de Gruyter, 1995). The number of manuscripts included varies as follows (the number of witnesses subsumed under "Byz" is given in parentheses):

	Continuous text MSS		Lectionaries	
Jas	163	(78)	19	(19)
1Pt	133	(44)	10	(10)
2Pt	131	(45)	9	(9)
1Jn	132	(41)	11	(11)
2Jn	131	(37)	5	(5)
3Jn	130	(37)	5	(5)
Jd	132	(37)	6	(6)

14. Leaving small fragments out of consideration, we are dealing with 34 out of 41 witnesses that contribute 140 variants not attested otherwise. Of these, 132 are singular variants, of which 28 are in minuscule 38 and 25 are in minuscule 631! Most of them are due to forms that are easily confused like the first and second plural of the personal pronoun, the initial vowel of αυτ-/εαυτ- and the like.

15. Comparison of the following figures for the individual letters and the whole corpus shows that the number of witnesses coming close to the majority text has no significant impact on the number of variants.

	Words	Variant Passages	Variants	Variants per Passage	Relative Frequency of Variant Passages
Jas	1743	761	2355	3.09	1.09
1Pt	1680	700	2243	3.20	1.04
2Pt	1100	417	1324	3.18	0.94
1Jn	2140	765	2082	2.72	0.89
2Jn	245	104	320	3.08	1.06
3Jn	219	95	275	2.89	1.09
Jd	458	204	691	3.39	1.11
Catholic Letters	7585	3046	9290	3.05	**1.00**

these writings. Hypotheses about coherence and ways of contamination now have to prove their value with regard to the full range of data assembled for the ECM.

5. The Need for Novel Methodological Considerations

For text-critical work in the Catholic Letters we now have the ECM databases at our disposal. They enable us to subject the material to very specific queries. There are databases containing evidence from patristic citations and the main early versions (Latin, Coptic, Syriac). In the center, however, there is the database containing every reading of each manuscript included in the ECM of the Catholic Letters. It consists of 563,195 sets of data.

Looking at this abundance of data, it is obvious that text-critical work cannot simply continue as before. It can be expected that the way we conceive of the textual history will profit from this comprehensive collection of evidence. Textual research into the Catholic Letters now requires making full use of this material. Such study will focus on two major aspects: (i) the individual features of witnesses and their relationships with each other, (ii) the genesis of variants. The first pertains to external criteria, the second to internal criteria.

It is without doubt a preeminent task of textual research to investigate structures inherent in the collated material. It is not recommended, for this purpose, to sort the material by types, families, or groups at the outset. The traditional text-type approach, in particular, should be avoided in favor of the structure that will emerge if we focus on the relationships between all individual witnesses and thus determine their places in the transmission history.[16]

---

16. The notion of a Hesychian and a Lucianic recension, carried out in about 300, is scarcely sustainable and cannot really draw on Jerome's often-cited *Epistula ad Damasum* as far as the New Testament is concerned. I agree with Klaus Wachtel completely, who discussed this issue in *Der byzantinische Text der katholischen Briefe*, 166–69. The corollary concept of text-types, however, is still current. The problem with this concept is that it will confirm itself once the basic pattern has been accepted as a classification criterion. Witnesses will be assigned to one of the supposed text-types unless they are too distant from the assumed core representatives. In this case, some may create a new text-type, while others presume a mixture (see the discussions about the "Caesarean text"). At any rate, we should not try to impose the concept of text-types on evidence that is far too complex to be adequately sorted by it. Doubts concerning the traditional view of the textual history arose already when the witnesses included in the ECM were

These relationships are characterized by agreement and disagreement of variants. The level of affinity is determined by the degree of agreement between witnesses. Divergencies result from textual development and are therefore potential sources of information about genealogical relationships between witnesses.

The combination of witnesses attesting the same variants changes from passage to passage. This is the consequence of two predominant features of textual development: contamination and multiple independent emergence of same variants. A text-critical method will not be able to master the problems of the New Testament tradition unless it can cope with both contamination and coincidence.

Consequently, the aim of the Coherence-Based Genealogical Method (CBGM) must be a comprehensive hypothesis concerning the transmission process and its genealogical implications based on affinities evidenced by agreement and concerning textual developments evidenced by divergence. A distinction between contamination, which can occur only in connection with genealogical dependence, and multiple emergence of variants is mandatory for CBGM procedures.

Tracing the ways of contamination will enrich the external criteria, while observing multiple emergence of identical variants will throw new light on internal criteria. Both internal and external criteria have to be applied with due caution in the beginning. The external ones are based on hypotheses that may need correction as a consequence of applying the CBGM. It is also likely that internal criteria will have to be revised where suppositions about certain tendencies in copying are proven to be wrong. Moreover, the well-known problem of circularity[17] needs to be tackled by

---

compared with the NA[27]/GNT[4] text of the Letters of Peter. See Gerd Mink, "Was verändert sich in der Textkritik durch die Beachtung genealogischer Kohärenz?" in *Recent Developments in Textual Criticism: New Testament, Other Early Christian and Jewish Literature. Papers Read at a Noster Conference in Münster, January 4–6, 2001* (ed. Wim Weren and Dietrich-Alex Koch; Studies in Theology and Religion 8; Assen: Royal Van Gorcum, 2003), 39–68, esp. 47–49.

17. Methodological problems with external and internal criteria cannot be overlooked. The circularity of arguments is obvious: witnesses are assessed as "good" if they contain "good" readings, while readings are assessed as good, if they are attested by "good" manuscripts. This circularity cannot adequately be controlled by internal criteria. They are never presented without due caveats; see Eldon Jay Epp's contribution to the present volume; Kurt Aland and Barbara Aland, *The Text of the New Testament* (2nd rev. and exp. ed.; Grand Rapids: Eerdmans; Leiden: Brill, 1989), 281; Bruce M. Metzger and Bart D. Ehrman, *The Text of the New Testament: Its Transmission, Corruption, and Restoration* (4th ed.; New York and Oxford: Oxford University Press, 2005), 302–4.

pondering all the text-critical decisions regarding priority or posteriority of variants in light of the overall picture produced by means of the CBGM. Although preferences for certain witnesses may influence the final results, the complexity of procedures and the differences in approach (see textual flow diagrams and optimal substemmata) preclude consistent bias in favor of a certain result. Since the final picture is not predictable, the role of circular reasoning is likely to be reduced. Scientific progress is often achieved this way: research cannot work without any presuppositions, but its results may change the presuppositions or even render them obsolete.

Consequently it is necessary to integrate two arrays of data into the overall picture: (i) the relations between witnesses as evidenced by agreements and divergencies and (ii) assessment of the genealogical direction of divergencies on philological grounds. It is to this end that the CBGM provides a means to describe coherence between texts, to search for genealogical structures inherent in the tradition, and, most importantly, on the basis of these structures, to formulate statements about the relationships between witnesses that are valid for all variant passages and thus for the entire text. The elements of this hypothesis are the texts and their variants which may converge or diverge. The task is to determine for each text a range of source texts, that is, sources of contamination, by which its features can be explained. This means that a genealogical hypothesis is also a hypothesis about sources of contamination. Ideally, the overall picture will take the form of a stemmatic representation, a graphical exhibit of a complex hypothesis about the genealogy of all included manuscript texts. Yet the complexity of the hypothesis surpasses what a traditional stemmatic graph can display. Therefore, a new concept of "stemma" had to be developed integrating the facts and the assessments on which the hypothesis is based.

In sum, the CBGM derives genealogical relationships between wit-

---

Arguments referring to internal criteria rarely claim that a variant x *must* derive from variant y. They usually just offer an explanation why variant x *may* go back to y. In many cases, however, internal reasons can also be found for the inverse statement that y may go back to x. Nevertheless, we cannot but resort to considerations according to external and internal criteria, if we strive to reconstruct a text for exegetical purposes from divergent strands of our manuscript tradition. Means to control circularity are provided by taking the whole picture into account while assessing a single variant passage. Hence, it is an important task of the CBGM to produce a comprehensive overview and to incorporate it methodologically in the text-critical procedures. To be sure, the overall picture develops while work is progressing. Therefore text-critical decisions must be open for revision.

For the character of the iterative process of assessing variants, see the Conclusion below.

nesses from genealogical relationships between their variants. The gist of the method is a way to map genealogical relationships between variants into coherent fields within a global stemma of witnesses. Principally, the basis of all this is the relationship between witnesses at each of the variant passages. A witness will either agree with or derive its variant from one of its immediate stemmatic ancestors. Therefore, local stemmata of variants are the elements on which a global hypothesis about the genealogy of their witnesses can be based.

6. Basic Assumptions

One of the objectives of the CBGM is an overall structure resting on genealogical relationships between the states of text contained in the witnesses included in the apparatus. Starting from the same set of witnesses, a vast number of overall structures are possible, all of which could be based on relationships between the witnesses. Whenever there are such multiple possibilities, rules must be agreed upon for the justification of concrete claims—rules that will govern the preferences for the work of both the philologist and the programmer. One rule that should have the highest priority in any quest for any hypothesis, and thus also for a hypothesis taking the form of a complex structure, is the rule of parsimony: the simpler hypothesis is preferable to the more complex. This rule must be observed in all phases of the work. Basic assumptions have to be formulated reflecting the factors active in transmission. These assumptions will not claim to be valid in every case—they actually cannot be universally valid—but they will apply more likely than their contrary. In each single case, an assumption can be regarded as true only until a different assumption can explain the situation with greater likelihood. There are four such basic assumptions:

1. A SCRIBE WANTS TO COPY THE *VORLAGE* WITH FIDELITY.

This assumption does not simply follow the principle of least effort but is supported by the fact that in the late, richly documented phase of transmission we can determine a close relative for nearly each witness. Witnesses preserved from earlier phases are by far fewer in number and hence are textually less similar to each other. Furthermore, in the earlier phase represented by witnesses from the first centuries, the frequency of copying was lower. With a higher frequency of copying it is easier for a copyist who feels uncertain about a passage in his exemplar to consult a different manuscript. Moreover, it is also more likely under such circumstances that a scribe unintentionally reproduces an already existing variant, because there is already a large pool of variants.

Most variants do not result from intentional tampering with the text.

In most cases they simply reflect the human factor in copying, and the scribe himself would probably have considered them errors. This does not mean that deliberate interpolations and even redactional reworking of whole texts never occurred. Moreover, in most cases by far, a variant emerged only once. From that moment on it was—correctly, from the point of view of the scribe—copied just like any other passage. This is confirmed again and again by textual flow diagrams showing the most closely related potential ancestor of a witness supporting the same variant (e.g., figs. 5, 27), in spite of so many links being lost. Yet the textual flow diagrams also show cases that can be explained only by the multiple emergence of a variant (e.g., figs. 9, 23, 24, 28). In a case of multiple emergence, the attestation will show two or more groups of witnesses connected by close relationship that share the same variant (coherence chains). Larger attestations scarcely feature poor coherence, which is typical of variants that are easily created by the smallest imprecision (e.g., if an itacistic change produces an intelligible text).

The first basic assumption means that in the context of the CBGM, each variant shared by highly similar witnesses—regardless of whether the variant appears significant—counts as an instance supporting their affinity, their genealogical coherence. In such witnesses minor agreements are not considered coincidental. Two examples from Jas 2:23 can demonstrate this. The text supported by the majority of witnesses reads επιστευσεν δε αβρααμ τω θεω ... και φιλος θεου εκληθη. Instead of φιλος several witnesses read δουλος (2:23/36 b), a significant variant. The particle δε at the beginning of the sentence (2:23/16) is omitted by a number of witnesses—a variant with little bearing on meaning. Now 1799 omits δε and reads δουλος, and the same is true for its most closely related potential ancestor, 206, and for the closest potential ancestor of 206, namely, 429, and for the next witnesses in the chain of coherence, 2200 and 1611, as well. This chain indicates a strand of transmission in which δε was lacking and a few words later δουλος occurred instead of φιλος. The copyist did not see a variant here. Hence the omission of δε and the presence of δουλος are both genealogical ties connecting the witnesses of these readings. Consequently, no difference is made between "important" and "unimportant" agreements of highly similar witnesses.[18]

---

18. If witnesses of inconspicuous variants are less similar, the question arises whether the instance of agreement occurred coincidentally. While constructing optimal substemmata (see below "14. Constructing Optimal Substemmata") we may exclude even highly similar relatives from ancestry, if their contribution to the explanation of the descendant's text is minute, for example, if the respective variants could be due to vowel interchange.

2. IF A SCRIBE INTRODUCES DIVERGING VARIANTS, THEY COME FROM ANOTHER SOURCE (I.E., THEY ARE NOT "INVENTED").

It goes without saying that copyists have created variants again and again. If a witness supports a variant differing from the one attested by its most closely related potential ancestor, the witness will usually share its variant with one of his other closely related potential ancestors. Thus the second basic assumption, like the first one, has in view that coherence between witnesses is evidenced by each instance of agreement. As long as no factor points to the contrary, we do not assume that a variant was "newly invented" by a scribe.[19]

Let us return to Jas 2:23. The witness 614 omits δε and supports δουλος. Its most closely related potential ancestor, 1292 (agreeing with 614 at 93.94%), omits δε, but reads φιλος in 2:23/36. However, the second most closely related potential ancestor of 614, namely, 1611 (agreeing at 93.74%), supports δουλος just as does 614. This reading then can hardly be seen as an independent "invention" of 614. The combination of both variants alone—the omission of δε, and δουλος instead of φιλος—would not indicate contamination, because in this verse 614 agrees completely with 1611. In the Catholic Letters, however, there are 58 passages, on the whole, where 614 agrees with 1292 against 1611. Thus, we may conclude that the text of 614 was formed by variants of 1292 and 1611, and in this case by δουλος in 1611.

It is a frequently occurring feature that a witness does not agree with its most closely related potential ancestor but with the closest potential ancestor of the latter. This indicates contamination with a highly similar text. It is characteristic of such relationships that descendants may contain a considerable number of variants that are prior to those of their immediate ancestors.[20]

3. THE SCRIBE USES FEW RATHER THAN MANY SOURCES.

This assumption follows from a realistic view of the copying process and from the rule of parsimony. This rule is important for the construction of optimal substemmata. Each optimal substemma is constituted by a descendant and its stemmatic ancestors. By definition the number of stemmatic ancestors of a witness is required to be as small as possible. If the entire text of a descendant can be explained by four stemmatic ancestors, a fifth one should not be postulated.

---

19. For potential restrictions, see the previous note.
20. Cf. the models of a simple and a two-stage contamination and the problems that may result from multistage contamination in Mink, "Problems of a Highly Contaminated Tradition," 49–51, figs. 18–20.

4. THE SOURCES FEATURE CLOSELY RELATED TEXTS RATHER THAN LESS RELATED ONES.

This rule is a corollary of the first. It does not exclude the possibility that contamination can go back to text forms with quite different characteristics. As a rule the witness in question will have a certain affinity to several distinct text forms. This applies to 323, for example, a witness studied more thoroughly below. It occurs more rarely that the source of contamination is likely to be a more remote potential ancestor. In this case the connectivity of the variant resting on its unusual character must be so strong that coincidental agreement can be excluded.

A typical case can be studied by returning to Jas 2:23, the verse that was transmitted with or without δε after επιστευσεν and with Abraham as φιλος or δουλος.

επιστευσεν αβρααμ τω θεω . . . και **φιλος** θεου εκληθη	1292
επιστευσεν αβρααμ τω θεω . . . και **δουλος** θεου εκληθη	1611 (most closely related potential ancestor of 1292)
επιστευσεν αβρααμ τω θεω . . . και **φιλος** θεου εκληθη	1448 (fourth most closely related potential ancestor of 1292)
επιστευσεν **δε** αβρααμ τω θεω . . . και **φιλος** θεου εκληθη	35 (most closely related potential ancestor of 1448)
επιστευσεν αβρααμ τω θεω . . . και **φιλος** θεου εκληθη	617 (sixth most closely related potential ancestor of 1448)

The potential ancestors agreeing most with 1448 share about the same distance from it (in the 92% range). 1448 agrees with 35 at 92.76%, with 617 at 91.87%. Thus, the sixth position in the list of potential ancestors of 1448 does not indicate irrelevance. 1292 completely agrees with 1448 in this verse. Consequently the variants of 1292 and 1448 in this verse alone do not indicate contamination. The next closely related potential ancestors of 1292 agree at about 95%. The potential ancestor 1448 reaches only 91.62%. There are 184 instances where 1292 agrees with 1611 against 1448. We may conclude that φιλος intruded into this strand of transmission by contamination via 1292 or one of its lost ancestors. 1448 agrees completely with 617 here, but there are 71 instances where 1448 agrees with 35 against 617.

These relationships indicate certain problems. Our example shows that the same combination of variants sometimes does not recur in the first or one of the most closely related potential ancestors, but in one that is in a still acceptable but lower position. On such a basis it is possible to hypothesize a way by which contamination intruded with good reasons. However, one cannot be sure at this point whether a potential ancestor viewed as a source here will also be represented in the relevant optimal substemma which is the final hypothesis about the sources of contamination by which a witness is affected. According to the third basic assumption and the definition of an optimal substemma, the number of stemmatic ancestors (i.e., presumed sources of contamination) should be as small as possible. Yet it will be necessary in many cases that because of variants that are connective on internal grounds the text of a descendant can be explained only if more distant potential ancestors are taken into account. Accordingly, some more similar witnesses will not be needed in the combination of ancestors in a substemma. In this case the third rule ranks higher, because it is the one that guarantees in the end that the rule of parsimony, which prohibits superfluous assumptions, is obeyed.

7. Contamination

Combinations of witnesses changing almost constantly from variant to variant are clear indicators of contamination. This is due to the fact that a copyist did not always follow his exemplar but sometimes preferred variants from another source. He may have preferred them for various reasons—perhaps because he considered the variant more apt linguistically or logically, perhaps because he had more confidence in the other source, or perhaps simply because his main exemplar was damaged or illegible at a passage. We do not have positive knowledge about this.

It is certainly most unlikely that a copyist consistently used several exemplars. Normally contamination seems to have had only minor influence on each individual copying process. It is a consequence of the loss of so many links between surviving witnesses that they appear to be heavily contaminated. The larger the distance from the Byzantine text the more links are missing. For the witnesses traditionally labeled "Alexandrian" this is true for virtually all the links. Even if contamination is progressing at a low level from copy to copy, the resulting contamination may be considerable after some time. Consequently, it appears to have been much stronger than it actually was historically, especially if most of the manuscripts are lost.[21]

The traceability of contamination depends on the degree to which the immediate genealogical environment of a witness has been preserved. In this regard there are extremes. On one hand, in the realm of the majority text there are always very closely related potential ancestors. Only some of these witnesses were selected for the ECM apparatus as representatives of the Byzantine text. On the other hand, there are witnesses exhibited as the most closely related potential ancestors, even though there are considerable divergences between them and their potential descendants.

In the following list, one of the witnesses of each pair is the most closely related potential ancestor of the other. The respective arrow points

---

21. See the figures in *Introductory Presentation*, 58–62.

to the descendant. The relationship is not directed (although quite close) in just one case: 876 – 1832.[22]

Pair of Witnesses	Agreement in %	Absolute figures
18 < 35	99.05%	3010/3039
93 > 665	98.43%	2694/2737
307 > 453	98.55%	2998/3042
326 > 1837	98.11%	2902/2958
614 > 2412	99.06%	2832/2859
876 – 1832	98.55%	2987/3031
1270 < 1297	98.75%	2990/3028
01 < 03	87.18%	2617/3002
02 > 1735	90.38%	2723/3013
03 > 04	89.30%	1878/2103
03 > 1739	89.13%	2689/3017
04 < 1739	90.92%	1913/2104
044 < 1739	85.82%	2608/3039
33 < 2344	93.29%	2502/2682
81 > 2344	90.06%	2656/2949
1739 > 323	95.46%	2902/3040

The high value of agreement with the last pair of the list is an exception, because as a rule higher percentages of agreement are rare where the witnesses compared share relatively few majority readings. The pair 044 < 1739, on the other hand, features a particularly low percentage of agreement. The reason is that 044 is a text with many peculiarities. It has 102 variants that have no further witnesses among those that are cited consistently in the ECM apparatus of the Catholic Letters.[23] 01, too, has quite a few such variants: 89. In comparison, 02 has 31, 03 has 36, 33 has 38, 1735 has 43, 1739 has 3 variants singular in this sense. Where agreement values are higher, such peculiar readings are relatively rare. For example,

---

22. In such a case a change of the genealogical relationship of the respective variants at only one passage would make one of the witnesses the potential ancestor of the other.

23. These 123 witnesses provide the basic material for our genealogical studies. Thus, it is reasonable to base the count of singular variants on the material actually compared. The statement that a variant is a singular reading necessarily refers to a defined pool of data. Since we have no positive knowledge about the historical singularity of a reading, one should not overestimate this category. If we assess the impact of this kind of variants on agreement values, only higher proportions of singulars may point to extraordinary textual character. Moreover, it makes no logical difference whether a witness has a singular variant or shares its reading with other witnesses coincidentally.

18 has 2, 1837 has 15 such singulars. The share of peculiar readings of this kind has an immediate impact on the distance from the next closely related potential ancestor. In the case of 1739 and C3 only 0.9% of the differences are due to singular readings in 1739. In the case of 33 and 2344 the percentage of singulars in 33 is 20.6% of the differences; in the case of 01 and 03 the percentage of singulars in 01 is 23.1% of the differences; in the case of 044 and 1739 the percentage of singulars in 044 is 23.7% of the differences. Thus, the peculiar variants are only one factor, and one of relatively small significance, leading to lower values of agreement. A far more important factor is the absence of all very closely related potential ancestors of this category of witnesses.[24] This, in many cases, is probably the reason why peculiar variants have no further attestation. Unfortunately, there is no criterion to distinguish inherited singulars from those created by the scribe of a preserved manuscript like 01 or 044.

8. Agreement of Variants as Indicator of Relatedness

Genealogical correlations between variants and between witnesses can be described in hypothetical form only. Yet it is certain that they exist. Collation shows agreements and differences. The number of agreements reveals affinity or distance between witnesses, but does not say anything about their genealogical relations. Differences, however, can provide such information, if a genealogical direction between differing variants can be determined.

Agreement as such has no specific genealogical implications. It helps to identify and determine pre-genealogical coherence, which can be expressed in percentages and absolute figures. Percentages allow for comparison of complete and fragmented witnesses. The more fragmented a witness is, the more important are the absolute figures, because fragmentation diminishes the validity of inferences on the manuscript as a whole. Evaluating percentages we must keep in mind that the average agreement of all pairs of witnesses is 87.6%.[25]

---

24. See the excursus "Values Determining Coherence" in *Introductory Presentation*, 280–97, esp. 283–94.

25. See *Introductory Presentation*, 280: "Which percentage of agreement is high or low? These values may show the range we find in the material collated for the Catholic Letters:
maximum: 99.1% agreement between 614 and 2412 (27 disagreements)
minimum: 77.9% agreement between 1241 and 1838 (624 disagreements)
average agreement: 87.6%"

Pre-genealogical coherence has an important part in preparing genealogical analyses.[26] It helps to answer two questions:

- Does the attestation show characteristics of unique or multiple emergence?

A variant is likely to have arisen only once if all the witnesses in its attestation are connected by high pre-genealogical coherence. A variant is likely to have arisen more than once if one or several witnesses show weak pre-genealogical coherence with the rest of the attestation. Multiple emergence is probable as well if the attestation consists of differing groups with strong coherence within themselves. Yet in spite of weak pre-genealogical coherence the unusual character of variants may argue in favor of relatedness.

- Which other variants are attested by close relatives of the witnesses supporting the variant in question?

Answering the first question helps to clarify whether a variant is likely to have only one source or multiple sources. The second question aims at identifying possible sources of a variant. Yet high pre-genealogical coherence does not provide a definite clue to which variant sprang from which. To answer this question requires that the customary text-critical methods be applied.

For assessing pre-genealogical coherence we need tables showing for each witness in each attestation which variants are supported by a defined number of close relatives.[27] With very large attestations pre-genealogical coherence is usually good,[28] and with small ones it can easily be checked. But it is relatively difficult to check pre-genealogical coherence of medium-sized attestations, because many comparisons have to be done for this purpose.

---

26. For the various possibilities of pre-genealogical coherence, see *Introductory Presentation*, 181–92.

27. Such tables are not yet available online. The values showing pre-genealogical coherence can be gathered from the tables produced by the *"Potential Ancestors and Descendants"* module of *"Genealogical Queries"* (see above under "References"), if the option "Show Descendants" has been selected. If the user studies the lists of potential ancestors and descendants, he or she will find the percentage of agreement for each witness compared and can infer a criterion for pre-genealogical coherence.

28. The following thought may illustrate the reason behind this: If there is no variation, the text is attested by all witnesses, and each witness has its most closely related potential ancestor within this attestation. Coherence is perfect.

9. Divergence between Variants as Indicator of Genealogical Relatedness of Witnesses

As one tries to determine the text that is directly or indirectly prior to all other variants in a passage, one may also try to find for each variant another one that is directly prior to it. Pre-genealogical coherence is of help in this attempt. It shows (1) which variants are unlikely to be genealogically related, because their witnesses are lacking close relatedness (= agreement).[29] Moreover, it shows (2) which attestations do not feature sufficient unity to exclude multiple emergence. Multiple emergence, however, that results in coincidental agreement will be relevant for further CBGM procedures only if it has arisen from different source variants.[30]

Genealogical relationships between variants are documented as local stemmata of variants. They comprise statements about variants (x, y) that take the form $x \to y$ or, if the source is questionable, $? \to y$. Even the initial variant of a passage may be left undefined, if necessary, and can be represented by "?" in a local stemma. For the sake of descriptiveness such statements about the genealogy of variants can be expressed graphically. Figures 1, 2, 3, and 4 show some examples:[31]

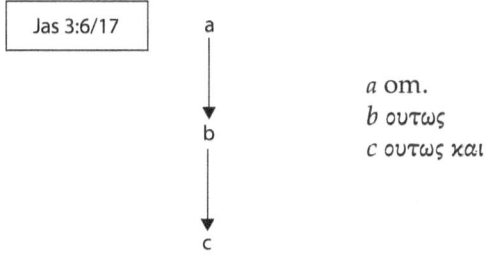

Figure 1. Local Stemma of Variants

---

29. See the example in *Introductory Presentation*, 190–92.

30. No matter whether agreements are coincidental or not, their number is the measure of relatedness and it is co-decisive for recognizing coincidence. Coincidental agreements do not change pre-genealogical coherence. Likewise they do not influence the genealogical direction between witnesses, if the agreements rest on the same source variants. Yet, in case of different source variants, genealogical direction may be affected.

31. "*Local Stemmata*" is a module of "*Genealogical Queries*" (see above under "References").

Figure 1 displays a simple local stemma featuring nothing exceptional.

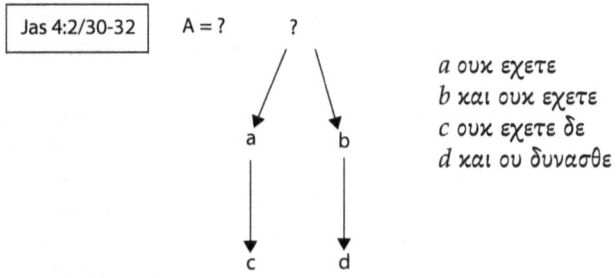

a ουκ εχετε
b και ουκ εχετε
c ουκ εχετε δε
d και ου δυνασθε

Figure 2. Local Stemma Whose Source (Initial Text) Is Unclear

In fig. 2 it is left open whether *a* or *b* holds the initial text. Thus, the source of the whole stemma is represented by "?".

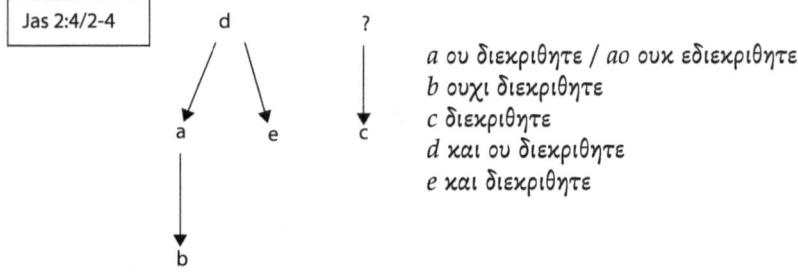

a ου διεκριθητε / ao ουκ εδιεκριθητε
b ουχι διεκριθητε
c διεκριθητε
d και ου διεκριθητε
e και διεκριθητε

Figure 3. Local Stemma of Variants One of Which Has an Unclear Source

In the local stemma presented in fig. 3, the source of variant *c* was left undefined, because linguistically each of the other variants would be a possibility.[32]

---

32. In this case variant *a* is no longer seen as the source of the stemma. The decision made for the ECM text at this passage was revised later, because variant *d* (και *apodoseos*) proved to be the *lectio difficilior* (see Mink, "Problems of a Highly Contaminated Tradition," 61). The arguments given there rest on the James material only, but the decision was confirmed by the data of all Catholic Letters.

In case of mixture, one variant can have several sources (fig. 4).

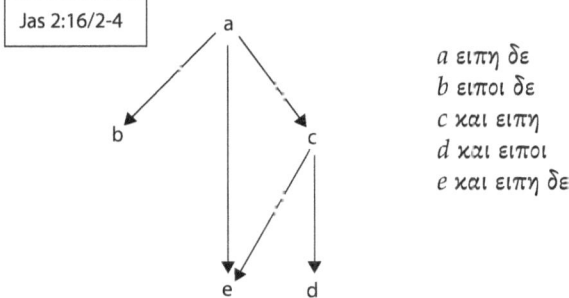

a ειπη δε
b ειποι δε
c και ειπη
d και ειποι
e και ειπη δε

Figure 4. Local Stemma with a Variant Originating from Two Sources

When in the initial phase of the editing process the local stemmata of variants are constructed for the first time, pre-genealogical coherence will be incorporated as an external criterion, while genealogical coherence of witnesses has to be explored in this very phase. The editor will bring along ideas about the value of certain witnesses, some of them well founded, others less so. To be sure, he or she will find very many combinations of witnesses that are not apt or can even be excluded as a possible attestation of the initial text. On the other hand, the best known, highly esteemed witnesses have to be treated with special caution. It is not least their text-historical position that has to be reexamined in the light of newly established genealogical coherence. This means that, in case of doubt, a decision has to be left open in this phase. Therefore the ECM editors treated B/03, a witness that tipped the scales in many previous text-critical decisions, with skepticism when they constructed the local stemmata.[33]

By relating the variants genealogically to each other in local stemmata the witnesses of these variants are brought into genealogical relationship accordingly. We describe the relationship between two witnesses x and y at each variant passage by one of five statements:

(i) x and y agree in the same variant.
(ii) The variant of x is prior to the variant of y.
(iii) The variant of x is posterior to the variant of y.
(iv) There is no direct relationship between the variants of x and y.

---

33. Nevertheless, it was confirmed that 03 is an outstanding witness agreeing more than any other with the reconstructed initial text.

(v) The relationship between the variants of *x* and *y* is unclear and has to be left open.

The appropriate statements will be stored in a database. From these data, tendencies reflecting the general relationship of witnesses *x* and *y* can be extrapolated. The resulting values will be found in the lists of potential ancestors.

10. Potential Ancestors

The above genealogical statements can be used to determine the position of each witness in relation to each other witness within a general textual flow that proceeds from older to younger states of text.[34] This is required for establishing *genealogical coherence* based on the genealogical relationship between variants in pairs of witnesses. The ultimate goal of this procedure is to find the *stemmatic ancestors* of a witness.[35] Because of contamination and loss of many witnesses, it is quite unlikely that ancestors will contain only variants agreeing with or being prior to those in a descendant. In fact, ancestors will also contain readings posterior to those in the descendant, and descendants will also contain readings prior to those in the ancestor. The ancestor, however, by definition has *more* priority readings than the descendant. Ancestors are called *potential* to distinguish them from *stemmatic* ancestors which will be included in an optimal substemma or a global stemma.[36] A witness may have many potential ancestors, but as a rule only a few of them will be required to explain its text and thus be needed for its optimal substemma. The rule of parsimony demands that the number of stemmatic ancestors be as small as possible. Potential ancestors constitute a pool from which the stemmatic ancestors have to be selected. An optimal substemma will consist of a witness (*stemmatic descendant*) and an optimal selection from the pool of its potential ancestors. In the selection process, potential ancestors with a high proportion of agreement, that is, stronger pre-genealogical coherence, with the witness in question will have a greater chance of becoming ancestors in an optimal substemma. If there are, on the other hand, several potential ancestors with high degrees of agreement with the descendant and similarity to each other, it is unlikely that all of them are needed in an optimal substemma.

---

34. For the concept of textual flow and potential ancestors, see Mink, "Problems of a Highly Contaminated Tradition," 31, 33–34; and *Introductory Presentation*, 109–26.

35. See *Introductory Presentation*, 133–34.

36. See ibid., 127–32.

The list of potential ancestors of 025 may serve as an example (table 1).[37]

Potential Ancestors of 025 (W1)
Data Source: Cath. Letters (excl. small fragments and extracts)

W2	NR	D	PERC1	EQ	PASS	W1<W2	W1>W2	UNCL	NOREL
A	1		92.437	2371	2565	181	0	6	7
468		0 -	91.096	2435	2673	92	92	48	6
1739	2		88.810	2381	2681	126	93	63	18
04	3		88.318	1701	1926	88	78	45	14
03	4		87.551	2342	2675	175	68	82	8

Table 1 Potential Ancestors of 025

In this list, 025 is compared with other witnesses under W2 (= Witness 2; W1 or Witness 1 is 025). Among these witnesses there is "A," the first entry in W2, representing the reconstructed initial text. Logically, it contains all the variants that are seen as source of the other variants in each variant passage. Thus, it is possible to compare each real witness with the reconstructed initial text A.

Let us now have a look at the five statements made according to the local stemmata containing the variants of the compared witnesses. The number of instances of statement (i), agreement in the same variant, is stored in "EQ" (equal); for example, 1739 agrees with 025 in 2,381 variant passages. This number has to be brought into proportion with the number of passages where 1739 and 025 are both extant. This number is found under "PASS" (passages).[38] The respective percentage is given under "PERC1" (percentage 1).

The entries in this list are ordered by the percentages of agreement. It is important, however, to take the absolute figures into account too, because the validity of percentages is lower with more fragmented texts. If larger portions of text are lacking in a witnesses, it would be misleading to extrapolate from what has survived the quality of what actually is not extant. The line with 04, a heavily fragmented witness, shows that it shares only 1,926 passages with 025. Thus, the EQ percentage of 04, although not much lower than the one of 1739, is less relevant, because the sample is much smaller in the case of 04.

The number of instances where statements (ii) or (iii) about priority or posteriority of variants applied is given under "W1<W2" or "W1>W2" respectively. 1739, for example, supports a variant assessed to be prior to

---

37. For an extensive legend with additional information, see the excursus "Values Determining Coherence" in *Introductory Presentation*, 232–54.

38. The maximum is 3,046, the total of variant passages recorded in the ECM apparatus. 025 is a palimpsest with many illegible passages; hence it is available in 2,681 passages only.

the one of 025 in 126 cases. In 93 cases the relationship was contrary: 025 was seen to be the witness of the prior variant.

As mentioned above, this phenomenon is typical of heavily contaminated traditions. In a non-contaminated, linear tradition, potential descendants could contain variants prior to those in the ancestor to a minor degree only. Agreements with an older state of text could occur only coincidentally, if the copyist knew just the text of his exemplar. However, if a text is the result of mixture of readings from two sources x and y, it is possible that in some cases the reading from x is the prior one, while in other cases it is the reading of y.

Statement (iv), no direct relationship between the variants of x and y, applies 18 times with 025 and 1739, as is shown by the figure under "NOREL" (no relation).

Finally the number of cases where statement (v) applies is stored under "UNCL" (unclear). When local stemmata were constructed in the first phase, the decision was left open at 63 variant passages in the case of 025 and 1739.

Potential ancestors are witnesses whose variants are more often prior as compared to the variants of a potential descendant. The respective figures constitute the genealogical direction between witnesses. Accordingly, the values under "W1<W2" must be higher than those under "W1>W2." In our example table this is not the case with 468, where both values are equal. Thus, 468 is not a potential ancestor of 025. Yet a genealogical reassessment at only one passage would make one of the witnesses the potential ancestor of the other. Consequently, the difference between the values under "W1<W2" and "W1>W2" has to be taken into account in a discussion of the relationship between witnesses. If the difference is low, as with 025 and 04, relatively few reassessments can bring about an inversion of the genealogical direction. In the present case this would happen, if in six of 88 instances now booked under "W1<W2" the variant of 04 would be derived from the one in 025. Where the differences are higher, as with 1739 or 03 in particular, the genealogical direction is less likely to change in consequence of a revision of the underlying text-critical decisions.

Each potential ancestor is given a ranking number under "NR" according to the degree of agreement with W1. In the present example 468 has a 0 in this field, because there is no genealogical direction between W1 and W2 in this case. In addition, a dash under "D" points to this fact.[39]

---

39. The ranking number will also equal 0, if a compared witness is too heavily fragmented to allow for conclusions regarding the genealogical relationship. If the value under "W1<W2" is sufficient to formally qualify the fragmented witness as a potential ancestor, this will be indicated by ">" under "D". Cf. P74 in table 2.

11. What Is the Use of Lists of Potential Ancestors?

As explained above, it is one important function of the list of potential ancestors to display all possible candidates for the optimal substemma of a witness. Moreover, the list of potential ancestors for each witness serves an important purpose before optimal substemmata can be constructed.

Potential ancestors can be determined in an early phase of the editing process, as soon as local stemmata have been produced at unproblematic places.[40] Before this step only pre-genealogical coherence can be taken into account. Once local stemmata have been constructed it is possible to derive genealogical information from them. Pre-genealogical coherence is strong if the degree of agreement between potential ancestors and descendants is high. The characteristic feature of genealogical coherence is the additional evaluation of differences. For the potential ancestor the value under "W1<W2" is higher than the one under "W1>W2." The size of the difference between these values shows how reliable the resultant direction of textual flow is. A minor difference demands caution, because the direction of textual flow can easily change in the course of a subsequent revision of local stemmata[41] Through such revision it can be determined whether extrapolation from "safe" cases throws light on problematic ones. It may also occur that the initial assessment of a witness proves to be wrong, for example, because possible relationships between variants were overlooked.

Two questions lead to features characteristic of the list of potential ancestors for each individual witness: (i) Which witnesses are found under "W2" in higher positions (with low ranking numbers) and what is their textual character? (ii) In which way do the percentages under "PERC1" decrease?

Let us take the potential ancestors of 025 (table 1) as an example. At the top there is "A," the hypothetical witness of the reconstructed initial

---

40. For the iterative CBGM procedures, see Mink, "Problems of a Highly Contaminated Tradition," 46; and *Introductory Presentation*, 19–22, 575; and esp. the "Conclusion" of the present article below.

41. Very large differences, however, are unfavorable as well, because they point to small (pre-)genealogical coherence; see Mink, "Was verändert sich in der Textkritik durch die Beachtung genealogischer Kohärenz?" 51: "Weist einer der Zeugen sehr viel mehr prioritäre als posterioritäre Lesarten auf, so ist eine unmittelbare genealogische Kohärenz sehr unwahrscheinlich. Der Grund dafür ist, dass eine hohe Zahl prioritärer oder posterioritärer Lesarten die Zahl übereinstimmender Lesarten, die eine enge Verwandtschaft zweier Zeugen begründet, einschränkt." Accordingly, see Mink, "Problems of a Highly Contaminated Tradition," 56: "The *priority value* need not to be high. Very high values argue against close relationships, as they lower the number of agreements."

text. We can see what kind of relationship 025 has with *A*. There is no potential ancestor, in fact no preserved witness at all, that agrees more with 025 than *A*.[42] We find *A* in the first position (ranking number 1) with several other witnesses: [43]

01	90.80%	81	92.30%	1735	91.20%
02	92.08%	436	90.55%	1739	93.80%
03	96.86%	442	90.19%	1852	91.35%
04	92.90%	468	92.55%	2344	90.77%
044	88.71%	1175	91.29%	2492	91.92%
5	91.51%	1243	91.40%		

A comparison of percentages enables us to assess the degree of agreement between 025 and *A*. 92.44% is not a peak value as found with 03 and 1739, but it can be assigned to the range of 02, 04, 81 or 468. 468, by the way, shows a profile of potential ancestry quite similar to that of 025 (table 2).

Potential Ancestors of 468 (W1)
Data Source: Cath. Letters (excl. small fragments and extracts)

W2	NR	D	PERC1	EQ	PASS	W1<W2	W1>W2	UNCL	NOREL
A	1		92.548	2695	2912	201	0	9	7
025	0	-	91.096	2435	2673	92	92	48	6
1739	2		87.652	2662	3037	150	120	86	19
03	3		87.633	2636	3008	190	77	92	13
04	4		87.220	1829	2097	96	95	63	14
P74	0	>	83.333	280	336	24	23	7	2

Table 2. Potential Ancestors of 468

If we regard the "initial text" as a plausible hypothesis, then we must conclude, by way of corollary, that 025 and 468 contain a considerable share of oldest text. The average percentage of agreement of all witnesses with *A* amounts to 90.17%, while the maximum is reached by 03 with 96.86%, the minimum by 1838 with 84.89%.

The distance of witnesses featuring an above-average share of non-Byzantine text from the most closely related real witness often is relatively large. For example, 01 agrees with 03 at 87.18%, 02 with 1735 at 90.38%, 04 with 1739 at 90.92%. The degree of relationship between 025 and 468 (91.10%) will be regarded as comparably significant because of

---

42. The most closely related real witness is 424 with 91.56% agreement; see table 10, i. Next relatives can be found by choosing the option "Show Descendants" in the module *"Potential Ancestors and Descendants."* The closest relative is the witness with the highest value under "PERC1" either in the list of ancestors or that of descendants.

43. Percentage values refer to agreements.

their large share of non-Byzantine text. Consequently, we will regard variants attested by just these two witnesses as genealogically relevant if they cannot be derived from other sources, although the genealogical direction between 025 and 468 could not yet be established.[44] In many textual flow diagrams they occur side by side in the same attestation where 468 is found at the top of a wide range of Byzantine witnesses.[45]

For an assessment of the textual character of witnesses listed under "W2" (see tables 1 and 2), comparison with other witnesses whose textual features are known better will be useful. An appropriate tool for this is the *"Genealogical Queries"* module *"Comparison of Witnesses."* Let us compare 468 with 35 on this basis (table 3).

W1	DIR	W2	WRIT	NR	PERC1	EQ	PASS	W1<W2	W1>W2	UNCL	NOREL
468	-->	35	Jas	7	95.263	724	760	12	13	6	0
468	-->	35	1Pt	3	93.857	657	700	16	17	9	1
468	<--	35	2Pt	6	95.444	398	417	9	7	3	0
468	-->	35	1Jn	2	97.625	740	758	6	8	4	0
468	-->	35	2Jn	2	97.115	101	104	1	2	0	0
468	-->	35	3Jn	7	95.789	91	95	0	1	3	0
468	<--	35	Jd	2	94.581	192	203	5	4	2	0
468	-->	35	CL	3	95.588	2903	3037	49	57	27	1

Table 3. Comparison of 468 and 35

The columns here are generally analogous to those found in tables of potential ancestors. The figures are displayed for each of the Catholic Letters individually and finally summarized for the entire corpus (CL). The arrow under "DIR" points to the witness with more posterior variants, in accordance with the values found under "W1<W2" and "W1>W2." Agreement with 35 is very high while the difference between the values under "W1<W2" and "W1>W2" is very low.

Let us compare the table for 025 and 35 (table 4). The absolute agreement figures are necessarily smaller now, because 025 is a partly illegible palimpsest. For James, 2 Peter, and 1 John the number of agreements between 025 and 35 is considerably lower than between 468 and 35, which points to a lower share of Byzantine variants in 025. It is an interesting question how 025 can agree with A at 92.44% (see table 1) and with 35, a straightforward Byzantine witness, at the similarly high rate of 91.16%.

---

44. See the section "Undirected Genealogical Coherencies" in Mink, "Problems of a Highly Contaminated Tradition," 63–67.

45. Examples are found in most places where "Byz" is part of the attestation, e.g., Jas 4:4/1b. In the *"Coherence in Attestations"* module, the textual flow diagrams do not display coherencies without direction. Thus, 025 and 468 frequently remain unconnected despite of their close relationship.

W1	DIR	W2	WRIT	NR	PERC1	EQ	PASS	W1<W2	W1>W2	UNCL	NOREL
025	-->	35	Jas	27	89.621	639	713	24	44	5	1
025	<--	35	1Pt	3	93.848	656	699	18	17	7	1
025	<--	35	2Pt	14	86.988	361	415	19	11	19	5
025	-->	35	1Jn	8	89.892	498	554	20	21	14	1
025	-->	35	2Jn	3	95.146	98	103	1	4	0	0
025	-->	35	3Jn	1	97.895	93	95	0	1	1	0
025	<--	35	Jd	4	97.059	99	102	2	1	0	0
025	-->	35	CL	5	91.160	2444	2681	84	99	46	8

Table 4. Comparison of 025 and 35

The key to the solution lies in the high degree of agreement between 35 and *A*: 92.26%.[46] The reconstructed text *A* shares a considerable number of readings with both 025 and 35 and thus the distance to both is about the same.

The values for the remaining potential ancestors of 025, that is, 1739, 04, and 03, seem to speak for themselves, because they are traditionally assigned to the (proto-)Alexandrian range. It is remarkable, however, how different they are. 1739 and 04 agree at only 90.92%, 03 and 04 at 89.30%, and 03 and 1739 at 89.13%.

Estimating the historical position of a witness regarding the provenance of its variants is not difficult with short tables like this. One may wonder why so many witnesses have *A* as their most closely related potential ancestor. The reason is that the manuscript texts that would have high positions in their lists of potential ancestors are lost. To be sure, if this list is short and agreement values are decreasing rapidly, then it is highly probable that the contemporaneous genealogical environment of the respective witness is lost. It is true for 025 and many other witnesses that even high-ranking potential ancestors will not necessarily qualify as stemmatic ancestors, because all priority variants of a potential ancestor may be contained in other potential ancestors.

In the case of 04 the table of potential ancestors is even shorter (table 5), and again agreement values are decreasing rapidly. The table referring to 18 is markedly different (table 6). 35, differing from 18 in only 29 out of 3,039 passages, holds the top position. At a distance of 2.7 percentage points, a series of entries from the 96-95% range begins: 2423, 617, 424, 319, 468. All of them, including 35, are outstanding carriers of Byzantine variants. The subsequent witness, 93, does not so clearly belong to this group, because it features considerably lower degrees of agreement in 2 John,

---

46. See table 10, iv. A similarly high value is found with other Byzantine witnesses, e.g., the potential ancestors of 18 in table 6.

3 John and Jude (within a range of 85-88%).[47] There is a distance of nearly two percentage points from the 92% array. There we find quite different witnesses: 1448 at a significant difference from the Byzantine text in James and notably in 1 Peter,[48] 307 (Byzantine text) and finally A, the hypothetical reconstruction of the initial text. Below rank number 11 there are only witnesses not regarded as Byzantine textually.

Potential Ancestors of 04 (W1)
Data Source: Cath. Letters (excl. small fragments and extracts)

W2	NR	D	PERC1	EQ	PASS	W1<W2	W1>W2	UNCL	NOREL
A	1		92.900	1871	2014	132	0	9	2
1739	2		90.922	1913	2104	78	70	35	8
03	3		89.301	1878	2103	116	48	55	6

Table 5. Potential Ancestors of 04

Potential Ancestors of 18 (W1)
Data Source: Cath. Letters (excl. small fragments and extracts)

W2	NR	D	PERC1	EQ	PASS	W1<W2	W1>W2	UNCL	NOREL
35	1		99.046	3010	3039	16	10	3	0
2423	2		96.346	2927	3038	48	42	18	3
617	3		96.117	2921	3039	57	41	14	6
424	4		96.111	2916	3034	53	40	22	3
319	5		95.930	2852	2973	51	49	17	4
468	6		95.776	2902	3030	58	43	26	1
93	7		94.143	2861	3039	73	67	31	7
1448	0	-	92.313	2798	3031	91	91	43	8
307	8		92.267	2804	3039	91	90	46	8
A	9		92.075	2684	2915	217	0	6	8
025	10		90.950	2432	2674	104	84	46	8
2298	11		89.397	2715	3037	117	116	70	19
323	12		89.350	2710	3033	118	112	75	18
81	13		88.657	2673	3015	130	127	61	24
1739	14		87.496	2659	3039	164	118	79	19
03	15		87.143	2623	3010	207	78	87	15
04	16		86.886	1822	2097	106	95	62	12
02	0	-	85.496	2570	3006	163	163	85	25
P74	0	>	82.196	277	337	28	23	6	3

Table 6. Potential Ancestors of 18

Looking at this table one may come to the conclusion that 18 is essentially shaped by Byzantine components. As there are so many closer relatives, a percentage of 90% agreements is relatively low. It can reasonably be expected that variants from this part of the tradition, if attested by 18, will also be found in its close relatives. It is possible, however, that 18

---

47. See the *"Genealogical Queries"* module *"Comparison of Witnesses"* and compare 18 with 93, one of the potential ancestors (under W2 in table 6) to observe changing textual character in individual writings.
48. Cf. the values shown in the *"Comparison of Witnesses"* module.

shares some variants exclusively with less closely related witnesses and that these variants are connective because of their unusual character. This will be found out in the process of constructing the optimal substemma.[49] The combination of ancestors in the optimal substemma for 18 is 35-2423-319-468. This result shows that no potential ancestor with less than 95% agreement is required to derive the entire text of 18. The substemma of 04, however, includes all potential ancestors: A-1739-03.[50] The percentage of agreements of 03 and 04 (89.30%) is rather low, but 03 has to be included, because for 04 there is no more closely related ancestor containing the variants contributed by 03. Other ancestors and possible sources of contamination are lost. Consequently, contamination in 04 appears to be more extensive than it presumably was when that manuscript was produced. For the same reason it is necessary to incorporate a more distant potential ancestor into the optimal substemma. Obviously it is necessary to relate the percentages of agreement to the kind of intervals by which they decrease.[51] Comparison of as many tables of potential ancestors as possible will be instructive here.[52]

Other tables of potential ancestors suggest a mixture of non-Byzantine and Byzantine sources. The potential ancestry of 2298 may serve as an example (table 7).

Potential Ancestors of 2298 (W1)
Data Source: Cath. Letters (excl. small fragments and extracts)

W2	NR	D	PERC1	EQ	PASS	W1<W2	W1>W2	UNCL	NOREL
1739	1		95.269	2900	3044	81	36	19	8
323	2		93.055	2827	3038	83	77	34	17
A	3		92.292	2694	2919	207	0	8	10
04	4		90.152	1895	2102	87	73	33	14
35	5		89.750	2732	3044	113	111	68	20
468	6		89.423	2714	3035	122	107	76	16
307	7		89.258	2717	3044	122	118	66	21
2423	8		89.123	2712	3043	124	119	70	18
424	9		89.075	2707	3039	126	117	74	15
617	10		88.962	2708	3044	133	122	68	13
025	11		88.914	2382	2679	115	106	61	15
93	12		88.798	2703	3044	134	128	63	16
319	13		88.617	2639	2978	128	126	66	19
03	14		87.529	2639	3015	199	79	83	15

Table 7. Potential Ancestors of 2298

1739, a clearly non-Byzantine witness, has the top position with a considerably high degree of agreement. The percentages decrease quickly to

---

49. See below "14. Constructing Optimal Substemmata."
50. See *Introductory Presentation*, 565.
51. See Mink, "Problems of a Highly Contaminated Tradition," 32.
52. Some examples are explained in *Introductory Presentation*, 255–80.

the range of 89%. In the second place there is a witness consisting of a mixture of predominantly non-Byzantine and Byzantine elements,[53] followed by the initial text, A, and 04, another non-Byzantine witness. In the range of 89% we see a sequence of Byzantine witnesses. In such a situation it appears possible that the entire text of 2298 can be derived from the first four potential ancestors, but it is more likely that Byzantine witnesses are required also. In fact it turned out that no combination of ancestors without Byzantine witnesses would be sufficient.[54] 323, on the other hand, is not required, because the relevant variants are covered by 1739. However, for a more precise determination of the extent of mixture it has to be taken into account that all potential ancestors, on the whole or as arranged in pairs, have an intersection of identical text.[55] In the process of determining the smallest possible combination of ancestors needed to derive the entire text of a witness, it is necessary to find out what each potential ancestor can contribute. The crucial question here is which variants can be explained only by incorporating specific ancestors into the substemma.[56]

The more posterior variants accumulated in a witness, the more likely it is that it has a major number of potential ancestors. By definition, a potential ancestor is a witness containing more priority variants than another one with which it is compared. Many witnesses have extremely long lists of potential ancestors. 1838 (eleventh century) has 123 potential ancestors—all the other witnesses consistently cited in the ECM of the Catholic Letters (including A). This seems to suggest that this is true only for witnesses produced toward the end of the textual history, but this is not the case. It is more likely that such a witness marks the end of a strand of transmission, because a high proportion of variants not preserved in other witnesses has in fact not been transmitted anymore.

Unexpectedly, even 01 has a long list of potential ancestors. The relevant table has 44 entries. The extract presented in fig. 8 shows the first 15. It does not come as a surprise that the immediate genealogical environment of 01 is lacking. The first real witness among the potential ancestors is 03 with not much more than 37% agreement. This is a value below the average of 87.6% for all pairs of witnesses.[57] The 85% range is already reached by 81 with ranking number 3. This is quite unusual. Moreover, while the

---

53. See below on "Constructing Optimal Substemmata." There, an additional example for a mixture of non-Byzantine and Byzantine text, 323, will be discussed extensively.

54. For the procedure, see below "14. Constructing Optimal Substemmata."

55. *Introductory Presentation* (164–78) may help in understanding the basic idea.

56. For the construction of optimal substemmata, see the discussion of that topic below.

57. See n. 24.

Potential Ancestors of 01 (W1)
Data Source: Cath. Letters (excl. small fragments and extracts)

W2	NR	D	PERC1	EQ	PASS	W1<W2	W1>W2	UNCL	NOREL
A	1		90.793	2623	2889	248	0	10	8
03	2		87.175	2617	3002	236	73	63	13
81	3		85.485	2556	2990	198	152	64	20
02	4		85.262	2557	2999	193	162	67	20
1739	5		85.254	2567	3011	216	131	80	17
623	6		85.234	2563	3007	187	158	67	32
04	7		85.175	1781	2091	144	101	56	9
468	8		85.143	2556	3002	199	146	75	26
1845	9		84.998	2544	2993	184	160	72	33
5	10		84.988	2559	3011	190	167	67	28
307	11		84.955	2558	3011	199	161	70	23
453	12		84.902	2553	3007	194	167	70	23
2423	13		84.884	2555	3010	198	163	68	26
617	14		84.822	2554	3011	203	154	73	27
35	15		84.723	2551	3011	205	157	73	25

Table 8. Potential Ancestors of 01 (extract)

first seven positions are occupied by non-Byzantine witnesses, the positions from NR 8 (468) are for the most part taken by Byzantine witnesses.

The distance of nearly 13 percentage points from 03 is caused by a surprisingly large number of differences between these prominent fourth-century manuscripts. 01 and 03 are at variance in 385 out of 3,002 passages. 89 of the differences (about 3% of the total of variant passages) are due to particular variants in 01.[58] This means that the percentages of agreement with all other witnesses are pushed down by 3 percentage points owing to the particular variants in 01.

The potential ancestors provide a part of the data by which the position of a witness in the history of transmission can be determined. They can tell us which sources had an impact on the formation of its text. The other part of the picture would show which part the witness played in the subsequent textual history. The starting points for this inquiry would be the positions with low ranking numbers taken by the witness as a potential ancestor of other witnesses.

In addition to the consideration of potential ancestry, a short remark on potential descendants is necessary.The module *"Potential Ancestors and Descendants"* will show close relatives of a given witness among its descendants, if the relevant option has been selected. One cannot infer,

---

58. See *Introductory Presentation*, 280–95, esp. 294. For the sake of comparison: 03 has 36 particular variants, 02 has 31, 04 has 29 (only two-thirds of the text being preserved), 1739 has 3, 35 being a typical Byzantine witness has none. 1838 has 80 particular variants. The witnesses, which are cited consistently in the Catholic Letters, are the basis for these numbers. See n. 24.

however, that this witness will have a low ranking number in the table of potential ancestors of a closely related descendant, because there may be ancestors agreeing more with that descendant. The first four entries in the list of potential descendants of 025 provide examples for this (table 9).

Potential Descendants of 025 (W1)
Data Source: Cath. Letters (excl. small fragments and extracts)

W2	NR	D	PERC1	EQ	PASS	W1<W2	W1>W2	UNCL	NOREL
424	1		91.555	2450	2676	88	91	40	7
2423	2		91.306	2447	2680	87	103	37	6
319	3		91.250	2388	2617	82	100	39	8
35	4		91.160	2444	2681	84	99	46	8

Table 9. Potential Descendants of 025 (extract)

Compare the different rank numbers of 025 (table 10) among the potential ancestors of its potential descendants 424, 2423, 319, and 35 which all share about the same level of agreement with 025.

(i)

W2	NR	D	PERC1
617	1		96.975
468	2		96.141
A	3		92.424
025	4		91.555
04	5		87.452
03	6		87.417
1739	7		87.373
P74	0	>	83.680

(ii)

W2	NR	D	PERC1
617	1		97.274
424	2		97.039
35	3		96.289
468	4		95.751
93	5		94.581
A	6		92.226
025	7		91.306
323	8		89.207
03	9		87.235
1739	10		87.192
04	11		86.923
P74	0	>	82.196

(iii)

W2	NR	D	PERC1
617	1		96.544
2423	2		96.509
424	3		96.471
35	4		95.906
468	5		95.355
93	6		94.430
A	7		92.090
307	8		91.980
1448	9		91.454
025	10		91.250
323	11		88.399
81	12		88.261
03	13		87.267
1739	14		86.946
04	15		86.782
P74	0	>	83.591

(iv)

W2	NR	D	PERC1
617	1		95.995
424	2		95.988
468	3		95.588
A	4		92.263
025	5		91.160
323	0	-	89.638
1739	6		87.853
03	7		87.272
04	8		87.262
P74	0	>	82.493

Table 10. Different Positions of 025 among the Potential Ancestors of 424 (i), 2423 (ii), 319 (iii), and 35 (iv)

12. Textual Flow Diagrams— How Coherent Are Attestations?

If a variant emerged only once and all subsequent copyists followed only their exemplars, then all witnesses of the variant would necessarily cohere genealogically. The result would be perfect genealogical coherence connecting all the witnesses with a potential ancestor within the same attestation. One witness, however, will not have a potential ancestor there, but constitute the source of all coherencies in that attestation (except when the variant is the initial text[59]). Thus, the potential ancestors of that one witness must necessarily be outside the attestation. They will attest one or more other variants, one of which will be the source of the variant in question.

In 1 Pet 3:16/32-42 there is a variant η υμων την καλην εν χριστω αναστροφην. It competes with 17 other variants, most of which differ in word order, sometimes additionally opting for another adjective. We might ask whether this variant emerged more than once. The relevant textual flow diagram (fig. 5) is accessible by the *"Genealogical Queries"* module *"Coherence in Attestations."*

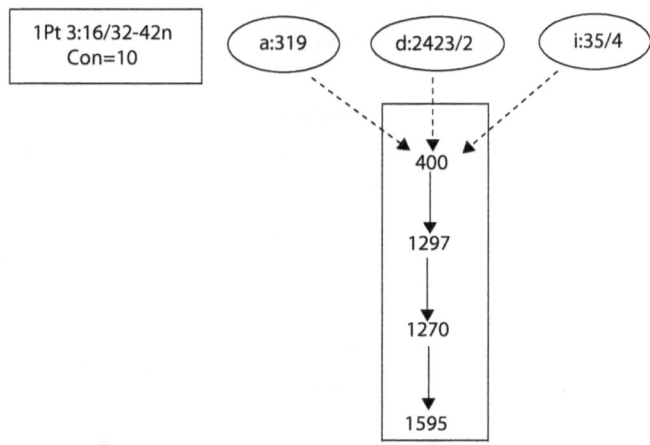

Figure 5. Textual Flow Diagram with Perfect Coherence

The textual flow diagram shows the attestation of variant *n* within the box.[60] It features perfect genealogical coherence.[61] Each witness is connected with its most closely related potential ancestor (rank number 1). If a potential ancestor within the same attestation has a rank number higher than 1, the number will be attached to the descendant with a slash.[62] 400

---

59. In this case, "A," the artificial witness of the initial text, is incorporated into the attestation as the hypothetical source of all coherencies.

60. The ECM apparatus lists 1270* for this variant. Generally, corrections are not taken into account in CBGM evaluations. Therefore no distinction is made in the present graph between 1270 and 1270*.

61. For perfect and imperfect coherence, see *Introductory Presentation*, 193–228. A full explanation of textual flow diagrams is given in ibid., 205–17.

62. See "1297/38" in fig. 7. On rank numbers, see the explanation of table 1 above. The rank numbers in textual flow diagrams are derived from the respective tables of potential ancestors. In textual flow diagrams, the rank number of a

has no potential ancestor within the attestation of *n*, but with other variants. The most closely related potential ancestor of 400 is 319 with variant *a*, the potential ancestor 2423 with rank number 2 reads *d*, 35 with rank number 4 reads *i*. When we consider which variant can actually be regarded as the source of *n*, *intrinsic* and *transcriptional probabilities* have to be taken into account. In this case the candidates indicated by potential ancestors of 400 have the following wording:

a) υμων την αγαθην εν χριστω αναστροφην
d) υμων την εν χριστω αγαθην αναστροφην
i) υμων τη αγαθη εν χρ στω αναστροφη

Variant *a* probably is the source of *n*, because it is most similar to *n* linguistically and because it is attested by the potential ancestor most closely related to 400.

The box in the top left-hand corner of the diagram shows the note "Con=10." It corresponds to the "Connectivity" option being set to "Average (1–10 ancestors)." With this setting, the potential ancestors of each witness of the variant in question are analyzed as long as their ranking number does not exceed 10. Technically this means that the application will look for potential ancestors of any witness within the same attestation up to rank number 10. If no such potential ancestor is found within the same attestation, then it will be looked for in the attestation of other variants of the passage. The option "Low (1–5 ancestors)" sets the limit to rank number 5; "Absolute" will include any potential ancestor regardless of its rank number. Finally, the user can set the limit to a value of his or her own choice.

If a variant emerged more than once coincidentally, then there will be no strong genealogical coherence comprising the entire attestation. The coherence will be imperfect. Nevertheless, it is possible that the attestation consists of several coherent groups. Each of these groups, however, has one witness for which no potential ancestor can be found within the same attestation and within the selected connectivity range. The example in fig. 6 shows small groups and single witnesses that are not genealogically linked to witnesses within the same attestation.

---

potential ancestor is attached to the descendant if both ancestor and descendant attest the same variant. If the ancestor attests another variant and thus is displayed outside the box, then the rank number is attached to the ancestor. Note that the rank numbers will match only if minor fragments are included or excluded in both modules. The relevant options are "Include/Exclude Minor Fragments" in "*Potential Ancestors and Descendants*" and "Catholic Letters incl./excl. fragments" in "*Coherence in Attestations.*"

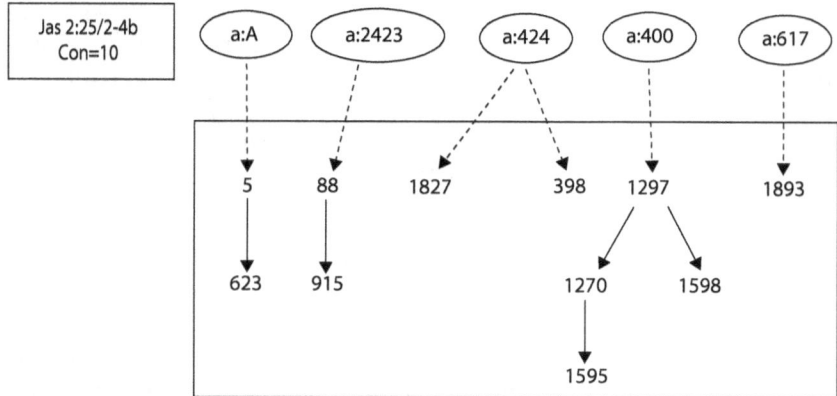

Figure 6. Textual Flow Diagram with Imperfect Coherence

In Jas 2:25/2-4 the variants in question are *a* ομοιως δε, *b* ομοιως, and *c* ουτως. Variant *b* has support from three coherent groups headed by 5, 88, and 1297 within the attestation of *b* (see the textual flow diagram, fig. 6). These and three single witnesses (1827, 398, and 1893) have immediate potential ancestors reading *a*. They are displayed outside the box accordingly. Connectivity was set to "Average," which may appear too high given the nature of the variant. However, setting it to "Low" would not make a difference here, because all potential ancestors involved have rank number 1. If connectivity is set to "Absolute," continuous coherence will be enforced, regardless of the distance between witnesses and their potential ancestors. The result is the diagram in fig. 7 to the left.

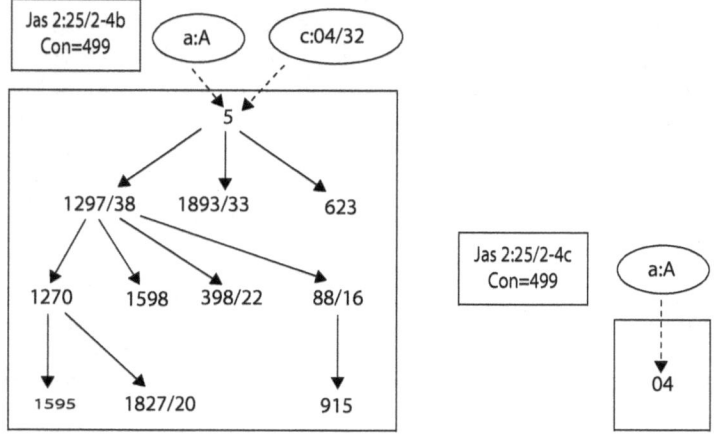

Figure 7. Textual Flow Diagram with Enforced Continuous Coherence (left) and Textual Flow Diagram Featuring One Source Exclusively (right)

Now high rank numbers are displayed with several witnesses. They refer to the potential ancestors from which they are derived. 1297 is now assigned to 5, which has rank number 38 in the table of the potential ancestors of 1297. The distance of 1297, 1893, 398, 83, and 1827 from their respective potential ancestors within the same attestation is far too high to indicate significant relationships. To be sure, potential ancestors with rank numbers like 16 or 20 may be taken into account, if the connectivity of a variant is high owing to its character or if percentages of agreement decrease slowly in the relevant tables. In this case, agreement percentages may be high enough to allow for genealogical relationship.

With connectivity set to "Absolute," only those witnesses which have no potential ancestor at all within the same attestation will be assigned to potential ancestors above the box. Here only 5 is in such a position. Its most closely related potential ancestor A reads variant a. The same is true for all other potential ancestors of 5 apart from 04, attesting c ουτως. Rank number 32, however, is far too high for a potential ancestor to be taken into consideration in spite of so many more closely related candidates reading a.

The diagram to the right (fig. 7) shows that 04, the only witness of variant c, has no potential ancestor in the attestation of b. They all (A, 1739, 03) are witnesses of a. Thus, it is likely that 04 omits δε independently from variant b. A, the hypothetical witness of the initial text, is shown outside the box, because it is the most closely related potential ancestor of 04.

If we would regard variant b as the initial text here, perhaps because it is *lectio brevior*, A would be incorporated into the b attestation. 04 would still be shown as depending from A, if we would set "Initial Reading" to b in "Coherence in Attestations." For variant b the resultant diagram would look like fig. 8 (with average connectivity).

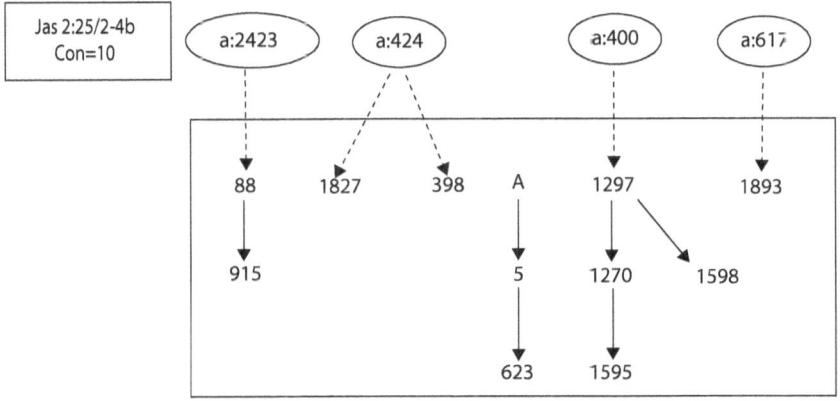

Figure 8. Textual Flow Diagram (cf. fig. 6)
When the Variant Is Assumed to Be the Initial Text

5 would stay connected with A, because A is its most closely related potential ancestor. For the rest, the diagram would look the same as before (fig. 6). 5 and 623 would now be the only real witnesses of the initial text; the remaining witnesses would just coincidentally have the same wording. To be sure, such a constellation of witnesses would not have much of a chance to be accepted as representing the initial text against all other witnesses, the less so with such a variant. 5 and 623 are often seen in the same attestation with A, but always in combination with many other witnesses.

In the case of Jas 2:25/2-4b, multiple emergence is likely, but the source would be one reading, a. For the global genealogical view, this would have no consequences. Multiple emergence from more source variants brings about a different situation. Jas 1:12/31 may serve as an example. According to the initial text a, there is no explicit subject for the predicate επεγγειλατο. As a consequence, different subjects were added: b κυριος, c ο κυριος, d ο θεος, e ο αψευδης θεος.[63]

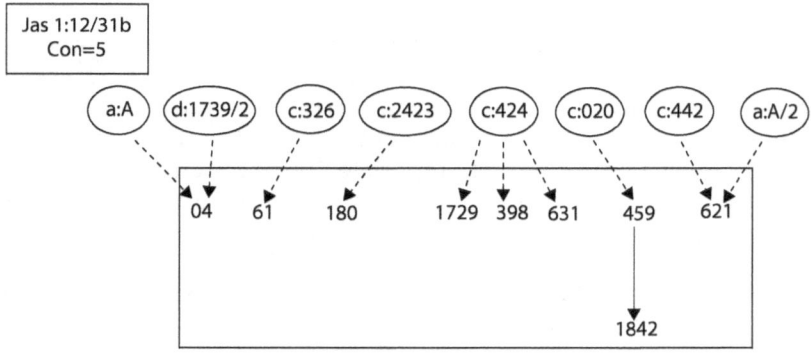

Figure 9. Textual Flow Diagram Showing Multiple Origins

The diagram for variant b (fig. 9) indicates multiple emergence for nearly all the witnesses, for the most part from variant c. In this case the reason obviously is haplography of one letter, επεγγειλατο ο κυριος becomes επεγγειλατο κυριος. Therefore connectivity was set to "Low." Probably 621, like most other witnesses of b, followed its most closely related ancestor, in this case 442, when its scribe committed the error. 04, however, does not have a potential ancestor with c. I think that variant a (with A and 03 as potential ancestors) is the more likely source, but variant d is a possible option as well. For a test we can set connectivity to "Absolute" to see the actual distance between the witnesses (fig. 10).

---

63. This passage is treated extensively in *Introductory Presentation*, 381–428.

CONTAMINATION, COHERENCE, AND COINCIDENCE 179

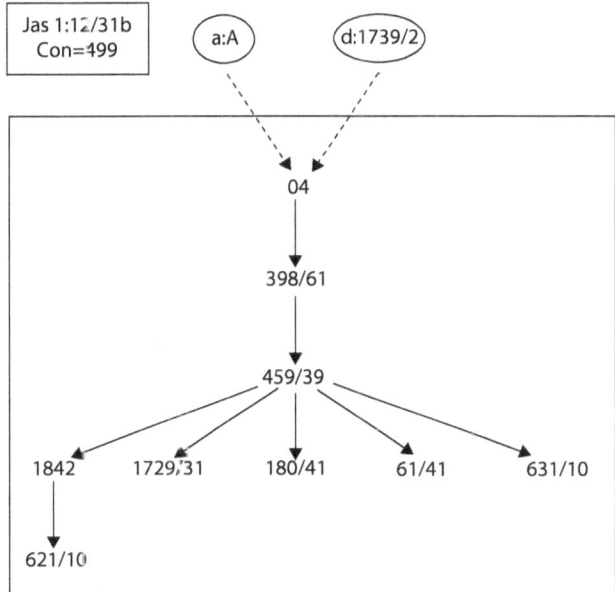

Figure 10. The Same Attestation as in Figure 9, but with Enforced Continuous Coherence

As a consequence, extremely high rank numbers occur, such as 61 for 04 as a potential ancestor of 398. Their percentage of agreement is extraordinarily low, 84.84%.

If several options for a variant's derivation are shown outside the box, this may indicate conflation. James 2:16/2-4e may serve as an example. Figure 11 shows the local stemma of variants side by side with the textual flow diagram for e. 2298 obviously conflates the readings of its most closely related potential ancestors.

Perfect genealogical coherence is a feature of many large attestations, particularly if the witnesses are predominantly Byzantine. Finally, I want to present Jas 2:13/20b (ελεον) as one of many astonishing examples for this. The only competing variant is a (ελεος). The preceding predicate is transmitted with variants as well (cf. Jas 2:13/18). Regardless of whether one prefers κατακαυχαται (majority text) or κατακαυχασθω, a following nominative is mandatory.[64] Therefore the Byzantine variant ελεον must be read as

---

64. 04C2 and 1739T have the grammatically impossible combination κατακαυχασθε ελεον. 323, 945, and 1241, whose closest potential ancestor is 1739, read κατακαυχασθω. Therefore it is very likely that the reading κατακαυχατθε, in 1739 at least, is due to a simple copying error.

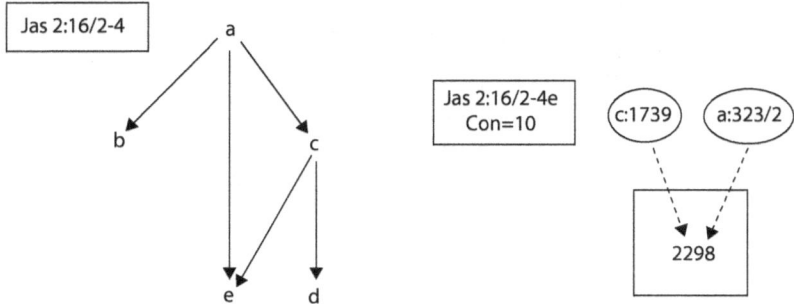

Figure 11. Conflated Reading *e* in the Local Stemma (left) and the Respective Textual Flow Diagram (right)

nominative. Both ο ελεος and το ελεος are well documented, but there is no second example for το ελεον in ancient and medieval Greek. Even if there were such references, it would appear unlikely that either the author or a scribe would (consciously or not) have used ελεον here, because shortly before ελεος is used (2:13/16).[65] Consequently, ελεον must be a well-transmitted error.

The textual flow diagram for Jas 2:13/20b (see figs. 21a-c [pp. 207–9]) displays perfect coherence, and what is more, with few exceptions the witnesses are assigned to their first potential ancestor within the same attestation. The picture looks even more self-contained, if we declare variant *b* to be the initial text (figs. 22a-b [pp. 210–11], option "Initial Reading": *b*). This variant (ελεον) obviously suggested correction to variant *a* (ελεος), as shown by the textual flow diagram for variant *a* (fig. 23 [p. 212]).

The tendency appears even clearer, if we declare *b* to be the initial text (see fig. 24 [p. 212]). Still, variant *b* is a striking example of an extremely difficult reading in the mainstream tradition, faithfully copied by Byzantine scribes through centuries. How could it come about? In the case of 018, 312, and 424 the reason may be adaptation to ελεον in 2:13/16.[66] The textual flow diagram for 2:13/20b (fig. 21c) shows 25 witnesses directly or indirectly related to 424, with 018 and 312 among them. These three witnesses, however, cannot be the ancestors of the entire attestation of *b*, because 424 and the strand deriving from it are subordinate to other manuscripts and because there are several other lines of transmission within

---

65. In 2:13/16, however, variant *b* ελεον is accusative and morphologically as correct as *a* ελεος. There are five witnesses for ελεον here. Only three of them combine it with ελεον in 2:13/20 (018, 312, and 424T).

66. See the variants there and the previous note.

the attestation of *b*. It may be worth considering that the reading emerged from the participle ελεων, as the result of an early ο/ω interchange. The contrasting juxtaposition of τω μη ποιησαντι ελεος and ελεων would make sense rhetorically. It remains to be discussed whether this would be stylistically plausible for the Letter of James and ελεων might be the initial text.

13. A Practical Example: Is ΠΑΣΑΝ ΨΥΧΗΝ the Initial Text in Jude 15/14-16?

Individual witnesses or groups of them within the same attestation sometimes are very different textually. In such cases coherence is weak, and one may ask whether agreement in these passages might be coincidental. The question refers to connectivity. A variant attested just by closely related witnesses can be regarded as connective, even if the variant as such allows one to suppose multiple coincidental emergence. If coherence is weak, then connectivity depends on the character of the variant. In such a case we would have to ponder whether the character of the variant suggests connectivity in spite of weak coherence.

The following example refers to cases where coherence appears to be strong only if the variant in question is regarded as initial text.

The context of the variants to be discussed now is ηλθεν . . . ποιησαι κρισιν κατα παντων και ελεγξαι <u>πασαν ψυχην</u> περι παντων των εργων ασεβειας αυτων ων ησεβησαν. These are the variants:

a πασαν ψυχην   P72. 01. 1852
b παντας τους ασεβεις   02. 03. 04. 044. 5. 33. 61. 81. 93. 94. 307. 321. 326. 330. 378. 431. 436. 453. 468. 623. 629. 630. 642. 665. 808. 918. 1067. 1127. 1243. 1292. 1409. 1448. 1501. 1505. 1611. 1678. 1735. 1751. 1837. 1838. 1845. 1846. 2138. 2147. 2186. 2200. 2344. 2374. 2412. 2544. 2652. 2718. 2774. 2805. 2818. L921. L938. L1141
c παντας τους ασεβεις αυτων   018. 020. 049. 1. 18. 35. 43. 88. 104. 180. 181. 218. 252. 254. 319. 398. 400. 424*. 429. 459. 467. 522. 607. 617. 876. 915. 945. 996. 1175. 1270. 1297. 1490. 1523. 1524. 1595. 1609. 1661. 1729. 1799. 1827. 1831. 1832. 1836. 1842. 1844. 1874. 1875. 1890. 2243. 2423. 2492. 2541
d παντας ασεβεις   6. 323. 424C. 1241. 1739. 1881. 2298
e τους ασεβεις   442. 621. L596.

The author introduces the passage as a citation from *Enoch*. In fact, it refers to *1 Enoch* 1:9, but it is by no means a precise quotation from any known version of the book.[67] Nobody can say whether there have been

---

67. See the synopsis of relevant versions with a discussion in Richard J.

more versions. At any rate, the Letter of Jude is the oldest reference to this passage from *Enoch*.

The wording of the Greek *Enoch* version is ερχεται . . . ποιησαι κρισιν κατα παντων και απολεσει παντας τους ασεβεις και ελεγξει <u>πασαν σαρκα</u> περι παντων εργων της ασεβειας αυτων ων ησεβησαν. . . .

To be sure, the *Enoch* versions that have come down to us differ considerably in detail, but, apart from the Aramaic version,[68] they feature a common sequence of actions: judgment, destruction of the impious, conviction of all flesh. In Jude, however, there are only two actions: judgment and conviction. The sequence of three is certainly prior to the one of two actions, because the sequence destruction—conviction is more than curious.[69] Did Jude omit the second action (destruction of the impious) and transfer its object (the impious) to the third action in the original sequence (conviction of all/all their/the impious according to variants *b*, *c*, *d* and *e*), thus replacing *Enoch*'s original object (all flesh)? Or did Jude completely omit "destruction of the impious" and replace "conviction of all flesh" with "conviction of every soul" (i.e., every individual)?[70]

The accumulation of words with the same root (ασεβεις, ασεβειας, ησεβησαν) in *1 Enoch* may have caused variation, in the authorial text of

---

Bauckham, *Jude, 2 Peter* (WBC 50; Waco: Word Books, 1983), 94–96; Henning Paulsen, *Der Zweite Petrusbrief und der Judasbrief* (KEK 12.2; Göttingen: Vandenhoek & Ruprecht, 1992), 75–76; Anton Vögtle, *Der Judasbrief – Der Zweite Petrusbrief* (EKK 22; Solothurn/Düsseldorf: Benziger; Neukirchen-Vluyn: Neukirchener Verlag, 1994), 71–77; Wachtel, *Der byzantinische Text der katholischen Briefe*, 358–59; Tommy Wasserman, *The Epistle of Jude: Its Text and Transmission* (ConBNT 43; Stockholm: Almqvist & Wiksell, 2006), esp. relevant in this context, 301–4.

68. The Aramaic version is too fragmentary for a reconstruction of the passage. There is just enough evidence to identify the equivalent of "flesh." Still, Carroll D. Osburn and Richard Bauckham are considering the possibility that the author of the Letter of Jude may have translated this citation directly from the Aramaic (Osburn, "The Christological Use of I Enoch I.9 in Jude 14, 15," *NTS* 23 [1977]: 334–41; and Bauckham, *Jude, 2 Peter*, 96). Bauckham, however, suggests a more differentiating view ("C" = Greek version): "The simplest explanation is that Jude *knew* the Greek version, but made his own translation from the Aramaic. Other possibilities are that the text in C is a corruption of the Greek version which Jude quotes, or that the translator of the Greek version was a Christian who knew Jude's letter (Zahn, *Introduction*, 287)." Vögtle (*Judasbrief*, 72–76) argues against an Aramaic source of the citation.

69. See Bauckham, *Jude, 2 Peter*, 94, 96: "'destroy,' (which comes rather oddly before 'convict' in *1 Enoch*)."

70. This reflects Vögtle's view: "Die Vorlage(n) des Jud bot(en) sicher 'alles Fleisch' als eine Bezeichnung des Gerichtsobjekts. Weil dieser Ausdruck aber sehr betont auf alle Menschen hinweist, ersetzte ihn Jud durch den Ausdruck 'jede Seele' (= jedermann), der individualisierenden Sinn hat" (*Judasbrief*, 78–79).

Jude as well as in the transmission. Thus, Jude 15/20-28, παντων των εργων ασεβειας αυτων, has ten more variants. In v. 15/14-16 all variants but *a* include ασεβεις. The word is more constrictive or specific than ψυχην[71] or may simply pick up the preceding phrase in Enoch (απολεσει παντας τους ασεβεις). Is πασαν ψυχην the initial text or does the expression derive from παντας (τους) ασεβεις (αυτων)? The latter case would apply if πασαν ψυχην was introduced to match *Enoch*'s text more adequately or to avoid too many words from the same root in one short passage.

The attestation of *a* has to compete with important witnesses supporting other variants. We can use the *"Potential Ancestors and Descendants"* module to find out how much the witnesses of *a* contribute to the attestation of the initial text in the Catholic Letters.

All three witnesses supporting variant *a* have A, the reconstructed initial text, as their most closely related potential ancestor. The amount of agreement, however, is very low with P72: 87.61%. This is just the average agreement value for all pairs of witnesses. The agreement of P72 with the most closely related real manuscript, 03, is even lower: 84.84%. 01 agrees with A at 90.80%. The agreement of 01 with its next closely related potential ancestor is considerably lower: 03 with 87.18%. The third witness of variant *a*, 1852, agrees with A at 91.35%. 04 is the potential ancestor with rank number 2 agreeing at 89.02%.

Let us compare the values of agreement with A reached by the top witnesses of other variants. Except for 617, they all have A as their most closely related potential ancestor:

b	03	96.86%
c	617	92.54% (*A* has rank number 2)
d	1739	93.80%
e	442	90.19%

Now the values of agreement with the most closely related potential ancestors among real witnesses:

b	03	no potential ancestor except *A*
c	617	95.62% (468)
d	1739	89.13% (03)
e	442	89.97% (323)

No witness of variant *a* has a high percentage of agreement with *A*. It is not unusual to find a considerable gap separating the most closely related real potential ancestor from *A*, where *A* has rank number 1. The

---

71. See Wachtel, *Der byzantinische Text der Katholischen Briefe*, 359.

gap is caused by loss of most of the close relatives of the witnesses in question. P72 and 01 are characterized by high shares of particular variants (P72 5.3%, 01 3%) which diminish agreement with A. The combination of P72, 01, and 1852 occurs nowhere else in the Catholic Letters within small attestations of the initial text, unless 03 joins them. In conclusion, the attestation of Jude 15/14-16a is not outstanding.[72]

A very simple test is applicable to such cases. Let us first view the textual flow diagram for variant a (fig. 12), supposing that it represents the initial text. Accordingly, the hypothetical witness A appears in the box containing the witnesses of a.

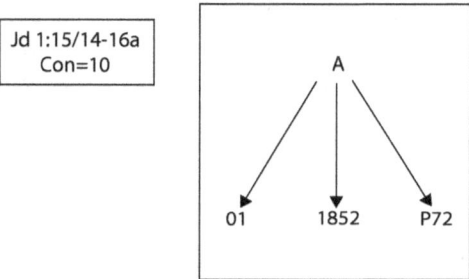

Figure. 12. Textual Flow Diagram for Jude 15/14-16a

In an optimal textual flow diagram, all real witnesses are related to their most closely related potential ancestors. Here A has this position for all three real witnesses of a. Figure 12 is not based on the hypothesis that 01, 1852, and P72 were copied immediately from A. It is very likely that in the past there existed many links that are now missing. However, all extant witnesses of variant a show a higher degree of agreement with A than with each other, hence this diagram. If we declare another variant to represent the initial text, then A will be incorporated into the relevant attestation and variant a would, if possible linguistically, be derived from that other variant. At least one witness of a would have to be related to A outside the attestation of a, because all the witnesses of a have A as their most closely related potential ancestor.

On the supposition that a is not initial text, the best candidates as a source of a are b (παντας τους ασεβεις) and d (παντας ασεβεις), because they do contain a form of πας but no αυτων. Supposing that b was initial text, the textual flow diagram for variant b would look as shown in fig. 25 (p. 213). Genealogical coherence is perfect. All witnesses of b have close potential ancestors within the same attestation with one exception: the

---

72. Wachtel (*Der byzantinische Text der katholischen Briefe*, 359) calls it relatively weak.

potential ancestors of 2774, with ranking numbers up to 10, support variant c (παντας τους ασεβεις αυτων). Yet, when connectivity is set to 11, 2774 is included in the perfect coherence and 468 is its potential ancestor with a fairly high agreement at 92 97%.[73]

If variant d is regarded as initial text, in the textual flow diagram all witnesses except witness 6[74] are derived from their most closely related ancestor, 1739, which in turn has "A," the witness of the initial text, as most closely related ancestor (see fig. 13, left diagram).

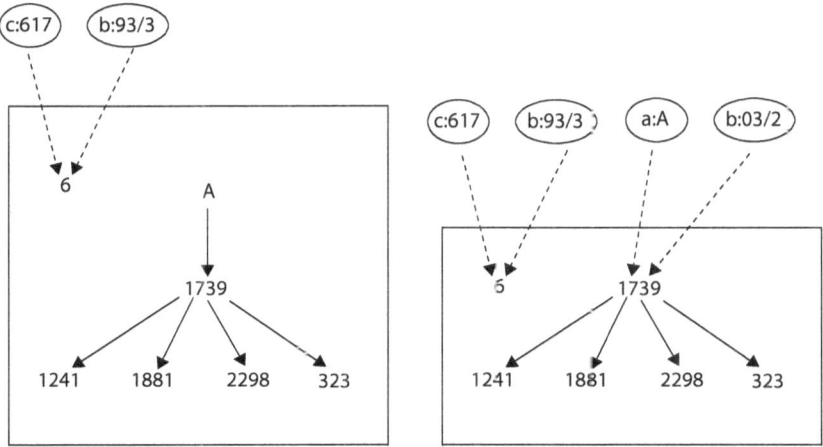

Figure 13. Textual Flow Diagrams of Jude 15/14-16d
When d (left diagram) or a (right diagram) Is Regarded as Initial Text

Provided that variant b is initial text, the textual flow diagram for a looks as presented in fig. 14.

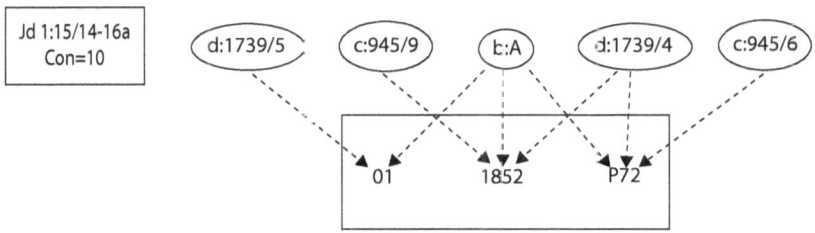

Figure 14. Textual Flow Diagram for Jude 15/14-16a, Not Being Initial Text

---

73. There is no potential ancestor of 2774 agreeing at more than 94.20% (1609).

74. Witness 6 can be derived from "A" when connectivity is set to 11 (instead of 10). Nearly all more closely related potential ancestors read variant c. 93 (rank number 3) reads b. In this case, b or c may be the preferable sources of 6.

With connectivity set to "Average" the application will retrieve the next potential ancestors of each witness up to rank number 10. On that condition there is no appropriate genealogical coherence at all within the attestation of *a*, if *b* is regarded as initial text. All relevant potential ancestors, as displayed above the box with their rank numbers, support other variants. For all witnesses of *a* the reconstructed initial text *A*, now identified as variant *b*, remains the most closely related potential ancestor and first choice for genealogical deduction.

Assuming that variant *d* is initial text, the textual flow diagram for *a* is rather similar (fig. 15). Again, genealogical coherence within the attestation of *a* is lacking completely when connectivity is set to 10.

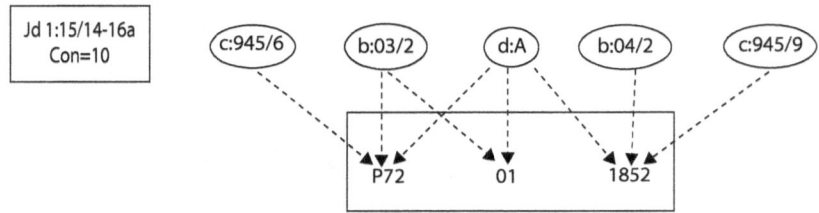

Figure 15. Textual Flow Diagram for Jude 15/14-16*a* While *d* Is Initial Text

If we want to find out whether a slightly higher connectivity rate would yield more genealogical relationships within the attestation of *a*, we can set connectivity to "Absolute" allowing for an extremely low rate of agreement, if necessary. With this option, the result is the diagram in fig. 16.

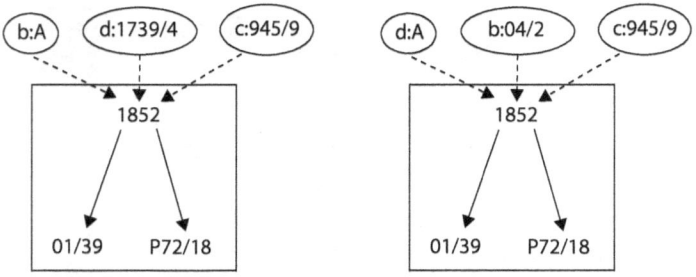

Figure 16. Textual Flow Diagrams for Jude 15/14-16*a* with Enforced Continuous Coherence (on the left: variant *b* initial text; on the right: variant *d* initial text)

No matter whether variant *b* or *d* is chosen as initial text, 1852 is still deducible from *A* as initial text in both diagrams. 01 and P72 derive from 1852, just because 1852 is listed as a potential ancestor for both, with rank number 18 for P72, with 39 (!) for 01. These positions relate to extremely low agreement values.[75] P72 agrees with 1852 at 80.71% (!) of the variant passages where they are both extant, 01 at 83.80%. One has to take into account the high number of particular variants, especially in P72, but for both witnesses there are several potential ancestors with higher agreement rates.[76]

Considering all relevant facts, acceptable genealogical coherence within the attestation of *a* will emerge only if variant *a* is regarded as initial text. Otherwise we would have to conclude that it arose more than once.[77] This assumption, however, does not appear plausible, because in that case we would hypothesize (i) that variant *b* would have been changed to *a* independently in three strands of transmission, or at least in the three preserved witnesses; (ii) that coincidentally the same wording πασαν ψυχην resulted with recourse to *Enoch*'s πασαν σαρκα—too many

---

75. The following values can be found via *"Potential Ancestors and Descendants"* or *"Coherence in Attestations."* For the latter option, have the textual flow diagram displayed and click 'Show Table." For the interpretation of the table, see the *"Guide,"* which is accessible from the start page of each CBGM module

76. For 01, see table 8 above. The most closely related potential ancestors of P72 are *A* (agreeing at 87.61%) and 03 (agreeing at 84.84%).

77. If variant *a* was not the initial text, it would be hypothesized to have emerged three times, because the witnesses are not genealogically closely related. Their agreement would be considered coincidental. With regard to this point, Timo Flink ("Reconsidering the Text of Jude 5, 13, 15 and 18," *Filologia Neotestamentaria* 20 [2007]: 95–125, here 116): "The problem with such an argument is that we have too few early witnesses to know for certain, which witnesses are related and which are not. It is possible that P72, ℵ and 1852 are indirectly related via now lost witnesses." However, the question is not whether these witnesses are at all related, because all witnesses are related somehow. We must ask whether their relationship is close enough to ascribe their agreement to genealogical ties rather than to coincidence. It is nothing unusual that links between preserved witnesses are missing. The earlier the states of text, the larger the gaps between them. For this reason it is most important to evaluate percentages of agreement taking into account the entire genealogical environment of a witness as shown by the list of potential ancestors (see the examples above in "11. What Is the Use of Lists of Potential Ancestors?" and *Introductory Presentation*, 280–96). Principally, the frequency of agreements is the decisive indicator of close genealogical relationship. The kinds of agreements may sometimes modify the picture, but in general there is no other evidence. The rank numbers in fig. 16 and the respective percentages are unambiguous.

assumptions.[78] It is a very simple hypothesis, however, that πασαν σαρκα in a supposed Greek exemplar was changed to πασαν ψυχην in the Letter of Jude.

In sum, there is good reason to accept variant *a* (πασαν ψυχην) as initial text.[79] The three witnesses are so different that *A* is required to achieve acceptable coherence. This leads to a new view of the traditional external

---

78. If influence from Rom 2:9 is taken into account (see Wasserman, *Epistle of Jude*, 304; or Flink, "Reconsidering the Text of Jude 5,13, 15 and 18," 117), then it should be regarded as easily possible that the passage influenced the wording three times independently (because of the poor coherence of the witnesses).

79. This is true, although the witnesses show several differences from *A* within the citation from *Enoch*. The citation is transmitted with a considerable degree of contamination, as shown by the high number of variation units in this passage. Among these Jude 14/28-32 and Jude 15/20-28 are particularly rich in variants (10 and 11). Contamination again is indicated by very different combinations of witnesses. P72, 01, 1852, and other prominent witnesses contribute to this phenomenon (e.g., 1739, 04, 81, 307, 468; it is interesting to follow their readings of the *Enoch* citation!).

In Jude 14/28-32 (*a* αγιαις μυριασιν αυτου) P72 alone reads αγιων αγγελων μυριασιν (*d*). 01 has another singular, μυριασιν αγιων αγγελων (*e*). Both take part in a wider strand of transmission (variants *c-h*) adding αγγελων—which seems an obvious choice. The coherence values suggest multiple emergence. Jude 15/20-28 (*a* παντων των εργων ασεβειας αυτων) is not extant in P72, because it omits 15/18-34, due probably to homoioarcton. 01 omits ασεβειας αυτων together with several other witnesses (*k*), due probably to homoioteleuton. 1852 derives *h*, a singular reading, from the initial text, omitting των due to haplography. In Jude 15/43 P72 stays with the initial text, while 01 and 1852 add a clarifying λογων—a variant that obviously emerged many times.

All these variants show clear marks of posteriority and likely emerged several times. They are of a character clearly different from the more dramatic shift from παντας τους ασεβεις to πασαν ψυχην, which can hardly have been introduced more than once.

πασαν ψυχην is the text on which the commentaries of Paulsen (*Zweiter Petrusbrief und Judasbrief*, without detailed text-critical discussion) and Vögtle (*Judasbrief*, mainly discussing internal criteria, 78–79) are based. Wasserman (*Epistle of Jude*, 301–4) prefers *b* (παντας τους ασεβεις) and qualifies this decision by {e>i}. In Wasserman's quite useful rating system, this means that "[e]xternal evidence favours the adopted variant readings, whereas internal evidence is ambiguous" (pp. 236–37). Flink is of the same opinion ("Reconsidering the Text of Jude 5, 13, 15 and 18," 118). Stylistic arguments are brought forward by Wasserman (p. 303) and Flink (p. 117–18), but they rightly are not considered decisive. We are dealing with a *citation*, after all, and it is a citation by an author of whom only one short writing has been preserved. Moreover, opinions will largely diverge as to what may be the definition of a "stylistically polished formula" (Flink, 117–18; cf. Wasserman, 303 n. 293).

criterion according to which a wide range of witnesses of diverse provenance constitutes a valuable argument in favor of the variant they share. Applying the concept of text-types to state such diversity will usually not stand the test of a coherence query, because, as in the case of variant *b* in the passage discussed here, a network of close relationships between individual witnesses will connect even very distant relatives representing different traditional text-types (see figs. 25 and 26 [pp. 213–14]). One should rather talk about a wide range of witnesses, if *A*, the hypothetical witness of the initial text, is required to establish coherence within an attestation. This would presuppose, however, that *A* has a high rank among the potential ancestors of the witnesses in question. Thus, we have one more reason to treat such witnesses with special attention. On the other hand, a wide range of witnesses may be the result of coincidental agreement.

If variant *a* is hypothesized to be the initial text, the textual flow diagrams for the other variants in Jude 15/14-16 show that variant *b* probably derives from *a*. The attestation of variant *c* is perfectly coherent. The diagram shows 617 as source witness within the attestation proposing *a*, *b*, and *d* as possible source variants. The most closely related potential ancestor of 617 is 468 with variant *b*, which suggests itself as source linguistically as well. In the diagram for variant *d* 1739 is shown as ancestor of all other witnesses within the attestation, except for witness 6.[80] For 1739 *d* variants *a* and *b* are suggested as sources. Yet only variant *b* is similar, and the connection can be established via 03, one potential ancestor of 1739 (rank number 2). Variant *d* in witness 6 can derive from *b* or *c*, while *e* can have arisen from variants *b-d*. Linguistically *b* appears to be the best option.

14. Constructing Optimal Substemmata

The construction of optimal substemmata is an advanced CBGM procedure. It is rather complex because it requires the frequent interaction of computerized procedures with philological assessments of intermediary results. The basics are explained in the *Introductory Presentation* of the CBGM, using witness 35 as an example.[81] Examples are essential for comprehending the method, not least because each witness has its own

---

80. Witness 6 is not included in the perfect chain of coherence (see fig. 13 [right diagram]) unless connectivity is set to 14. Yet the percentage of agreement with the most closely related ancestor within the attestation (323, 90.50%) is poor, regarding the ancestors with higher rank numbers. Most of them are agreeing in the 93-94% range and read variant *c* (see n. 73).

81. *Introductory Presentation*, 475–574.

peculiar features. For this present study the mixed text of 323 (preserved in a twelfth-century manuscript) provides a suitable sample.

Potential Ancestors of 323 (W1)
Data Source: Cath. Letters (excl. small fragments and extracts)

W2	NR	D	PERC1	EQ	PASS	W1<W2	W1>W2	UNCL	NOREL
1739	1		95.461	2902	3040	70	33	26	9
A	2		92.284	2691	2916	206	0	13	6
35	0	-	89.638	2725	3040	111	111	76	17
04	3		89.323	1874	2098	89	76	46	13
93	4		89.276	2714	3040	121	119	70	16
617	4		89.276	2714	3040	124	116	73	13
307	6		89.145	2710	3040	123	120	68	19
468	6		89.145	2702	3031	123	113	77	16
424	8		89.028	2702	3035	121	116	80	16
025	9		88.262	2361	2675	121	115	62	16
03	10		87.811	2644	3011	195	75	88	9

Table 11. Potential Ancestors of 323

Let us begin with the potential ancestors of 323 (table 11). Obviously there is a very close relationship with 1739, a non-Byzantine witness. This brings about a high share of agreement with the reconstructed initial text A. This share is on a level characteristic of the important representatives of the Byzantine text. In the list of potential ancestors, 1739 is separated from the next real witness, 35, by six percentage points. Yet, between 323 and 35 there is no genealogical direction (cf. the "-" under D and the equal numbers of posterior and prior variants under W1<W2 and W1>W2). Therefore 35 is not the next potential ancestor, but 04 (rank number 3).[82] In the range of 89% agreement we see several core witnesses of the Byzantine text which are closely related to one another.[83] This may suggest a mixture of Byzantine and non-Byzantine variants. Otherwise we would have to assume that the text of 323 could be explained as deriving from 1739, A, 04, and perhaps 03, although the distance from the latter is relatively large. The search for the optimal substemma will show which potential ancestors are actually needed and to what extent mixture affected the text of 323.

---

82. In the actual case, it is not necessary to consider the undirected coherency between 323 and 35 because the text of 35 is well represented by other Byzantine witnesses in table 11. It agrees with 617 at 96.00%, with 424 at 96.00%, and with 468 at 95.59%. See also the next note. For undirected genealogical coherencies, see Mink, "Problems of a Highly Contaminated Tradition," 63–67.

83. 468 is the most closely related potential ancestor of 617 (95.62% agreement) and 307 (94.21% agreement). 617 is the most closely related potential ancestor of 424 (96.98% agreement) and 35 (96.00% agreement).

A computer program (not yet available online) helps with this search. First, all possible combinations of the potential ancestors in question are calculated. In the case of 323 we have 10 potential ancestors and 1,023 possible combinations.

Next, the program examines these combinations and registers how many variants of the witness in question, here 323, would be explained by agreement with or dependence on a variant in one of the witnesses included in the respective combination. This process reveals four possibilities:

(i) The witness, here 323, agrees with at least one potential ancestor of the combination at a certain number of passages. The relevant variants in 323 are considered as explained by these agreements. There will usually be a remainder of variants not covered by agreement with a potential ancestor.

(ii) Variants in 323 differ from variants in all potential ancestors of the combination and are posterior to at least one of them. Such variants support the ancestor–descendant relationship.

(iii) Variants in 323 differ from all variants in the combination of potential ancestors, but the relationship of one or more variants in 323 with a variant in one of the potential ancestors has been classified as unclear in the local stemma. In this case it has to be reconsidered whether the variants in question can be derived from variants in the potential ancestors.

(iv) There are passages where the variant of 323 definitely cannot be derived from a variant in one of the potential ancestors. In this case the respective combination is not suitable for the construction of an optimal substemma.

If no combination of potential ancestors is able to explain all the variants of a witness, then there are two possible options:

(a) Variants of the witness can be derived from variants documented only in witnesses that are closely related but do not qualify as potential ancestors, because the number of variants considered prior to those of the witness in question equals the number of variants considered posterior.[84]

(b) Variants of the witness can be derived from variants attested by non-ancestors only. This can happen with witnesses contain-

---

84. See the section "Undirected Genealogical Coherencies" in Mink, "Problems of a Highly Contaminated Tradition," 63–67.

ing very old text, if the common ancestor of the two seemingly unrelated witnesses is lost.[85]

The program arranges the results for all combinations by the number of agreements and derived variants in descending order. Accordingly, it suggests the following combination of ancestors for the substemma of 323:

1739–04–617–93–307–025–03

Of 3,046 variant passages in the Catholic Letters 323 has text at	3,040
Covered by agreement with at least one of the suggested ancestors (case i)	3,006
Covered by prior variants in one of the suggested ancestors (case ii)	26
Decision still pending (case iii)	8
Definitely unresolved (case iv)	0

Now the question is whether these witnesses, and especially those with lower agreement rates, contribute substantially to explaining the text of 323 or, if this is not the case, whether their contribution consists of connective variants.

Let us begin with 03. This witness exclusively agrees with 323 in one passage only: 1 Pet 5:2/16. All other witnesses of the combination (except

---

85. See the section "Prior Variants Found Only in Non-ancestors," in Mink, "Problems of a Highly Contaminated Tradition," 59–63. To illustrate this scenario: At a passage variant a is prior to variant b. Variant a is supported by witness z, variant b by witness y. Witness z is not a potential ancestor of witness y, because y contains more variants prior to those in z. Consequently the common source x of witnesses of y and z is lost (fig. 17).

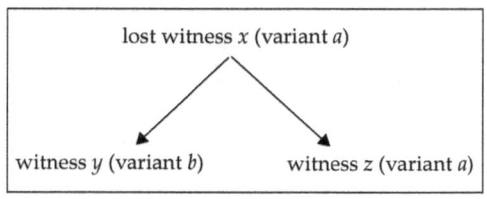

Figure 17. Genealogical Relevance of a Lost Witness

04 with lacuna) read variant *a* (επισκοπουντες), while 323 and 03 omit the word (variant *d*, together with 01* only). I consider this variant as connective, because there is no obvious reason for this omission. Therefore, 03 must be included in the substemma.

025, too, agrees in only one passage exclusively with 323: Jas 5:7/44*b* (αν λαβη). All remaining witnesses of the combination (again except 04 with lacuna) read variant *a* (λαβη). With default parameters, the textual flow diagram for variant *b* indicates strong genealogical coherence within its attestation.[86] Yet it is striking that for many witnesses of *b* the closest potential ancestor is not part of this attestation.[87] This is true also for 323, derivable from 025 with rank 9. The insertion of αν is grammatically correct and suggests itself in a prospective temporal clause. Linguistically this does not appear to be a connective variant, and the moderate degree of agreement between 323 and 025 confirms this view. However, this is a matter of philological assessment.

Witness 93 agrees with 323 exclusively only in Jas 2:13/8*b* (ανιλεως). In 025 only]λεος can be read, which may be the ending of variant *a* or *b*. All other witnesses of the combination read *a* (ανελεος) It is a matter of philological assessment again whether or not this variant is considered connective. There is a marked contrast between the textual flow diagrams of variants *a* and *b*, in that within the attestation of *a* only 10 times does a witness have no connection with its closest potential ancestor, while within the attestation of *b*—the number of witnesses is a little greater—this happens 40 times.[88] Ultimately, this is not decisive. It has to be borne in mind that the alignment of witnesses in a textual flow diagram is based on the tables of potential ancestors. Even the closest potential ancestor does not necessarily qualify as a stemmatic ancestor because the optimal coverage of variants may be produced by a combination of witnesses without it. If a

---

86. See the *"Genealogical Queries"* module *"Coherence in Attestations"* for this variant.

87. This becomes clear, if the user sets connectivity to "User Defined: up to 1." With this option all the witnesses that do not have their closest potential ancestor within the same attestation are connected with witnesses outside the box containing the attestation in question.

88. See *"Coherence in Attestations"* for this variant. These numbers depend on which variant is considered as initial text. If *b* were the initial text, 21 witnesses of *a* would not be connected with their closest potential ancestor, because *A*, the witness of the initial text, which is the closest potential ancestor of 12 witnesses in this attestation would be included in the attestation of *b*. In this case the number of witnesses of *b* not connected with their closest potential ancestor would diminish to 34. Witness 323 would be derived here from *A*, and 93 would no longer be required for the substemma of 323.

textual flow diagram shows a witness depending on a potential ancestor with a relatively low percentage of agreements, this may indicate multiple emergence of the variant due to coincidence. 025 and 93 are border cases. At any rate, the variant ανιλεως is not necessarily connective. Both of them would exclusively contribute only one passage, and the variant is certainly less significant than 1 Pet 5:2/16d in 03.

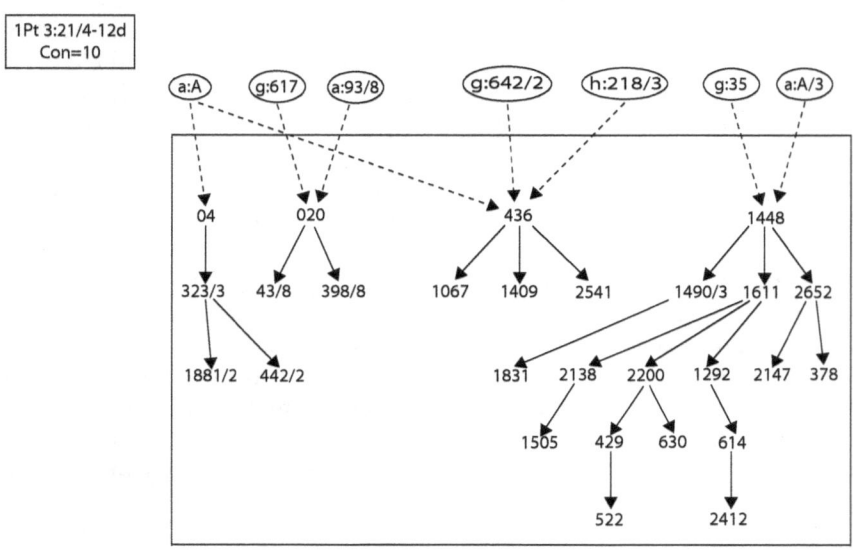

Figure 18. Textual Flow Diagram for 1 Peter 3:21/4-12*d*

For 04, we have to discuss two passages. 04 reads 1 Pet 3:21/4-12*d* (και ημας αντιτυπον νυν σωζει) exclusively with 323. The closest potential ancestor, 1739, supports variant *a* (και υμας αντιτυπον νυν σωζει), while other witnesses of the combination read *g* (αντιτυπον νυν και ημας σωζει). The textual flow diagram also suggests multiple emergence, partly from variant *a* (e.g., with 04 and 323), partly from variant *g* (see fig. 18).[89] The second passage is Jude 19/9. 04 and 323 add εαυτους (variant *b*). Copyists may have missed an object with the preceding αποδιοριζοντες. If connectivity is considered low, the textual flow diagram suggests coincidental multiple emergence.[90] I decided therefore not to incorporate 04 into the substemma, but this, again, is a matter of assessment.

---

89. For 436 variant *h* is indicated as a possible source along with *g*, but linguistically and genealogically variants *a* and *g* are better options.

90. See *"Coherence in Attestations"* or *Introductory Presentation*, 540.

If 307 was removed from the combination of ancestors in the sub-stemma (1739–04–617–93–307-025–03), then five variants of 323 could no longer be explained by agreement; without 617 there would be nine such variants, and without 1739, finally, there would be 60. These figures would increase if the combination was restricted to 1739-617-307-03: with 307 to 10 passages, with 617 to 19, with 1739 to 104. This happens because in the respective passages agreement with 025, 93, and 04 would not count anymore. If 04 was reinstalled into the combination, then only the figure for 1739 would remain considerably higher than before reducing the combination: 75 instead of 104. For 307 there would be 9 instead of 10, for 617 there would be no difference.

If we opt for the combination 1739-617-307-03, discarding 04, 025, and 93 from the initial combination, there will be one more case where the source of the variant is doubtful (1 Pet 3:21/4-12), and three more cases where the variant of 323 has to be explained by a prior variant in at least one of the witnesses in the reduced combination (Jas 2:13/8; Jas 5:7/44; Jude 19/9).

The following list contains the 29 passages where 323 has a variant posterior to at least one ancestor in the combination 1739-617-307-03.

	variant		source variant[91]	
Jas 1:25/24	d	323	a	03. 1739
Jas 1:25/28	b	323	a	03. 307. 617. 1739
Jas 2:4/2-4	e	323	d	307. 617
Jas 2:5/22-26	c	323	a[92]	03. 1739
Jas 2:8/12-16	c	323	a	03. 307. 617. 1739
Jas 2:11/20-28	e	323	b	617
Jas 2:13/8	b	323	a	03. 307. 617. 1739
Jas 4:17/6-8	d	323	a[93]	03. 307. 617. 1739
Jas 5:4/26	b	323	a	03. 307. 617. 1739
Jas 5:7/44	b	323	a	03. 307. 617. 1739
1Pt 1:3/26-32	b	323	a	03. 307. 617. 1739
1Pt 2:4/6	b	323	a	03. 307. 617. 1739
1Pt 2:21/30	c	323	a	03. 307. 617. 1739
1Pt 4:7/4	b	323	a	03. 307. 617. 1739
1Pt 5:10/38-44	d	323	h[94]	307

---

91. Only witnesses contained in the relevant combination are quoted

92. Hitherto, variant e was seen as the source here (cf. "Local Stemmata"), but variant a is the better option linguistically.

93. Variant d (καλον) could derive from b (καλον πο ησαι) or c (ποιειν καλον), if we just look at linguistic probability, but if genealogical coherence is taken into account, variant a is the most likely source.

94. Variant d features a strange mixture of verbal forms (καταρτισαι στηριξει σθενωσει θεμελιωσει). Variant h is the only one in question as its source (καταρτισαι υμας στηριξει σθενωσει θεμελιωσει). The omission of υμας could result from an influ-

2Pt 2:20/2	b	323	a	03. 307. 617. 1739
2Pt 2:20/44	b	323	a	03. 307. 617. 1739
2Pt 3:5/24-34	h	323	a	307. 617. 1739[95]
1Jn 2:1/36-40	c	323	a	03. 307. 617. 1739
1Jn 2:7/22	b	323	a	03. 307. 617. 1739
1Jn 3:7/22-28	d	323	a[96]	03. 307. 617. 1739
1Jn 3:17/8	b[97]	323	a	03. 307. 617. 1739
1Jn 4:20/32	b	323	a	03. 307. 617. 1739
1Jn 5:20/36	b	323	a	03. 307. 617. 1739
2Jn 7/32-44	c	323	a	03. 307. 617. 1739
2Jn 9/22	b	323	a	03. 307. 617. 1739
2Jn 12/4	b	323	a	03. 307. 617. 1739
3Jn 13/2-4	d	323	a	03. 307. 617. 1739
Jd 19/9	b	323	a	03. 307. 617. 1739T

All of these instances are covered by the combination 1739-617-307-03 or a subset, leaving a remainder of 9 questionable passages:

Jas 2:18/42-52g   τα εργα μου εκ της πιστεως   322. 323

Potential ancestors of 323 support variants *a* (εκ των εργων μου την πιστιν) and *d* (εκ των εργων μου την πιστιν μου), but the μου lacking after πιστεως is an analogy with *a*. 03 and 1739, both essential members of the combination presently studied, support *a*.

---

ence of variant *a* (καταρτισει στηριξει σθενωσει θεμελιωσει) with 1739T among its witnesses.

95. Variant *a* is rendered incorrectly by 03 (συνεστωσης for συνεστωσα, the latter leading to συνεστωτα in 323).

96. The omission in 323 (homoioteleuton) could theoretically derive from variant *c*, but there is genealogical coherence with variant *a* only. No potential ancestor of 323 supports another variant.

97. The variants in question are *a* (εχη) and *b* (εχει) in a prospective relative clause with αν. In light of the textual flow diagram of variant *b* (see "*Coherence in Attestations*") it may be doubted that the scribes of this variant felt any difference between these readings. With the option "Connectivity: Low," the coherence within the attestation proves to be very weak. Moreover, it occurs only rarely here that a witness is connected with its closest potential ancestor. We may assume that one of the readings frequently arose from the other. Thus, it is a matter of different orthographical rendering resulting from itacism rather than real variation. In the ECM apparatus, however, such interchanges of moods are treated as variants, because it is debatable whether or not they are grammatically equivalent. Those cases of doubtful indicative/subjunctive interchange occur frequently, especially so in 1 John. (See ECM IV, 28*, esp. n. 3.)

1Pt 1:17/8e αιτεισθε 323

Theoretically, all other variants of this passage can be the source of *e*, but *a* (επικαλεισθε) is the only one supported by potential ancestors of 323, with 03, 307, 617, and 1739 among them.

1Pt 1:24/18e om. 323

Of course, all other variants can be the source of this omission. But only *a* (αυτης) and *c* (ανθρωπου) have support from potential ancestors of 323. 03, 307, and 1739 read *a*, and 617 reads *c*, thus both possibilities would be covered by the combination presently studied.

1Pt 3:21/4-12d και ημας αντιτυπον νυν σωζει   04. 020. 43. 323. 378. 398. 429. 436. 442. 522. 614. 630. 1067. 1241C. 1292. 1409. 1448. 1490. 1505. 1611. 1831. 1881. 1890C. 2138. 2147. 2200. 2412. 2541. 2652.

This variant was discussed above. It was not considered necessary to include 04 in the combination of stemmatic ancestors just to cover this variant by agreement. The textual flow diagram suggests multiple emergence of this variant.[98] The most likely source is *a* (και υμας αντιτυπον νυν σωζει), supported by 03 and 1739 from the combination presently studied.

1Pt 5:9/32f επιμελεισθε 323. 1241

Variant *b* (επιτελεισθε) is most similar graphically. Phonetically, *b* is equal to *a* (επιτελεισθαι). The textual flow diagram for variant *a* (fig. 27 [p. 215]) shows an attestation coherent in itself, while variant *b* obviously arose several times from *a* (fig. 28 [p. 216]).[99] Thus, variant *b*, with 03* among its witnesses, is an option as a source for 323, but *a* has to be taken into consideration as well. Perhaps it even has to be preferred, because many of its witnesses are relatives of 323, among them 1739, 307, and 617 from the combination of stemmatic ancestors presently discussed. At any rate, the combination 1739-617-307-03 would fit both options.

---

98. See fig. 18.
99. For both of the textual flow diagrams, "Connectivity" was set to "Low." The diagram for *a* shows a perfect, consistently strong genealogical coherence. Almost all witnesses are connected with their closest potential ancestors. Quite to the contrary, the coherence of the witnesses of *b* is far from perfect, which indicates multiple emergence.

2Pt 1:4/8-18k μεγιστα ημιν και τιμια επαγγελματα δεδωρηται
323. 398. 2805

There are 15 very similar variants in this passage, differing for the most part in word order and the choice of the pronoun ημιν or υμιν. Accordingly, genealogical coherence is not very distinct. The witnesses of *k*, as well, do not feature significant coherence with each other (fig. 19).

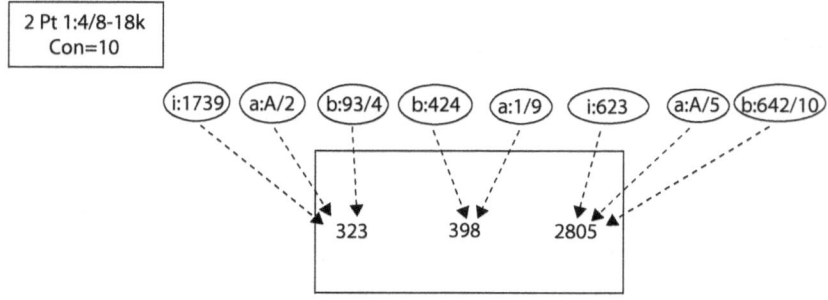

Figure 19. No Adequate Coherence in 2 Peter 1:4/8-18*k*

The textual flow diagram shows that it would be possible to derive *k* from *a* (τιμια και μεγιστα ημιν επαγγελματα δεδωρηται), *b* (τιμια ημιν και μεγιστα επαγγελματα δεδωρηται) or *i* (μεγιστα και τιμια ημιν επαγγελματα δεδωρηται). Among these variants only *i* has μεγιστα as the first word; thus it is a good option as a source variant of *k*.[100] 307 and 1739 from the combination presently studied are among the witnesses. Some may prefer variant *b* as source. In this case stemmatic ancestor 617 would support the source of the variant in 323.

2Pt 2:12/10-14c ζωα γεγενημενα φυσικα   01. 02C. 18. 33. 35. 69f. 218. 254. 323. 442. 522. 621. 630. 642. 808. 945. 1127. 1241. 1448*. 1505. 1524. 1611. 1852. 1881. 2298. 2344. 2374. 2464. 2805. L696

There are 10 variants at this passage, several of which are very similar to each other. The textual flow diagram for variant *c* shows imperfect coherence. The genealogical relationships suggest three possible sources for 323, namely, *a* (ζωα γεγεννημενα φυσικα), *e* (ζωα φυσικα γεγενημενα) or *f* (ζωα γεγενημενα). Variant *c* differs from *a* by just one letter. One might even argue that the difference between single and double ν could be due to phonetic identity. But while the textual flow diagram for variant *a* does

---

100. Eye skipping from *a* in μεγιστα to the one in τιμια may have caused the transposition of και τιμια.

not indicate multiple emergence, the diagram for variant *c* does. 03 and 1739 from the combination of ancestors presently studied support *a*.

3Jn 9/4c   αν τι   6f. 323. 424Z. 1611*V

This passage appears among the problematic cases because it was hitherto left open whether *a* (τι) or *d* (om.) is more likely the initial text. Variant *c* probably is a mixture from *a* and *b* (αν). Witnesses in the combination presently studied support *a* (03, 1739) or *b* (307).

3Jn 12/34-42d   αληθης εστιν ημων η μαρτυρια   323. 442. 621. 1241V. 1243. L596(*f)

The textual flow diagram suggests variants *a* (η μαρτυρια ημων αληθης εστιν) and *b* (αληθης ημων εστιν η μαρτυρια) as possible sources. Variant *b* is without doubt closer to the text of 323. 1739 from the combination presently studied is among its witnesses.

The combination of ancestors 1739-617-307-03 stood the test at all problematic passages. Thus, it is able to explain the whole text of 323. The respective optimal substemma is shown in fig. 20.

Figure 20. Optimal Substemma of 323

The initial combination of seven ancestors has now been reduced to four. This could be achieved by taking philological arguments into consideration. The next step is a comparison of the present with other combinations of four witnesses, executed by a program written for this purpose. The purpose is to check whether there is any combination that would explain more variants in 323 by agreement. The result is negative.

The procedure of reducing the initial combination requires philological assessment. This implies that scholars may differ in opinion and, accordingly, arrive at different results. For instance, somebody may prefer to include 04 in the optimal substemma. This would not be a matter of true or false but of evaluating arguments. Regarding the small additional contribution which may be ascribed to 04, both the substemma in fig. 20 and one including 04 would describe the place of 323 in textual history without differing in anything substantial.

323 is characterized by a typical mixture of non-Byzantine and Byzantine elements. The percentage of agreements with 1739 is considerably higher than with Byzantine witnesses, which shows a preponderance of the non-Byzantine stratum. The following figures confirm this conclusion. In 185 passages 323 shares a variant with 1739 but not with 617 or 307, while in 51 passages it agrees with 617 against 1739 or 03. With posterior variants of 323 we almost always find the entire combination of ancestors supporting the prior variant. This is no surprise. 1739, 617, 307, and 03 agree with each other in 2,576 of the 3,046 variant passages listed in the ECM apparatus of the Catholic Letters.

One might ask whether the mixture of non-Byzantine and Byzantine readings is homogeneous throughout the Catholic Letters. The *"Genealogical Queries"* module *"Comparison of Witnesses"* can help to find out. Let us compare 323 with 1739 on the one hand (table 12) and 617 on the other (table 13).[101]

W1	DIR	W2	WRIT	NR	PERC1	EQ	PASS	W1<W2	W1>W2	UNCL	NOREL
323	<--	1739	Jas	10	90.802	691	761	36	21	6	7
323	<--	1739	1Pt	1	95.552	666	697	11	8	10	2
323	<--	1739	2Pt	1	96.643	403	417	5	3	6	0
323	<--	1739	1Jn	1	98.427	751	763	11	0	1	0
323	<--	1739	2Jn	1	97.115	101	104	3	0	0	0
323	<--	1739	3Jn	1	93.617	88	94	2	1	3	0
323	<--	1739	Jd	1	99.020	202	204	2	0	0	0
323	<--	1739	CL	1	95.461	2902	3040	70	33	26	9

Table 12. Comparison of 323 and 1739

W1	DIR	W2	WRIT	NR	PERC1	EQ	PASS	W1<W2	W1>W2	UNCL	NOREL
323	<--	617	Jas	1	94.087	716	761	21	17	3	4
323	-->	617	1Pt	20	87.374	609	697	30	32	22	4
323	<--	617	2Pt	17	88.010	367	417	22	11	16	1
323	-->	617	1Jn	6	89.384	682	763	29	33	18	1
323	-->	617	2Jn	25	82.692	86	104	7	10	1	0
323	<--	617	3Jn	9	87.234	82	94	5	2	4	1
323	-->	617	Jd	38	84.314	172	204	10	11	9	2
323	<--	617	CL	4	89.276	2714	3040	124	116	73	13

Table 13. Comparison of 323 and 617

---

101. A comparison of 323 with 03 yields low numbers of agreement in all Catholic Letters: 85.23 – 88.46%, 90.72% only in 1 John.

CONTAMINATION, COHERENCE, AND COINCIDENCE   201

In the Letter of James, the percentage of agreement (PERC1) with 1739 is significantly lower than in all other Catholic Letters. Table 13 shows values exactly complementary to those for 323-1739.[102] The different textual character of 323 stands out even more clearly, if we compare the list of potential ancestors as based on data for all Catholic Letters (table 14, left) with the one based exclusively on the data for the Letter of James (table 14, right [excerpt]).

W2	NR	D	PERC1	EQ	PASS
1739	1		95.461	2902	3040
A	2		92.284	2691	2916
35	0	-	89.638	2725	3040
04	3		89.323	1874	2098
93	4		89.276	2714	3040
617	4		89.276	2714	3040
307	6		89.145	2710	3040
468	6		89.145	2702	3031
424	8		89.028	2702	3035
025	9		88.262	2361	2675
03	10		87.811	2644	3011

W2	NR	D	PERC1	EQ	PASS
617	1		94.087	716	761
2423	2		93.947	714	760
424	3		93.693	713	761
18	4		93.430	711	761
319	5		93.017	666	716
35	0	-	92.904	707	761
468	6		92.895	706	760
93	0	-	92.773	706	761
312	0	-	92.593	700	756
642	0	-	92.510	704	761
2186	7		91.402	691	756
307	8		91.327	695	761
5	9		91.196	694	761
453	10		90.802	691	761
1739	10		90.802	691	761

Table 14. Potential Ancestors of 323, Based on Data for the Catholic Letters (left) and the Letter of James Only (excerpt, right)

In the table on the right, all higher ranking positions are held by clearly Byzantine witnesses, while 1739 is number 10.[103] Accordingly, 70 of 138 differences between 323 and 1739 are in James. This follows from the difference between the numbers under "PASS" and "EQ" for 1739 (table12). In the remaining Catholic Letters there is more agreement between 323 and 1739. In Jude they agree in 202 of 204 passages [104] Remarkably there is only one passage in the last three Catholic Letters where 323 agrees with 617 or 307 against 1739: 3 John 1/8a (together with 03).

---

102. With 323-307 the percentage of agreements in James is lower: 91.33%. Unlike 617, 307 differs quite often from the Byzantine mainstream in James.
103. The complete list ends with rank number 28.
104. The differences are at 1/24b and 19/9b. This can be found out easily choosing "View Differences" in the *"Comparison of Witnesses"* module.

15. Conclusions: How the CBGM Copes with Contamination: The Character of the Iterative Process

It is impossible to trace the real filiation of surviving manuscripts in a contaminated tradition whose witnesses have largely been lost. All we can realistically aim at is finding genealogical structures in relationships between preserved witnesses, that is, between texts as transmitted by manuscripts, not between manuscripts as historical artifacts. The texts feature chains of passages with and without variants. The genealogical relations between variants do not simply correspond to genealogical relations between texts. The reason for this is contamination. If we compare two witnesses x and y from a heavily contaminated tradition, we will usually find variants in x that are older and others that are younger than those in y. A genealogical or stemmatic hypothesis can reflect such a situation only if it assumes more than one stemmatic ancestor of a witness. These stemmatic ancestors must be able to explain the text of a descendant as a whole by offering a textual basis with an optimal share of agreements and with plausible source variants where there are differences.

The basis of all further procedures is created by determining priority or posteriority of variants in local stemmata. Ideally, the relations between witnesses would be taken into account as external criteria in assessing the relations between variants, but in practice we can only know the relation between witnesses after assessing the relations between variants. In the beginning, there is no conception of the genealogical relationship between most witnesses. There are relatively few witnesses that from the outset can be said to obtain an important or even exceptional role in the textual history, but they, too, cannot be finally judged before all the relevant evidence has been included.

Thus, the initial set of local stemmata can only be constructed with differing degrees of certainty and therefore remain tentative in many cases. In a considerable number of cases it will not be possible to determine the source variant. In the beginning, a lack of pre-genealogical coherence of witnesses is the most reliable indicator of a correspondingly deficient genealogical coherence and hence suggests not to assume a genealogical relationship between respective variants.

Consequently, many initial local stemmata have a preliminary status. On the other hand, most of the passages can be assessed with reasonable certainty. From the latter genealogical data are derived that can be used for a revision of the first results. Some genealogical statements made in the first phase will need correction, some previously unclear relations between variants will now become assessable. Many cases that had to be left pending altogether in the first phase will now be settled. It may also happen, however, that new problems occur at passages that were thought to be resolved.

The revision will improve the genealogical data and thus modify the overall result. In this context I have sometimes used the terms "iterative process" and "process of approximation."[105] This is correct insofar as new insights often lead to a revision of previous assessments. It has to be emphasized, however, that ambiguous evidence must not be cleared by simply continuing a recognized trend. This would mean something like coming to a decision at passages with unclear initial text by following 03 consistently, because it generally comes closest to the initial text.

How many iterations have to take place? This depends on the quality and number of local stemmata arrived at initially. Moreover, the completeness of the data basis itself is important here. When we prepared the ECM of the Catholic Letters, we could draw on pre-genealogical data only. As we progressed, genealogical data referring to separate letters became available.

Now that the full set of genealogical data for the Catholic Letters is accessible and differences regarding the textual character of single witnesses within the corpus can be taken into account, a final revision of local stemmata and at the same time of the reconstruction of the initial text is being carried out. Each revision will produce new data, of course. These changes, however, will have little impact on the overall picture. It may happen that occasionally the relationship between very similar witnesses will be inverted, if the number of prior and posterior readings is nearly equal. These are cases, however, for which a genealogical hypothesis is weakly founded anyway. Additional corrections at a few places may be necessary here. For the next projects, the Acts and the Gospel of John, I presume that just one thorough revision will be sufficient, because all relevant data will be available for the entire writings before the reconstruction of the initial text will begin.

In the CBGM, statements about the genealogy of variants lead to statements about the genealogical position of witnesses, and these statements result from very different procedures.

On the one hand, there are the textual flow diagrams. Based on lists of potential ancestors they display at each variant passage the respective relations between witnesses. Among the relations possible in a passage they indicate the ones that occur most frequently in the Catholic Letters (or optionally in a single writing). Such textual flow diagrams provide important help with a revision of local stemmata, because the degree of coherence within an attestation indicates whether a variant is likely to

---

105. See *Introductory Presentation*, 20–22, 575; Mink, "Problems of a Highly Contaminated Tradition," 46

have arisen once or several times. Moreover, the arrows emanating from potential ancestors outside the attestation of a variant indicate its possible source. In the course of a revision it will be checked carefully whether a relationship between variants that appears to be philologically and genealogically plausible was overlooked or whether a previously favored relationship conflicts with the overall picture. In such cases strong philological reasons will be required to sustain the original assumption.

On the other hand, there are the optimal substemmata as parts of the global stemma. They result from completely different procedures and make a completely different claim. They are meant to establish relations between witnesses that are valid at each variant passage and to provide the simplest hypothesis about a witness and the smallest possible combination of stemmatic ancestors that can plausibly explain its variants. This combination maps the simplest paths of contamination. While for textual flow diagrams those relations are retrieved that occur most frequently in the entire stock of data, the construction of an optimal substemma is based on testing all combinations of potential ancestors of a witness with the aim of explaining its text as a whole. The result may be a combination of witnesses containing, among others, more remote potential ancestors. In this case it has to be checked whether the agreements are such that a genealogical connection must be the reason or whether coincidental agreement, such as one based on a change in the text of a more closely related potential ancestor, is a preferable explanation.

Philological plausibility is the criterion in instances in which the question of the origin of a variant is definitely left open. In such cases it is possible that a variant in a witness cannot be connected with a source variant in one of its potential ancestors if it does not agree with any of them. Even in an optimal substemma such uncertainties cannot be ruled out completely. It is, however, a criterion for the acceptability of a substemma that even in unclear cases a deduction from a variant in a witness included in the combination of ancestors is at least philologically possible.

16. Outlook

For the reconstruction of the initial text and for studies of the textual history the relevant data will be made available beyond the printed edition in a database format. This is already the case for the Catholic Letters. Systematic inquiries can now be executed by the reader. The printed edition is just *one* form of the ECM. An electronic complement is now being developed, comprising the database and query programs like the ones used for the present study. This means a big leap forward in terms of editing methodology. New perspectives are opening up, not least for the reader, that were beyond the horizon of the editors themselves when the first fascicles appeared.

When the ongoing revision has been completed, the updated material will be accessible via "*Genealogical Queries*." The next step will be to provide users with a truly interactive workspace where they can put their own textual decisions to the test so that they can see what impact such decisions would have on the genealogical data and thus on the overall picture.

The current challenge, however, is the construction of optimal substemmata for witnesses with large numbers of potential ancestors. In many cases overwhelming numbers of possible substemmata emerge.[106] Testing the capacity of them all to explain the text of a given witness requires enormous computing power. In 2010 Münster University began to implement a new high performance computing cluster that will enable massive parallel processing. The Institute for New Testament Textual Research takes part in the workgroup of future users. In the long run, external CBGM clients will probably be able to use the new technology for their own attempts to construct optimal substemmata.

---

106. Just to illustrate the increasing numbers of combinations: 10 potential ancestors result in 1023 possible combinations (which do not pose any computing problems even on a PC), 20 result in 1,048,575 combinations, 30 in 1,073,741,823. It is not only the number of combinations that increases, but also the number of witnesses included.

Appendix

Figures 21–28

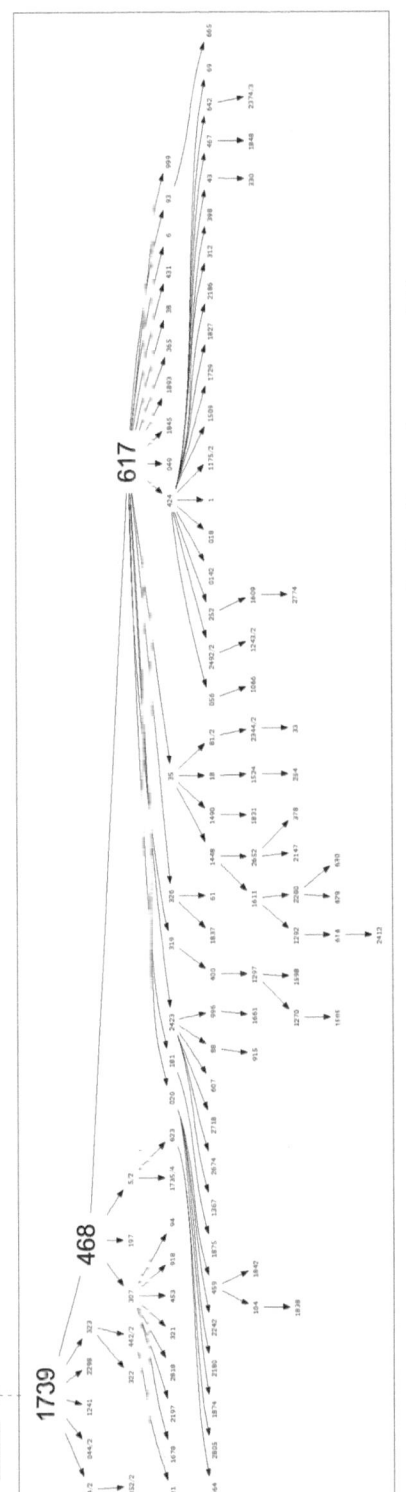

Figure 21a. Perfect coherence in the textual flow diagram for Jas 2:13/20b (overview, for details see figs. 21a and b)

-207-

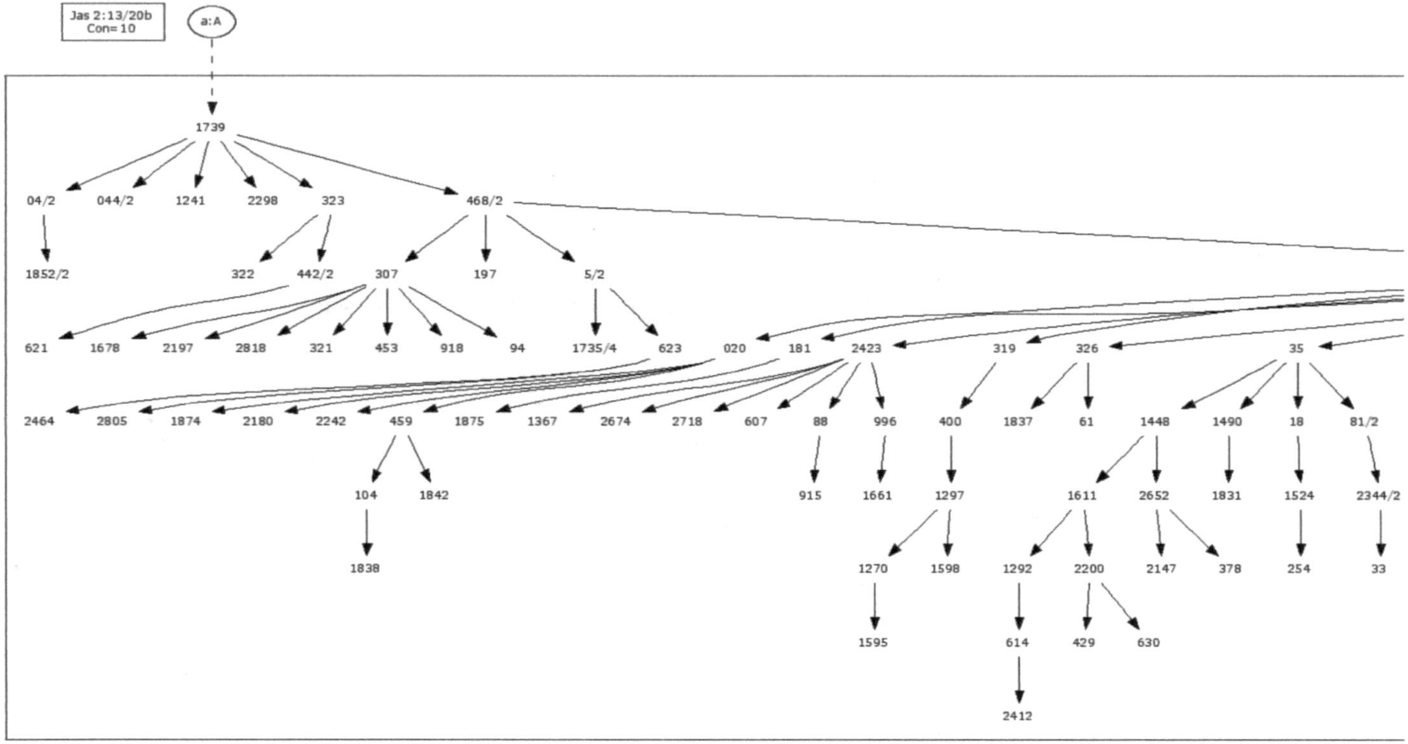

Figure 21b. Details of fig. 21a (left part)

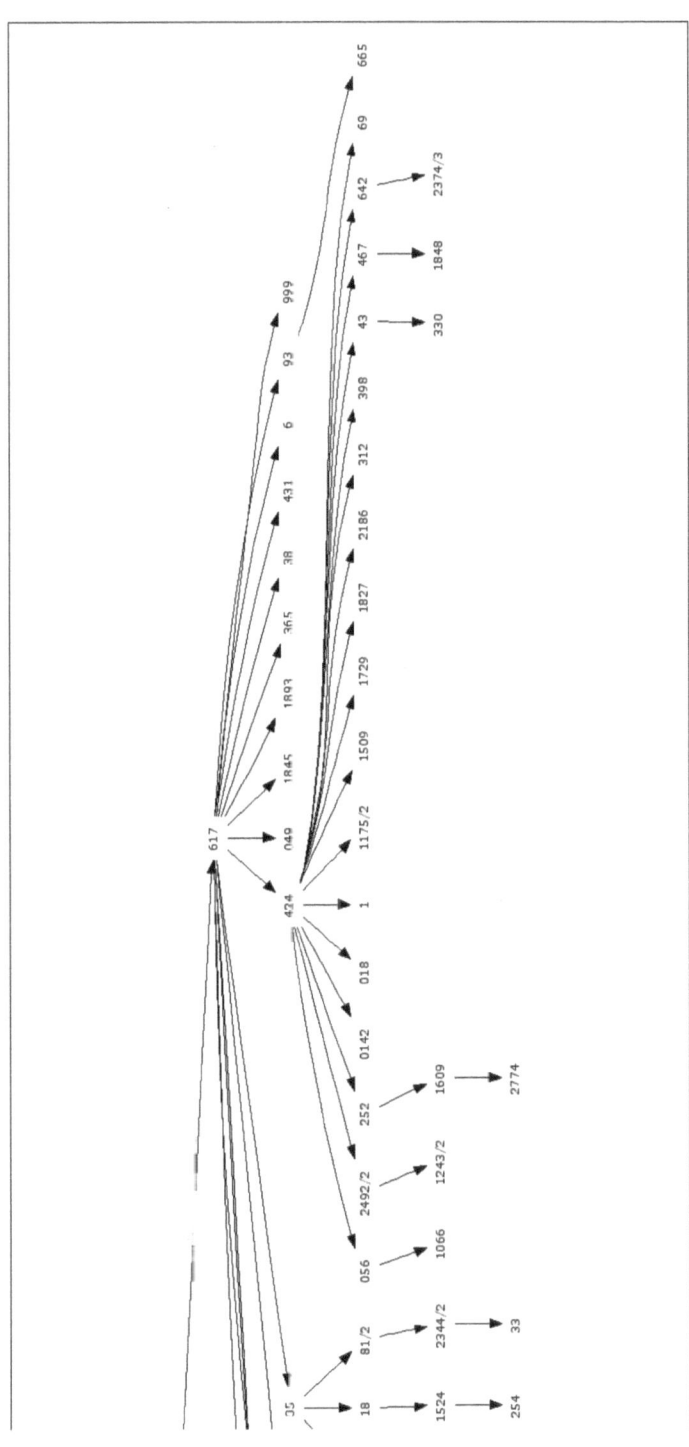

Figure 21c. Details of fig. 21a (right part)

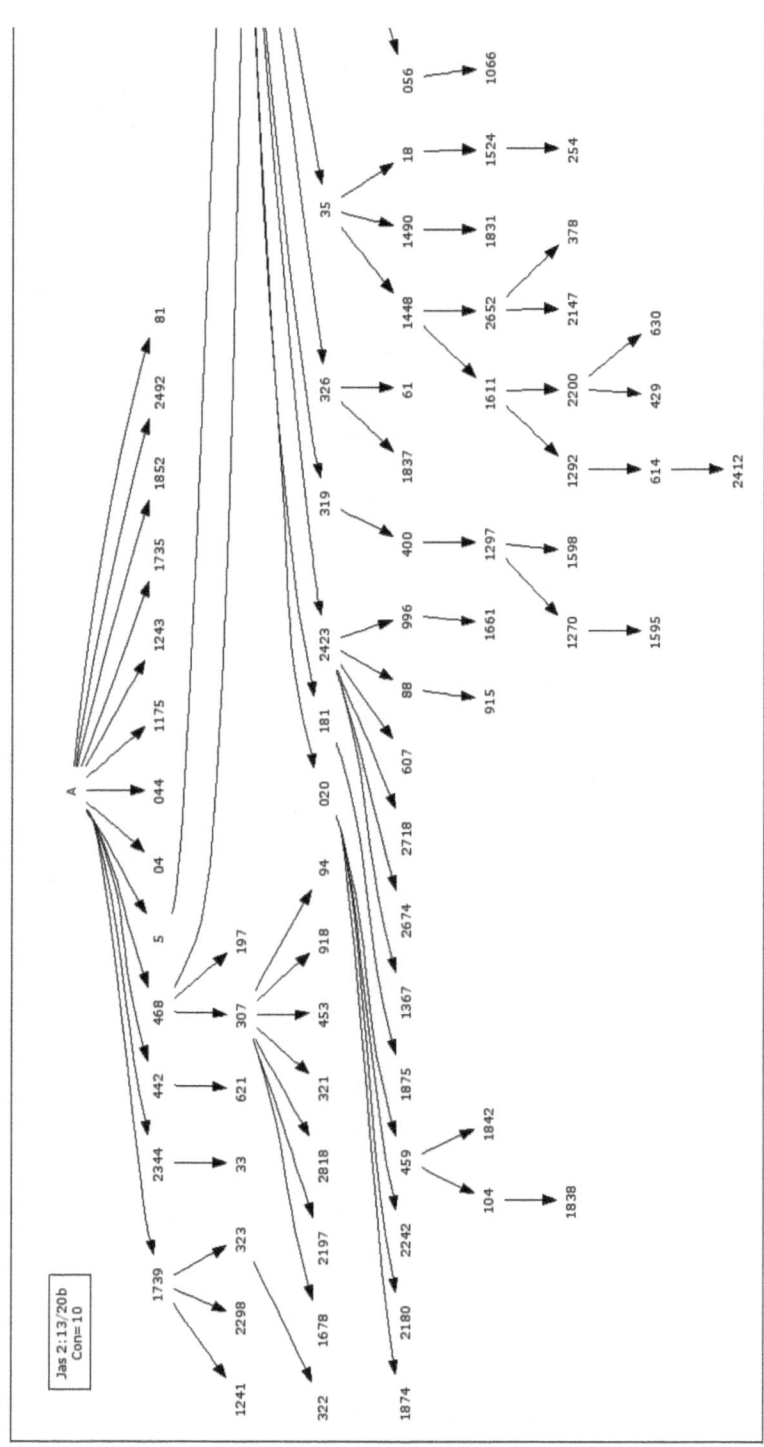

Figure 22a. The same attestation as in figs. 21a-c when the variant is regarded as initial text (left part)

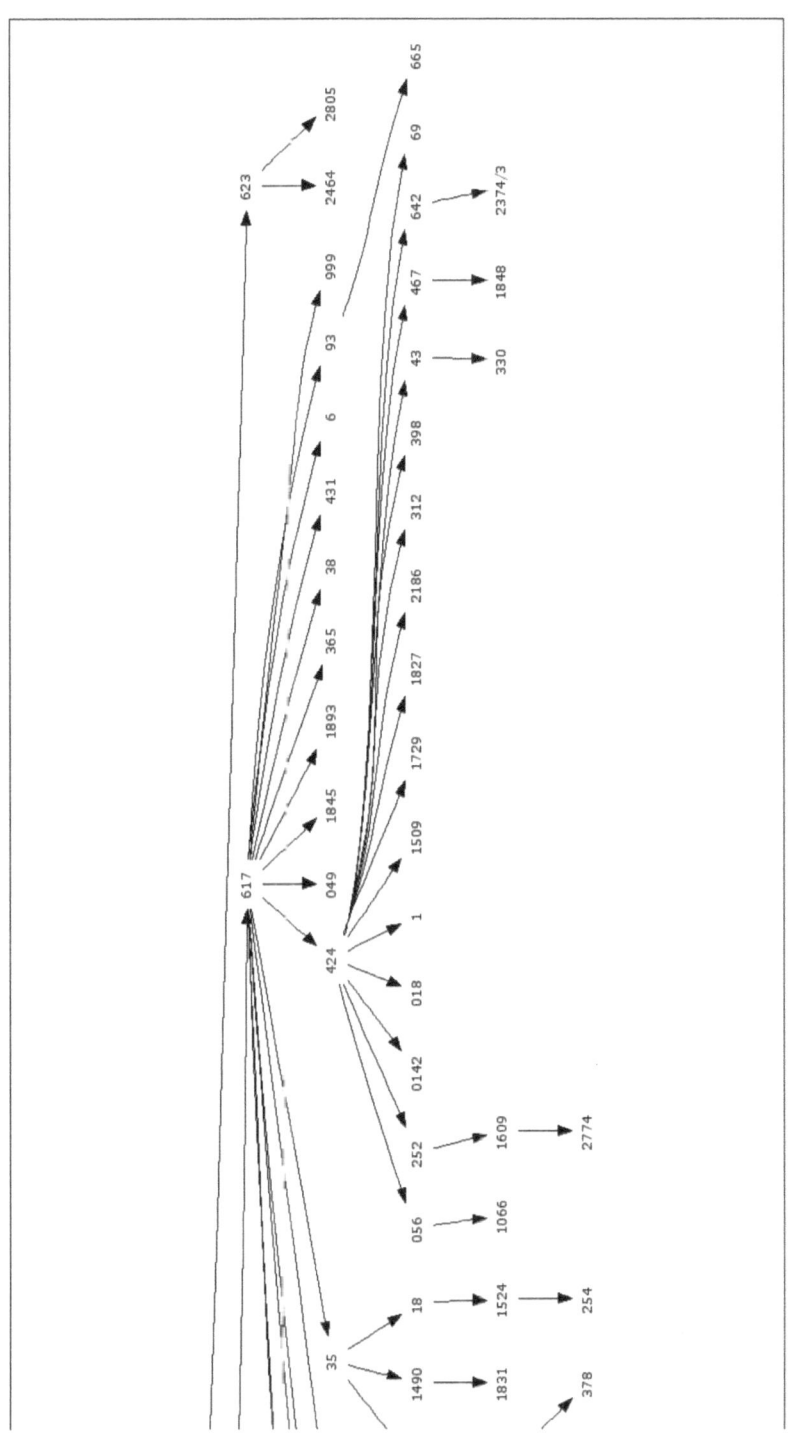

Figure 22b. The same attestation as in figs. 21a-c when the variant is regarded as initial text (right part)

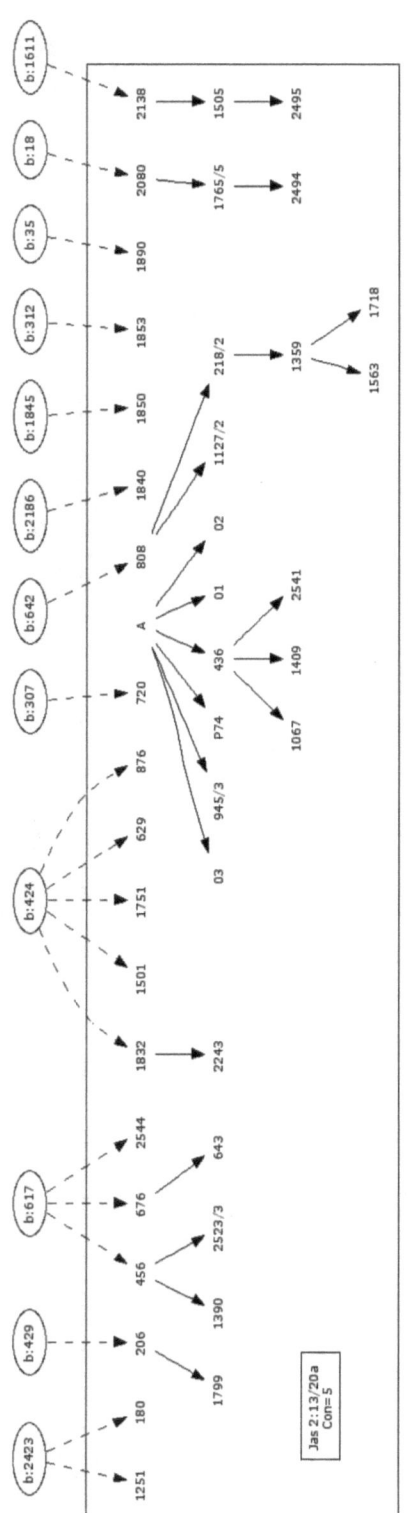

Figure 23. Textual flow diagram showing multiple origins of a variant regarded as initial text

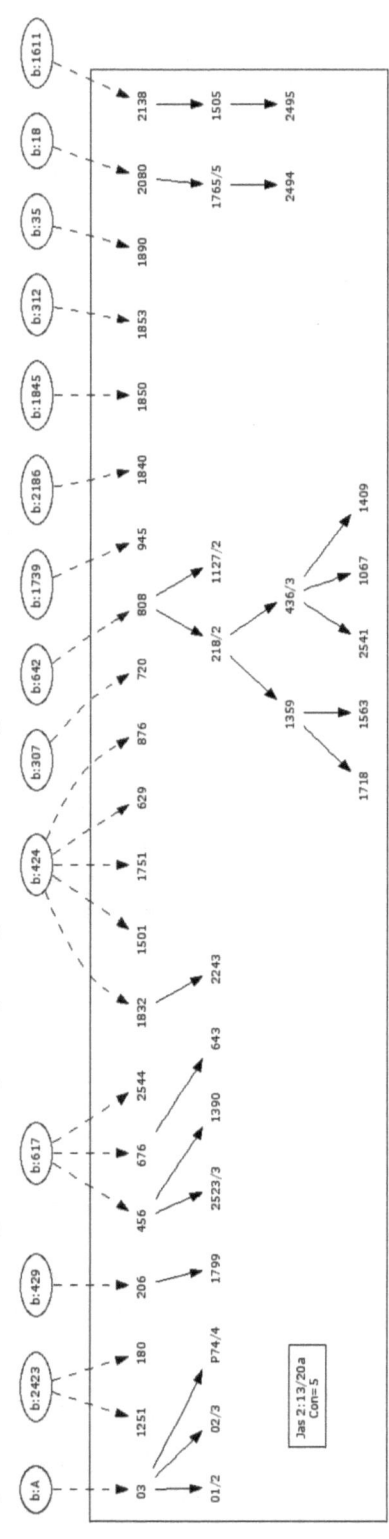

Figure 24. The same attestation as in fig. 23 if the variant is not regarded as initial text

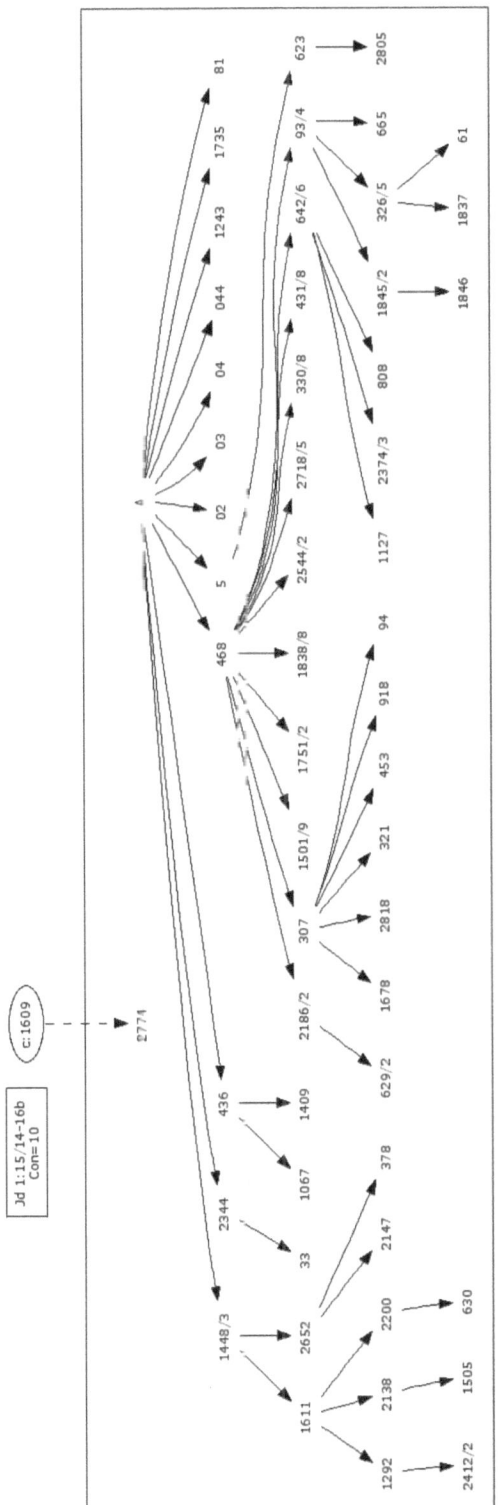

Figure 25. Textual flow diagram for Jd 15/14-16b if the variant is regarded as initial text

-213-

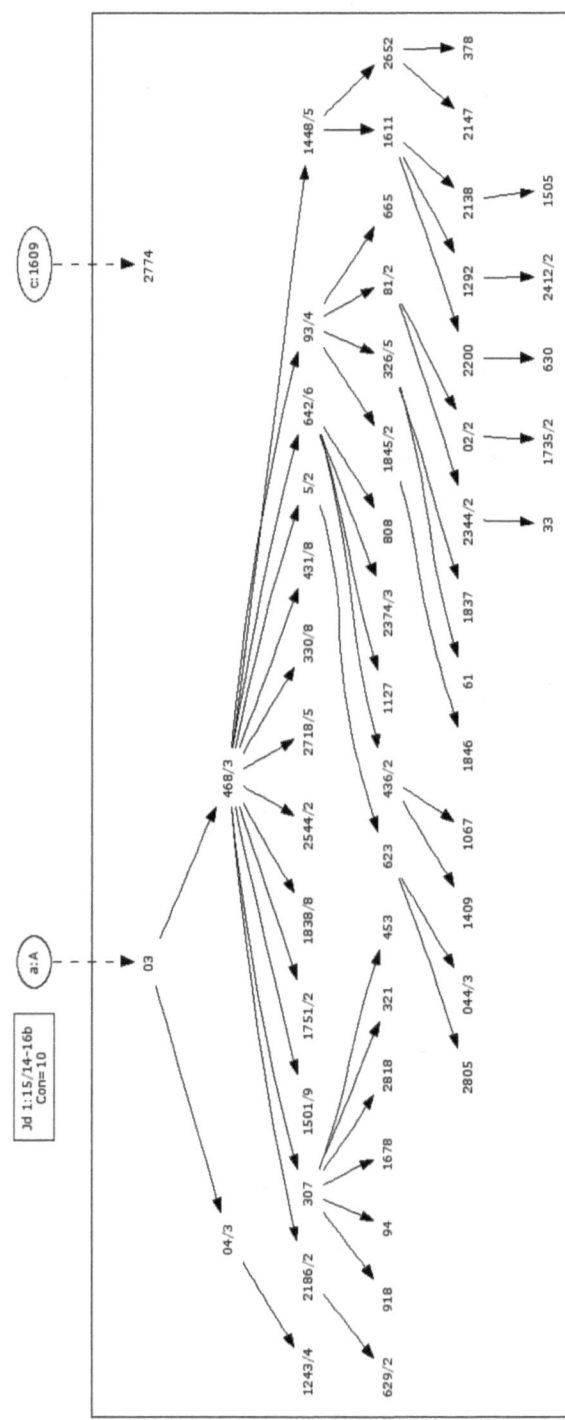

Figure 26. Textual flow diagram for Jd 15/14-16b if variant *a* is regarded as initial text

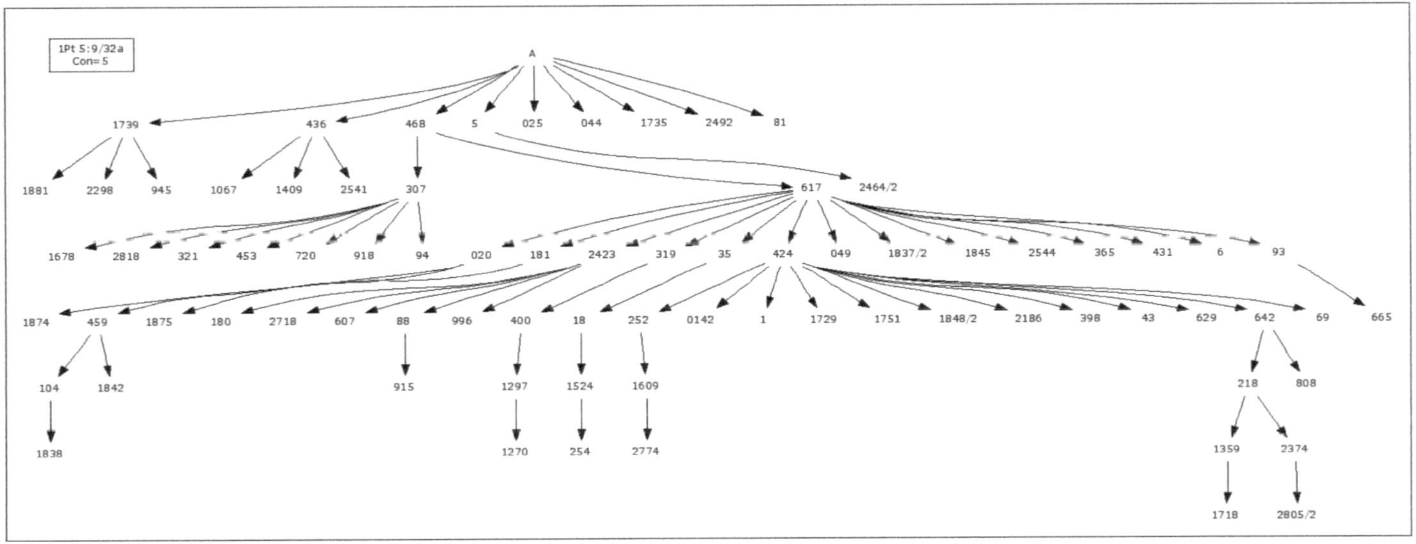

Figure 27. Perfect coherence in 1Pt 5:9/32a

-215-

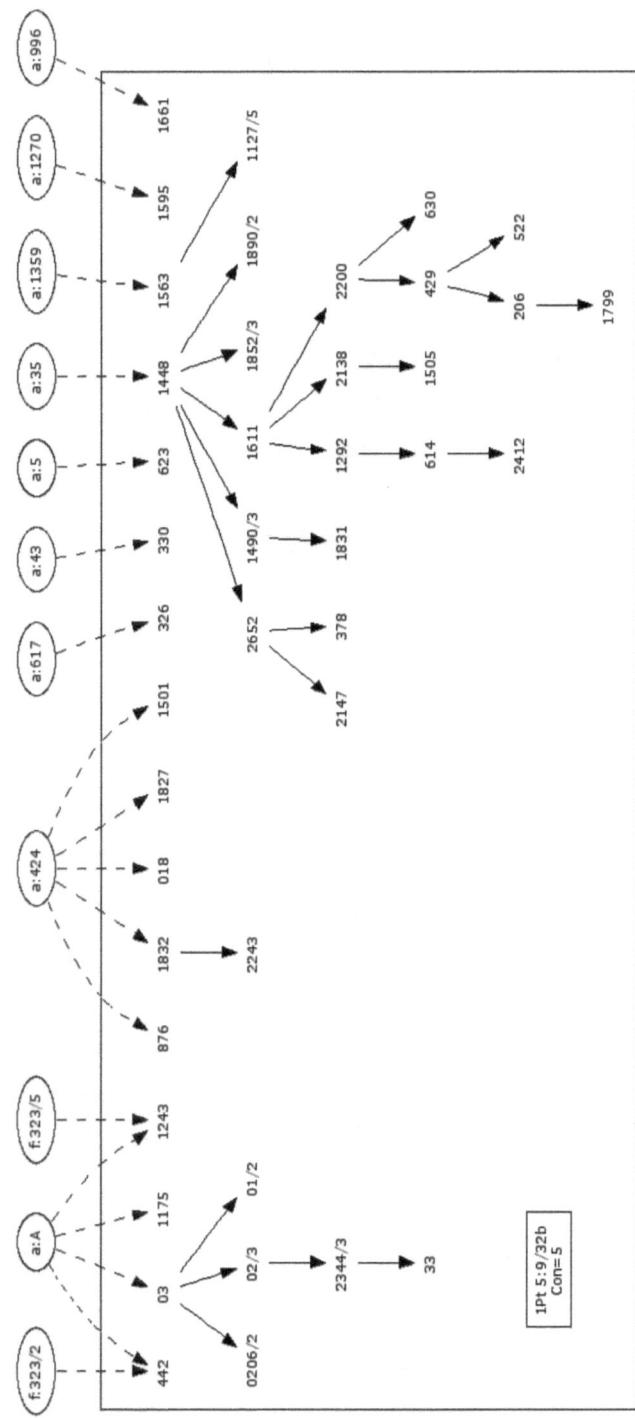

Figure 28. Imperfect coherence in 1Pt 5:9/32b

CONCLUSIONS

Klaus Wachtel

1. The Initial Text

The first two speakers of the colloquium, David Parker and Holger Strutwolf, represent institutions that for decades competed against each other in the aim of a comprehensive edition of the Greek New Testament. In the recent past the International Greek New Testament Project (IGNTP) and the Institut für Neutestamentliche Textforschung (INTF) agreed to work together in editing one *Editio Critica Maior* (ECM). This development is certainly advantageous for both parties. Yet, on the other hand, there doubtless is the risk of "consensus textual criticism," the danger of losing the mutual accountability brought about by academic competition, to which Parker rightly points in his contribution. So let us have a close look at the positions defended by the two partners in the ECM project, point out the differences as clearly as possible, and confront the question of whether they are compatible.

The terms "initial text" and "living text" denote two theoretical concepts of dealing with the manuscript tradition in editing ancient writings. The originals are lost, and what we actually have of the books of the New Testament are copies that date, for the most part, from the Middle Ages. The living text concept focuses more on the description and exegetical study of the textual variation rather than on the genealogical or historical assessment of it, particularly if this variation shows signs of the interpretation of the scriptural tradition in early Christianity. The attempt to reconstruct the initial text may lead (and in fact has often led) to an uncritical use of the reconstruction and a neglect of the manuscripts themselves, despite the claim that the initial text was based on evidence drawn from them.

Moreover, according to Parker it appears methodologically unclear what to do with variants known mainly from patristic sources predating the manuscript tradition, and hence not descended from the initial text. For example, a variant in the Lord's Prayer, 'Your Holy Spirit come upon us and cleanse us' (Luke 11:2, in place of 'Your kingdom come'), reflects the wording as it was known to Tertullian and possibly Marcion. The reading turns up in two medieval manuscripts, but very likely it was not in the archetype from which the extant manuscript tradition began. If our text-critical considerations led to the result that the wording known to Tertullian survived from the primitive form of the Lord's Prayer, would we include it in our edited text even though it could not be reconstructed as the initial text from the manuscript tradition?

Another problem of definition arises if we look at a passage like the pericope of the woman caught in adultery. It is widely accepted that it is not an authentic part of John's Gospel and was not in it when the manuscript tradition started. However, as it has an extensive manuscript attestation, how do its origins and its initial text relate to the initial text of the Gospel?

Strutwolf concedes in plain language that the term "original text" has become problematic, but he abides by it as the ultimate goal of critical editing of the New Testament, although this goal cannot be attained in the final analysis. Like Parker, he uses the Lukan form of the Lord's Prayer to show the problems and to suggest a solution. He identifies the short version that remains after purging the text of influences from the Matthean parallel as the oldest recoverable form: the initial text.

This passage certainly is one of those that would be utilized by CBGM as clear cases to build the foundation for reconsidering more problematic passages in light of tendencies that emerge from the first phase of coherence analyses. In most cases, Strutwolf argues, the initial text is likely identical with the archetype of the manuscript tradition. It would take us back to the middle of the second century when, according to Trobisch, the redaction of the first edition of the full New Testament took place. Moreover, it appears to be likely that we get back to the authorial texts by this reconstruction as long as there is no evidence pointing to a radical break in the transmission.

It is exactly this step that needs to be taken when it becomes important in text-critical and exegetical reasoning to know what the author is likely to have written. Strutwolf does this when he refers to the replacement of the coming of the "Holy Spirit" instead of the "kingdom of God" in Luke 11:2. He explains the early variant as being due to theological thinking that was not prepared to accept the idea of the coming of the kingdom of God. As the Gospel of Luke does not show this tendency at all, there is no reason to assume that the variant, although it is demonstrably earlier than the archetype, can be claimed to be part of the initial text. Yet in principle there is no reason why a reading with such attestation could not be accepted in the initial text, although it was not in the archetype. Let us suppose for the sake of the argument that Tertullian's reading of the second demand of the Lord's Prayer had the manuscript attestation that in reality supports the commonly accepted reading. In this case it would be incompatible neither with CBGM nor with the notion of the initial text as used in the theoretical framework of CBGM to accept the reading "Your kingdom come," in spite of its scant manuscript support, simply because of its intrinsic advantage. The CBGM reveals tendencies both in the objective structure of the material (pre-genealogical coherence) and in its interpretation by the editor (genealogical coherence), but it does allow for exceptions to those rules.

The conjecture-like decision in the ECM in favor of a reading that is supported by only a few Coptic and Syriac manuscripts, οὐχ εὑρεθήσεται in 2 Pet 3:10, offers a more concrete example. Intrinsic probability can be strong enough to enforce a textual decision against the external criteria.

This means that the definition of the term "initial text" must be carefully distinguished from the archetype of the tradition, on the one hand, and from the original text of the author, on the other. The archetype of the tradition was a real manuscript, the copy by which the transmission started that put forth the manuscripts we have—and many more that are lost. The original text of the author predates the manuscripts we have by more than a century in most cases. The initial text is the hypothetical reconstruction of the text as it was before the archetype of the tradition emerged. The initial text is the result of methodical efforts to approximate most closely the lost text of the author based on all relevant evidence, not excluding any trace of transmission predating the archetype. This theoretical presupposition is all the more necessary, as variants like Tertullian's reading of the second demand of the Lord's Prayer show that remnants of a part of the early textual tradition that did not find its way into the archetype may have been picked up by single scribes into individual copies.

The methodological consequence can only be that the "living text" respect for variant wordings of Scripture is not only compatible with but indispensable for the quest of the original text. Scholars, however, who are engaged in this quest have to be aware that all they can achieve is a hypothesis about the original, and this is what is called "initial text" in the context of the CBGM.

Regarding the early variant of the second demand of the Lord's Prayer, this means that it could theoretically be accepted as part of the initial text, although it antedates the archetype of the manuscript tradition or even the initial text as it can be reconstructed from the manuscript tradition alone. The distinction between archetype and initial text is of great importance here. The pericope of the woman caught in adultery, however, may have its own initial text, but this would not affect the reconstruction of the initial text of the Gospel, because according to literary and textual criticism it cannot be seen as an integral part of the authorial text.

2. Causes and Forms of Variation

According to David Trobisch, the most important task of a critical edition of the New Testament is to facilitate the reconstruction of its first edition, which he dates to the second half of the second century in his *First Edition of the New Testament*.[1] If we accept Trobisch's theory, this first edition identifies the archetype of our manuscript tradition. Thus, we are confronted with another compatibility problem. Can the ECM aim for a reconstruction of the archetype and the initial text at the same time? As was demonstrated above, the ECM claims to achieve a state of text preceding the archetype. This presupposes that all the relevant evidence is included in its apparatus, in fact everything that a scholar needs for the reconstruction of the archetype. The ECM editors, however, will not hesitate to incorporate readings into their text that predate all extant manuscript evidence, if the variation found in the tradition can be explained best as deriving from this evidence.

Trobisch's theory helps to explain why the manuscripts are so much alike. Their common source, the archetype of the tradition, gets a clear shape. It is also consistent with one of the basic assumptions on which the theoretical framework of the CBGM is based: a scribe wants to copy the *Vorlage* with fidelity. This assumption is primarily substantiated by the fact that nearly all witnesses have very close next relatives. The presence of common features in all the manuscripts points in the same direction.

Yet on the other hand, there is a high number of variants that require explanation. An observation important for determining causes of variation is the fact that most variants diverging from the text of the next potential ancestor of a witness are found in other manuscripts closely related to the same witness. This suggests that the scribes did not "invent" the variants but found them in their exemplars. Trobisch and Schmid each describe a possible way how certain kinds of variants found their way into the manuscript tradition. One is editorial activity. Trobisch reminds us of the possibility that the "Western" text of Acts may derive from a revision by the author himself. Schmid points out that readers' notes are likely sources for variants that can be traced back to textual parallels. Both confirm that the role of the scribe in the process of pre-modern book production was that of a copyist, not of an editor.

Another issue posed by Trobisch refers to the possibility that it may

---

1. David Trobisch, *The First Edition of the New Testament* (Oxford: Oxford University Press, 2000).

be difficult, or impossible in the case of the Acts of the Apostles, to make a clear distinction between archetype and author's text. However, this is only a theoretical explanation of evidence that for the most part shows clear signs of secondary emergence. Hence, the easiest way will probably be to treat those variants like all the other ones, regardless of whether they may possibly go back to the author.

3. Contamination and Coherence

The CBGM is not the philosopher's stone that produces a reliable reconstruction of the initial text automatically. Yet it makes visible and evaluates *coherence*—a class of evidence that could not be reliably gathered and surveyed before the adoption of database technology. Now that we can compare any manuscript text with any other text at all variant passages contained in our apparatus, we are able to express by concrete numbers how similar the preserved states of text are, in spite of the large number of variant passages that emerged.

The following figures impressively demonstrate the degree of coherence between New Testament manuscripts. The lowest percentage of agreement between two manuscripts of the Catholic Letters is 77.864% (2,195 out of 2,819 variant passages shared by minuscules 1241 and 1838). Most manuscripts included in the ECM apparatus agree at more than 85%. Above all, we are able to nominate for each manuscript text potential ancestors that agree at a level exceeding this average value by far. There are only four manuscript texts whose peculiarities make them differ at more than 10% of the variant passages they share with their closest potential ancestors, but none that differs by more than 13%.[2] This evidence enforces the conclusion that the efforts of scribes to copy their exemplar as precisely as possible was, on the whole, successful. A chain of closely related copies connects the single manuscript texts with the source of the tradition, the initial text.

However, textual criticism is about the cases where scribes either failed or deliberately opted for readings different from those they found in their exemplar. There can be no doubt that contamination or—to use the more neutral term preferred by Michael Holmes—"mixture" considerably impedes the construction of a way back from the later stages of transmission to the beginning. Holmes describes the difficulty in some detail, distinguishing three main manifestations:

- successive or block mixture, if the scribe used one exemplar for one part of the copy and then a different exemplar for another part

---

2. 044, 048, 629 and 1751; see "Genealogical Queries: Potential Ancestors."

- simultaneous mixture, if the copy was produced from two exemplars used eclectically
- incidental mixture, if a manuscript copied from one exemplar was corrected against another

One might object that the last label would better fit the intrusion of readers' notes and the recourse of scribes to copies different from their main *Vorlage*, where they encountered readings that appeared strange or were illegible. Systematic correction against another exemplar might rather be regarded as editorial. In addition, the situation may be complicated by the possibility of independent emergence of the same variant. At any rate, the problem posed by mixture principally is that "a derivative manuscript can appear instead as a source manuscript."

What remedy is offered by CBGM? In the discussion after his and Holmes's papers, Mink surprised the audience with the remark that his method does not address the problems as they were pointed out by Holmes. In the light of the CBGM, contamination is viewed in a perspective fundamentally different from that afforded by traditional methodology. Indeed, CBGM has no remedy to offer against contamination if the aim is a reconstruction of the manuscript tradition *more geometrico*. A stemma that would adequately represent the transmission history in terms of the traditional approach would display a complex system of extant manuscripts and reconstructed hyparchetypes—by far more hyparchetypes than manuscripts, in fact. The CBGM characteristically dispenses with hyparchtypes. Moreover, it does not aim at a stemma of manuscripts. The distinction made between the manuscript and its text is crucial for the CBGM approach. Its objective is to disclose structures within the transmission as extant in the states of text that came down to us.

To this end, it first indicates where contamination occurred. This is achieved by establishing tendencies and probabilities derived from the figures by which similarity can be objectively measured (*pre-genealogical coherence*) and from summarizing assessments of ancestry and descent of variants (*genealogical coherence*). Second, the analysis of genealogical coherence between witnesses is based on two figures indicating the number of priority readings attested by each of them. These priority indicators represent opposite directions of textual flow, one from potential ancestor to descendant and one from descendant to ancestor. Their proportion helps to assess genealogical relationships between attestations of variants and hence between the variants themselves in spite of contamination. One might say that the CBGM does not provide a cure of contamination but a way to live with it without giving up the evaluation of genealogical relationships between single witnesses.

4. The Canons of New Testament Textual Criticism

On the blog of James M. Leonard, one of the participants of the Münster Colloquium, Maurice Robinson, was cited as opposing CBGM for the following reason: "Prof. Robinson . . . claimed that if he were to feed his presuppositions into the computer's programming, the Münster method would spit out a Byzantine Priority schema."[3]

It is interesting that Robinson determines as the fatal flaw of the method that it might confirm the consistency of his own theory. However, it is, in fact, a decisive strength of CBGM that it is indifferent toward the scholarly approach of its users. Its usefulness is in the capability of confronting the user with tendencies derived from summarizations of his or her own assessments at all the other variant passages of a writing. It would not even be necessary to change the code of the CBGM programs to get output mirroring the presuppositions of a user. All we would have to do in the case of Maurice Robinson would be to mark the Byzantine variant as the source of the other readings at all variant passages in the appropriate database table. In most instances, the *"Coherence in Attestations"* module of CBGM would display perfectly coherent support for the Byzantine readings, all with A at the top, because Maurice Robinson decided accordingly. Yet coherence as such is not the decisive argument if it reflects a consistency that was reached by the presupposition that the Byzantine text is initial at any rate. This conclusion can be reached only if the rules known as internal criteria are largely discarded. It is necessary, however, for the formulation of a convincing hypothesis on the initial text that these rules, *intrinsic and transcriptional probabilities,* as Hort put it, are applied as thoroughly as possible in assessing the genealogy of readings and constructing the local stemmata. The CBGM is an instrument for organizing and systematizing text-critical analyses. In a way, it may be compared to bookkeeping software. If the numbers entered into it are false, it will produce inaccurate balances, although the calculations are entirely correct. Moreover, the CBGM is not an instrument meant to confirm one's presuppositions but to put them to test. If one is sure that the Byzantine reading is the initial reading at each variant passage, then there is no need to apply a method designed to keep track of every single assessment.

In analogy with Lachmann, the CBGM does not claim to reconstruct the original text as written by the authors. A fundamental difference lies

---

3. "Developments in Textual Criticism and the Münster Colloquium," posted Monday, August 11, 2008, at http://treasuresoldandnewbiblicaltexts.blogspot.com/.

in the foundation of external criteria. While Lachmann aims for *recensere sine interpretatione*,[4] the CBGM starts by assessing each variant passage, applying internal criteria predominantly, and derives tendencies regarding ancestor–descendant relationships on this basis.

In his knowledgeable presentation, Eldon Epp draws the balance of the development of method in the long history of textual criticism of the New Testament and arrives at the criterion or probability of local genealogical priority as the preeminent touchstone of textual decisions. Moreover, he points out very clearly that it is a matter of probability and interpretation whether a variant meets this criterion so that it is regarded as "able to account for the origin, development, or presence of all other readings in its variation unit." Text-critical decisions are part of the hermeneutical process, and everyone working at the text of the New Testament needs to be aware of this. Epp takes this argument even a step further by stating that "in reality the exegete becomes the final arbiter in text-critical decisions." This means that textual criticism and critical editing take on the role of an ancillary discipline again. Yet it is important to note that this means a considerable challenge for both text critics and exegetes. Text critics, the more so if they are also editors, need to communicate their results so that it becomes rewarding for exegetes to not just pick the reading from the apparatus that best fits their exegetical interpretation. The critical apparatus, with its cryptic symbols and principles, has been a device that is hard to use. In the digital age it is becoming a gateway to the sources rather than just a repository of readings. But it also has to be said that the exegetical task does not get easier with this development. Exegetes need to get involved with procedures required by the CBGM in order to learn to weigh the probabilities in favor of or against variants in the apparatus of the *Editio Critica Maior*.

5. ECM and CBGM: Future Prospects

If Lachmann's aim was *recensere sine interpretatione* and reasoned eclecticism stands for *recensere cum interpretatione*, then G. D. Kilpatrick's and J. K. Elliott's "thoroughgoing eclecticism" means *interpretari sine recensione*. But after Mink's presentation of results achieved by the CBGM, the existence of coherence, that is, of measurable structures inherent in the transmission of the New Testament text, cannot be denied.

---

4. Karl Lachmann, ed., *Novum Testamentum Graece et Latine*, vol. 1 (Berlin: G. Reimer, 1842), v. On the discrepancy between claim and reality in this regard in Lachmann's actual editing work, see Sebastiano Timpanaro, *The Genesis of Lachmann's Method* (Chicago and London: University of Chicago Press, 2005), 88-89.

Following Hort's terminology, one might say that the CBGM starts from intrinsic and transcriptional probability. A new element is pre-genealogical coherence, which contributes to both transcriptional evidence and internal evidence of documents. The analysis of genealogical coherence leads to genealogical evidence, yet in a far more differentiated form than was possible with Hort's "texts," labeled Western, Syrian, and Alexandrian. The CBGM approach takes into account the relationship of each manuscript with any other and thus arrives at a very detailed assessment of attestations. The aim is a redefinition of external criteria by extrapolating trends and probabilities on the basis of assessments achieved by reasoned eclecticism.[5] At the present time, the CBGM is brought into its final form by reducing the number of witnesses that have to be taken into account when analyzing the genealogy of readings by constructing optimal substemmata for each manuscript included.

From the beginning, the *Editio Critica Maior* has been a product of transition into the digital age. The collation of manuscripts for the Letters of James and Peter were still carried out on paper. However, when work on the realization of the edition was taken up in the mid-1990s it was clear that database technology offered the means to control the mass of data brought together for the critical apparatus and to prepare it for computer-aided analyses. Therefore, the paper collations were keyed into a database.

Since 1997, when the first installment of the ECM appeared, the procedures of editing have changed fundamentally. Manuscripts are still collated, that is, compared with a base text, but this is now done by a computer program on the basis of full transcriptions. The base text can be chosen according to the preferences of the editor or to practical requirements. The stable elements in the process are the transcriptions; the collation is carried out by a computer program with a set of variable parameters. The editor constructs a critical apparatus from the output resulting from automated collation. For this purpose, data irrelevant for the reconstruction of the initial text (such as spelling conventions and scribal blunder) can be filtered out, while the transcriptions preserve such individual features for those who want to study them.

It is true already now that the printed *Editio Critica Maior* presents just an extract of the critical apparatus whose full-fledged form exists in a database. The database also contains genealogical information assembled

---

5. On this aspect of the CBGM, see Klaus Wachtel, "Towards a Redefinition of External Criteria: The Role of Coherence in Assessing the Origin of Variants," in *Textual Variation: Theological and Social Tendencies?* (ed. H. A. G. Houghton and D. C. Parker; Texts and Studies, 3rd series 6; Piscataway, N.J.: Gorgias. 2008), 109–27.

while the initial text was edited. This enables quantitative and genealogical analyses of the full material that before the advent of database technology were impossible to perform. The *"Genealogical Queries"* suite of programs now allows external users to view the results of the CBGM as applied to the Greek manuscript tradition of the Catholic Letters.[6] This is a first step toward interactive use of the method. At present, however, the tools for constructing local stemmata, for deriving lists of potential ancestors, and textual flow diagrams can be used only by specialists at the Münster Institute. Yet it is technically possible now to give external scholars the means to work with ECM data according to their own methodological and theoretical presuppositions. This is planned to happen in a workspace of the developing "Virtual Manuscript Room," NT.VMR.[7]

This website demonstrates that digital editing has begun to offer a virtual way from the apparatus entry to the reading in the original document. In the framework of the NT.VMR the NT transcripts website[8] features a full apparatus based on the most important manuscripts with a link from each apparatus entry to the full transcription of the source and to an image of the source itself, if available online.

The scene is set for a new call *ad fontes*. When the humanists, and Erasmus in particular, proclaimed this motto, it was meant to focus the attention of the scholarly world on the ancient Greek sources of science and philosophy. Today it is the historicity of these sources that can and should be fully taken into account. The digital age finally provides the technical means to accept this challenge.

---

6. See http://intf.uni-muenster.de/cbgm/en.html.
7. See http://intf.uni-muenster.de/vmr/NTVMR/IndexNTVMR.php.
8. See http://nttranscripts.uni-muenster.de/.

www.ingramcontent.com/pod-product-compliance
Lightning Source LLC
Chambersburg PA
CBHW031709230426
43668CB00006B/167